THE RED BOOK
A True Extension of the Black Book Series

DWAYNE M. ADAMS

THE RED BOOK
A True Extension of the Black Book Series

WHY EXPLAIN THE TRUTH, WHEN MOST WILL ONLY ARGUE. FOR NOTHING IS TO BE GAINED BY THIS, AND NOTHING IS TO BE LOST. PLEASE EXCUSE ME WHILE I KISS THE SKY

Book III

WEMERGE

The Red Book | www.TheRedBookSeries.com
Copyright © 1979-2064 by Dwayne M. Adams
All rights reserved. No part of this book may be reproduced or transmitted
in any form or by any means without written permission from the author.

ISBN: 978-0-9906145-0-0
Published by: WeMerge, Inc.
www.WeMerge.com

Modern poetry is boring.
Usually it is just some person whining and trying desperately to be a writer.

Modern photography is lame.
Usually it is just some person with a camera trying desperately to be an artist.

Please note, the key word in both of the above sentences is "usually".

The book you hold in your hand right now and are about to read (once you get past this ridiculous forward) blows away the modern world of poetry and photography. The Red Book is an impressive juggernaut of words and images that the world needs to witness. It is not even close to the "usual" garbage that the recent cyber generations have mustered up. This is art in it's truest most savage, yet polished form.

The poetry in The Red Book isn't even close to boring. The poetry is vivid. The poetry is sincere. This poetry wants to be your friend. It is almost as if it is an extension of Dwayne's soul reaching out to say "Hello there... this is for you." His writing is truly a gift worth cherishing.

His photography captures life on earth in a dramatic fashion that is invigorating. Photographers of every level should take note- this is how it is done. The composition and timing is nothing less than perfect. The textures and emotions he captures fit hand in hand with the poetry with in the book. Ask any editor, this is no easy task.

I've known Dwayne personally for years. I always knew he had an artistic eye, but thought it was only for graphic design. (He flawlessly demonstrated his skills in that arena with in the 20+ issues of his magazine WeMerge.) The Red Book proves he is not some one trick pony, but more a leader and prime example of what an author and photographer should be. Even his abstract ink pieces at the end of every poem deserve praise for they bring it all together. A line of hope here, a dash of despair there, a gentle strike of love and a brutal dab of hate- all these emotions can be found in the line work. They stand out like an ancient language once forgotten, now deciphered as whatever your heart may choose.

In a world were everyone is trying to be Bukowski because they had 3 Pabst Blue Ribbons or a professional photographer because they got the new iphone9 and an Instagram account, it is refreshing to stumble upon The Red Book.

There is a living, beating heart with in this book. It is a book that properly defines the triumphs and tragedies of being a human. Dwayne has found his formula to creative genius and wrapped it up in a book for all of us to enjoy. Let's hope the world can recognize the gift Dwayne has given us all and grow from it.

Thank you for reading this and all my best, cheers....

Justin INVI Vilonna
-Creator of ZippyCakes and SnotMuffin,
The Holy Awesome, Deadly Woe and A Boy Can Dream.

DEDICATION

There have been many books I have read and enjoyed. There have been countless dedications I've come across and I always felt it was something every book created should have. There are many people who have touched my life. There are spiritual dedications as well as freinds and family to dedicate this book to. But there is one person in my life who I hope is enlightened by this book. One person who always brings joy to my life, either in a hug or a story. For this I love you.

This book is dedicated to my sister, Nicole. I decided to dedicate the first book I created to my sister to show her that anything you decide to do, can be done. As many would say, "if you put your mind to it, you can do anything." This book is a true testament to that statement. Starting out as just basic thoughts or writings, and which now have become a well created book of true emotion and thought. Holding nothing back and letting all that is felt be expressed in these pages.

When I watch my sister play hockey with such heart and skill from her constant practice, it gives me the inspiration to never let anything hold you back and just do what you love. Not only to do it, but to do it well. This is the reason I dedicate this book to my sister. Inspiration.

So, with this book I too hope to inspire and help people to realize their talents. To show people that anything can be done as long as you put forth the effort.

The second dedication of this book is to my mother.

Like most mothers, mine made sacrifices only a mother would make. She raised her children to the best of her ability and taught them all she knows. My mom is also known as Dr. Deb, because she always has a diagnoses for the tiniest sneeze.

This woman has always been there for me and supported me in what ever adventure I took on. The kind of support someone can only ever dream of. I would not be who I am today if it was not for the morals and amazing teachings she has shown me.

Always there for a hug and a high five when ever you need it. There aren't enough words to express how much I love her. She is the rock in my corner and the tender guidance needed when I am down.

I want to thank her for all she has ever done for me and with this tiny tribute, I want to share with the world the love a boy has for his mother.

Love ya ma. You're the best!

Dwayne M. Adams

PROLOGUE

The writings you are about to read were first created in my early twenties. I had a job at that moment in my life that gave me plenty of time to read. After reading a couple of books I decided that I needed to write my own. So I headed to the bookstore and looked for a journal that I could fill with all the thoughts that were running through my head. At the time it didn't seem like they were anything but meaningful thoughts. They more just seemed to be something that rambled, and while writing them, all I could think of was the song "*Ramble On*" by *Led Zeppelin*. So that's exactly what I did, I began to fill an entire book of ramblings.

The first book started out as the black book and was basically just a book that was going to be full of thoughts and journal entry type writings. But it turned out that I could fill up a lot more pages than I had anticipated. I first tried writing a story but found that it just kept going and going and really had no structure. Then I realized I needed to get a little more education on becoming an author and or writer. So after that I just began writing things that came to my mind and I would just list them in order, sentence structured, thought after thought after thought.

Once the first book was completed I realized how much I enjoyed writing in these books. Heading back to the store where the first book was acquired I found another one that had more lines. My first thought was to make the writings take longer so I could have more ability to be creative and not be constrained by the number of lines to express these thoughts. After the first couple pages I came to realize this was going to be a huge undertaking. But as I said before, the job that I had, gave me plenty of time, so I decided to use this time to my advantage. With that, the second book was complete.

After completing the second book I headed back to the bookstore. To my surprise all the black journals were just gone. Astonished I went to the front to ask the manager if there were any books on back order and to my surprise he said, "They took them all!" the bookstore had been bought out and was going to close. He asked if I had a second to wait and he would check in the back for me to see if there was any left over. After about five minutes and a wealth of anticipation he returned with a red book in hand. With this exchange of money for goods the red book series began.

Contained within these pages you will find the thoughts of an aspiring writer who really has no other way, but to ramble on. Please enjoy these writings and with all due respect most of them are just lies to be told, for this I will let you be the judge. This is the first book published and basically will begin the legacy of Mr. Adams as a writer, author and publisher, but most of all...creative. Each writing contains an image of photography that was taken by myself as well as a piece of art in the right-hand corner which I produced with watercolor. These elements were brought to each page to not only help the eye and brain read but also the heart and soul understand. As explained before, enjoy the ramblings. Thank you for your time.

Dwayne M. Adams

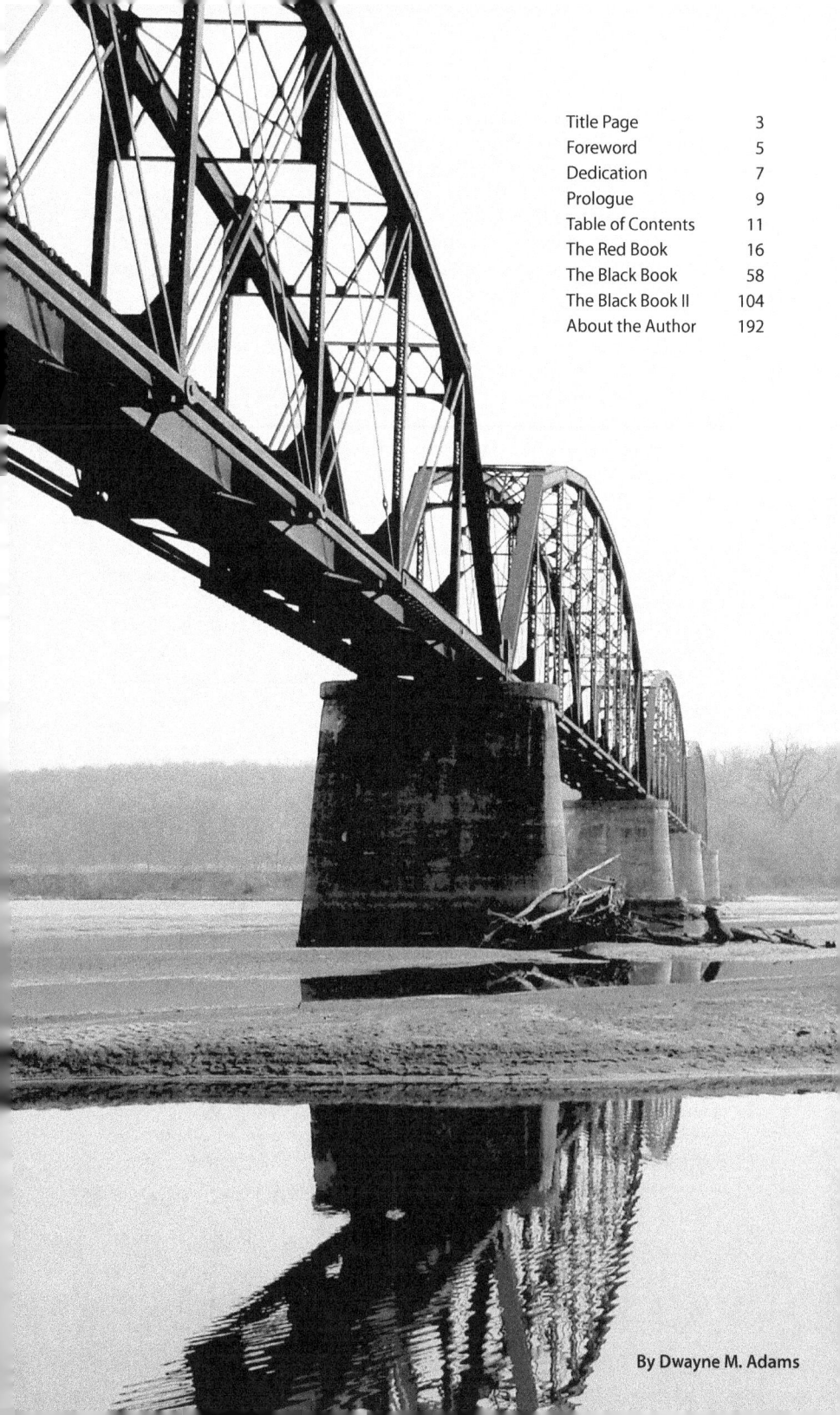

By Dwayne M. Adams

THE RED BOOK

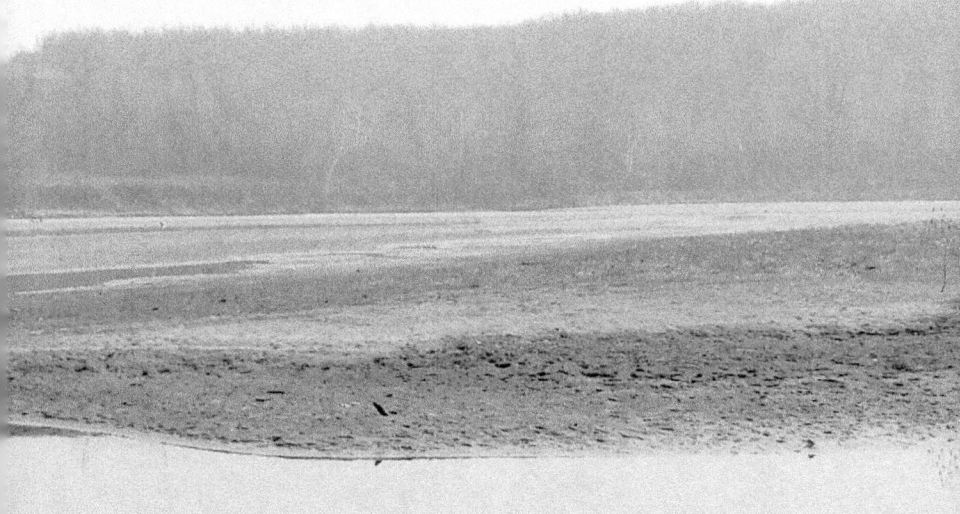

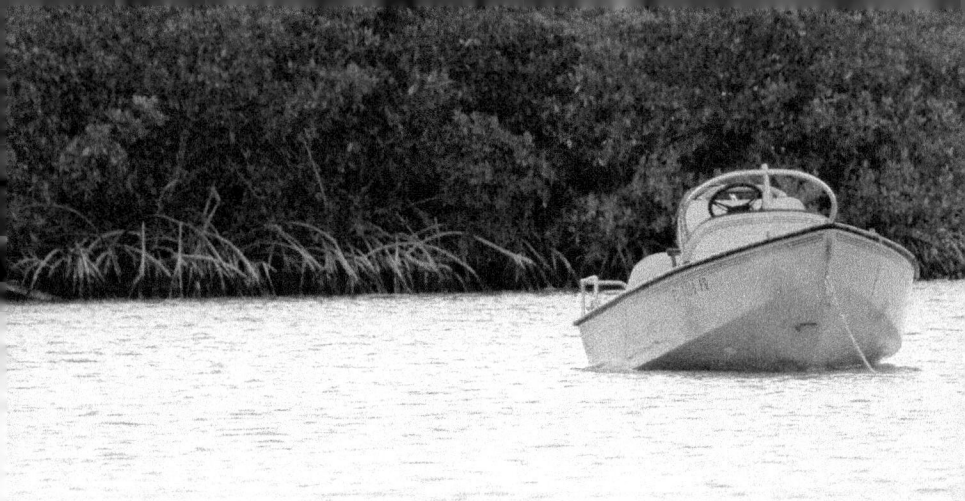

By Dwayne M. Adams

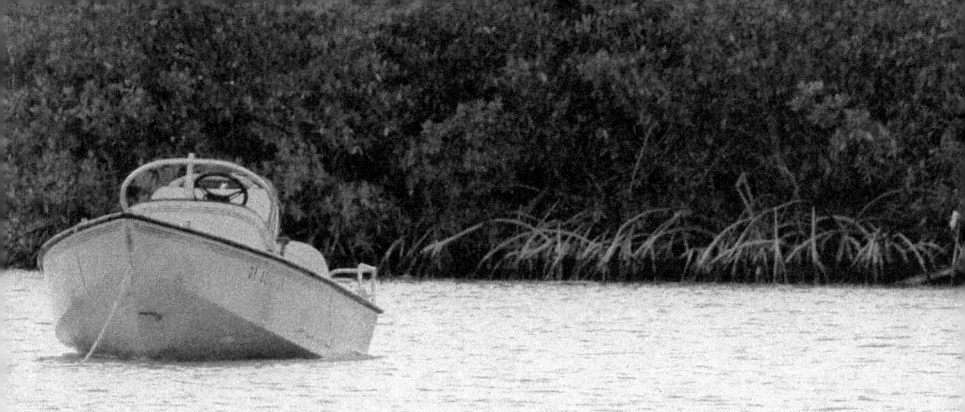

THE BLACK BOOK

By Dwayne M. Adams

THE BLACK BOOK II

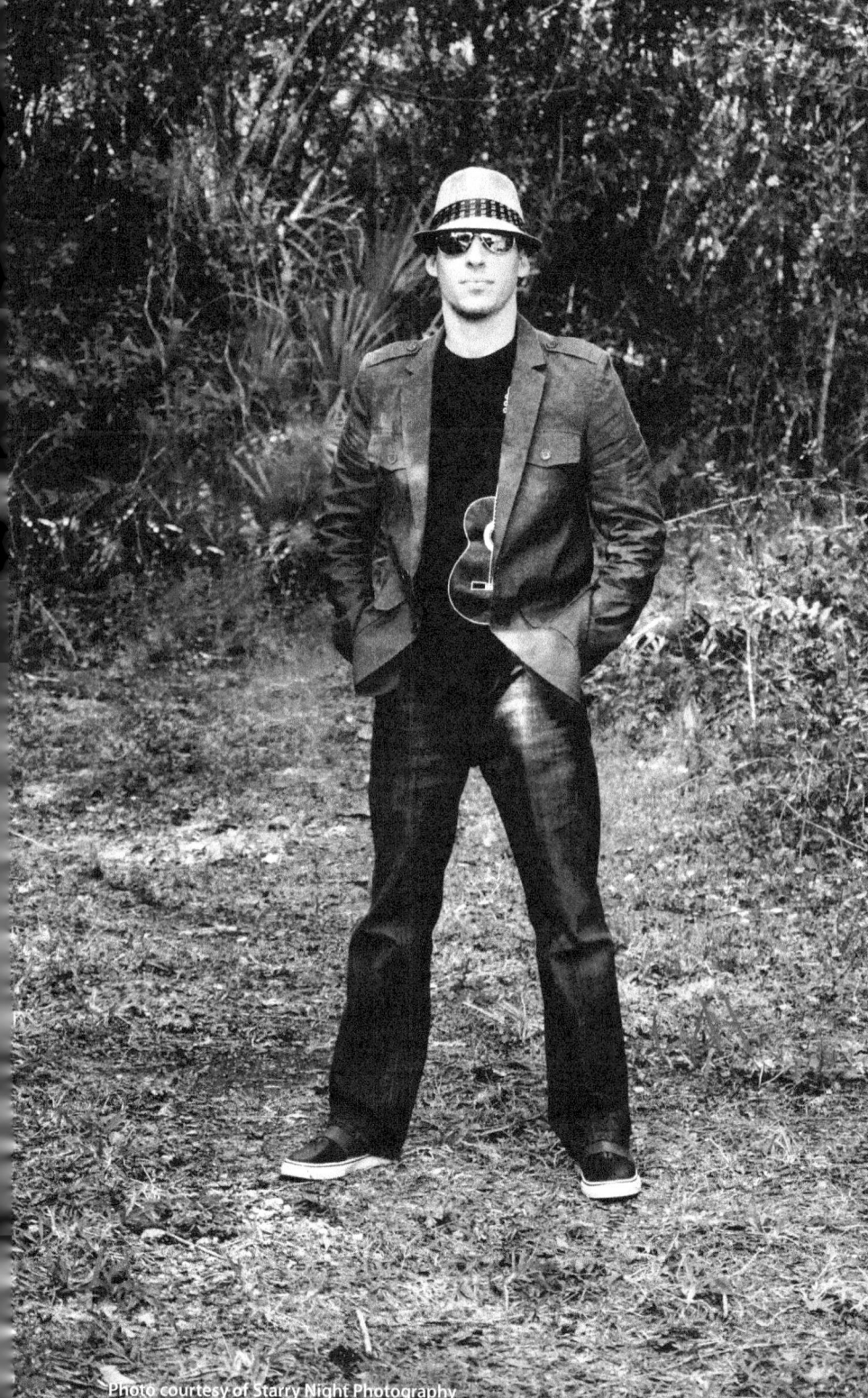

A ONCE LOST LION

Beautiful angel songs of a dancing breeze
Dull roar of a lost lion among men
To which way was the wind felt in haste
Covering the mountain of sacred knowledge
Which master will hold thy throne
Forgotten realities become true to nature
Only He posses true knowledge of a hidden past
So then to a man hidden amongst men
This be thy day which glory shines
Heaving great stones upon evil followers
A song is set forth as a horn of faith
A tremble seems to shake frozen grounds
Light of a supreme has been revealed
Will our souls be accepted as true to be
Alone a fate will be made into existence
Paths which have the way you must go
Warmth of a different kind begins to fill you
Soft music is heard in backgrounds of light
An embrace from a love that's been known
Realizing that you are one with the light of glory
Eternity of bliss awaits a once lost lion.

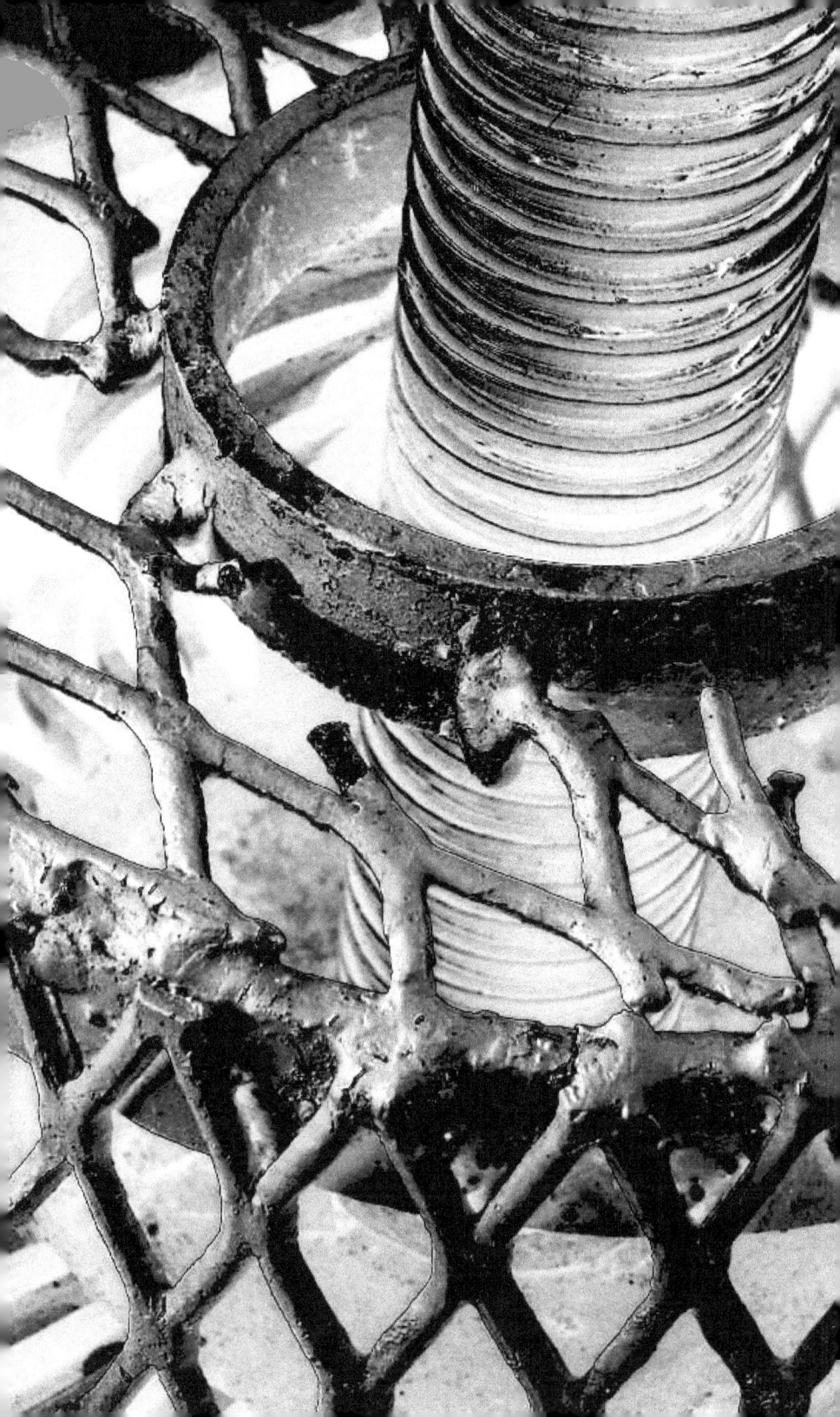

CRAZY.

Like Lizards dancing on lily pads
Sunflowers blowing in warm winds
Crystal clear rain falling from heavens
For this is where the joker plays his games
With the moon gleaming where the sun has no shade
While wicked animals tear at rotten flesh
Sweat beads up on a dead man's brow
Littering dense air with a foul smell of death
The monkey screams sounds of an angels cry
Who were meant to breathe the weather of hail
Jackals come with attitudes of rage
Rambling about as if to say something
Then spring autumn hits and no one knows
People stare at the spectacle in amazement
As if to understand what it all means
Volcanoes erupt lost souls of our past
Strangers walk by in amazement of this
Spider monkeys swing from metal rails of trains
Green eyes dart around unseen black hallways
Armies of tribes battle fatal wars together
Will the old man push the lines in our defense
Or will our dragons of pray never fight
Our existence depends on the orbit of our being
Carousels of stallions spin about in confusion
As we wonder around rooming for a ray of light
Sparks burst in hot air to cool our desire
Masquerades hide even dark secrets been gone
Even the joker has no real name of fame
While dragonflies walk by asking how to fly
The lion tells them to hide their tales
While secret agents make a run for it
Start here they say
Start Here.

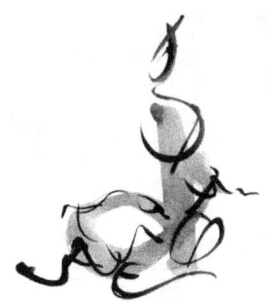

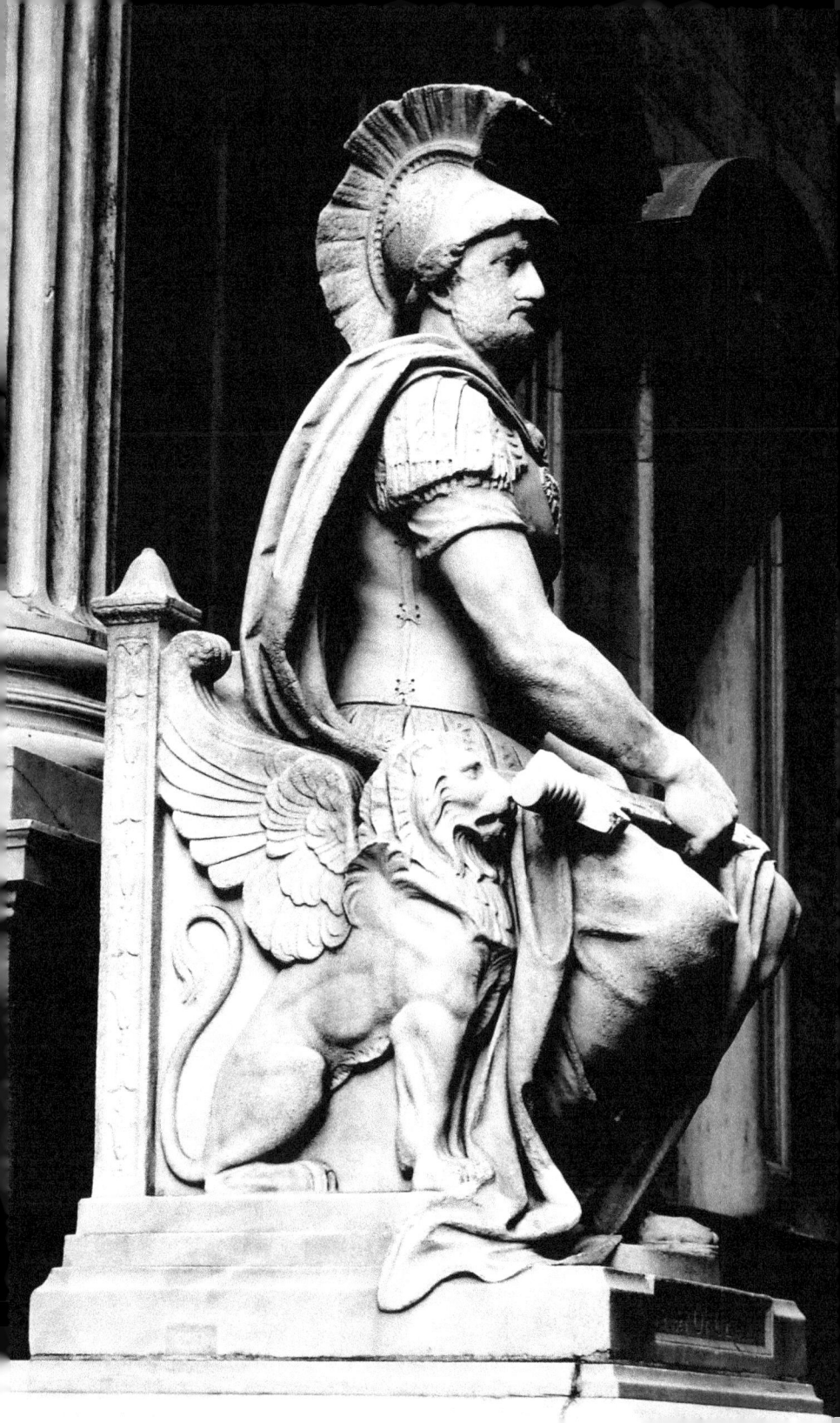

KING LION

Gasping creatures of a theater so grand
Mesmerized by the huge glowing pictures
Sitting and gasping at a moment with release
Awaking in a pool of cold sweat from reality
Knowing that which was taken, wasn't ours
Beauty to the moon of Shakespeare and foes
An angel lies in innocence amongst the cotton
Morning dawn shows her magnificence
Halos of light gather around her soft hair
Casting a beautiful frame making time stand
Sharp cold air tightens the Lions muscles
Growls are heard through morning air
The angel dozes in comfort of the jungle
Chaos is heard through slivers between cement
Smells of a nectar float in the sweet air
A gathering of tribes will meet to calm nerves
Smiles are greeted with a handshake of lost friends
A circle is formed for the bonding of tribes
Melodies of drums play in the background soft
Helping the day to relax easier in the chaos
A warm breeze blows through stirring the nectar
Hunger of a different kind haunts our thoughts
Meals of great kings are made to enjoy
The mighty castle is now filled with excitement
Happiness and joy is brought to the Land of Friends
The meeting has helped to bring knowledge
Understanding of a quest once forgotten
So if ever in the Land of Kings ruled
Then stop by the hidden castle to help see
Magic of other worlds of mysterious beings
Brought as gifts of wealth to experience
The King Lion will show you the great jade
Sit in his company for he knows a truth once lost.

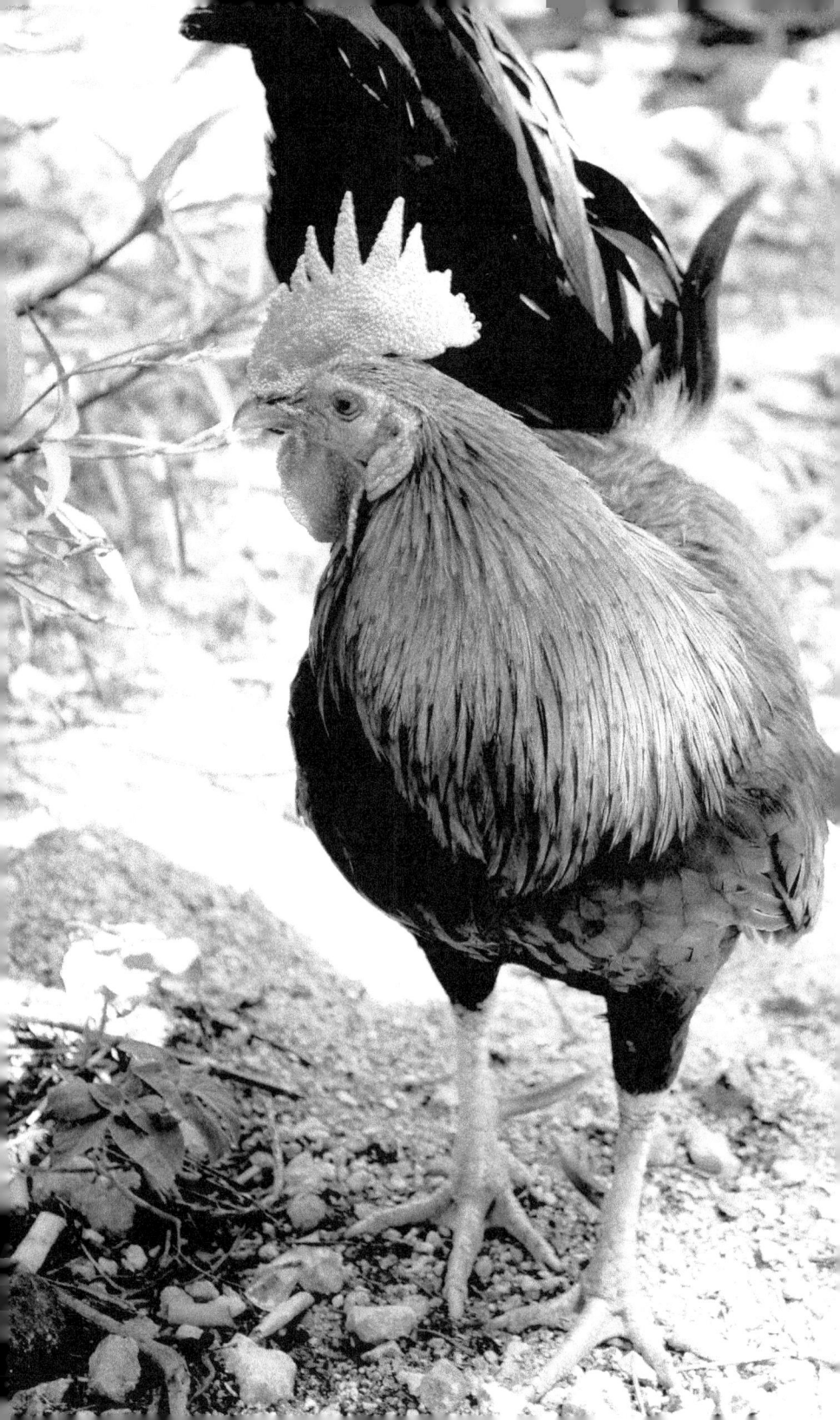

KNIGHT OF LIGHT

The size of these monstrous little devils
Making a gasp of air from a breathless chest
Grabbing for the surface of a bottomless pit
You begin to feel cold hands of armless creatures
Their claws slice your steel skin of armor
From your side you pull a sleek silver destroyer
Eyes of miles poke through the bright darkness
Your arms ache with undying weight of massive feathers
A voice tells you that you cannot fly without experience
Then from the corner of your eye is a light
A beautiful angel appears in fogy mist before you
Moist air around her is sweet with nectar rain
Darkness is afraid of the brightness she brings
Overwhelmed by the amazing power of her beautiful eyes
She takes away your destruction and your demise
With the powerful hands of her trusted grace
You are placed upon the precious clouds of Avalon
Only the great god will be able to watch over
No evil, nor demise will come to be ever again
The mighty silver destroyer will be laid to rest
Angels will stay for the time, till death
Your name with greatness, will lie in a castle of honor
Many children of your seed will carry on your legacy
Men will speak of the bravery you held against evil
Stone warriors will sit upon your grave as keepers
Gargoyles will lay by their feet to ward off evil
As evil will send its vicious villains and creepers
But the mighty power of our Lord will cast light
For the tyranny of evil men will be corrupted
And the fall, will be marked by a foul year of our lord
Only then will you fully understand the knowledge
Which will extinguish all devilish desires
Then all will be united as one being under light.

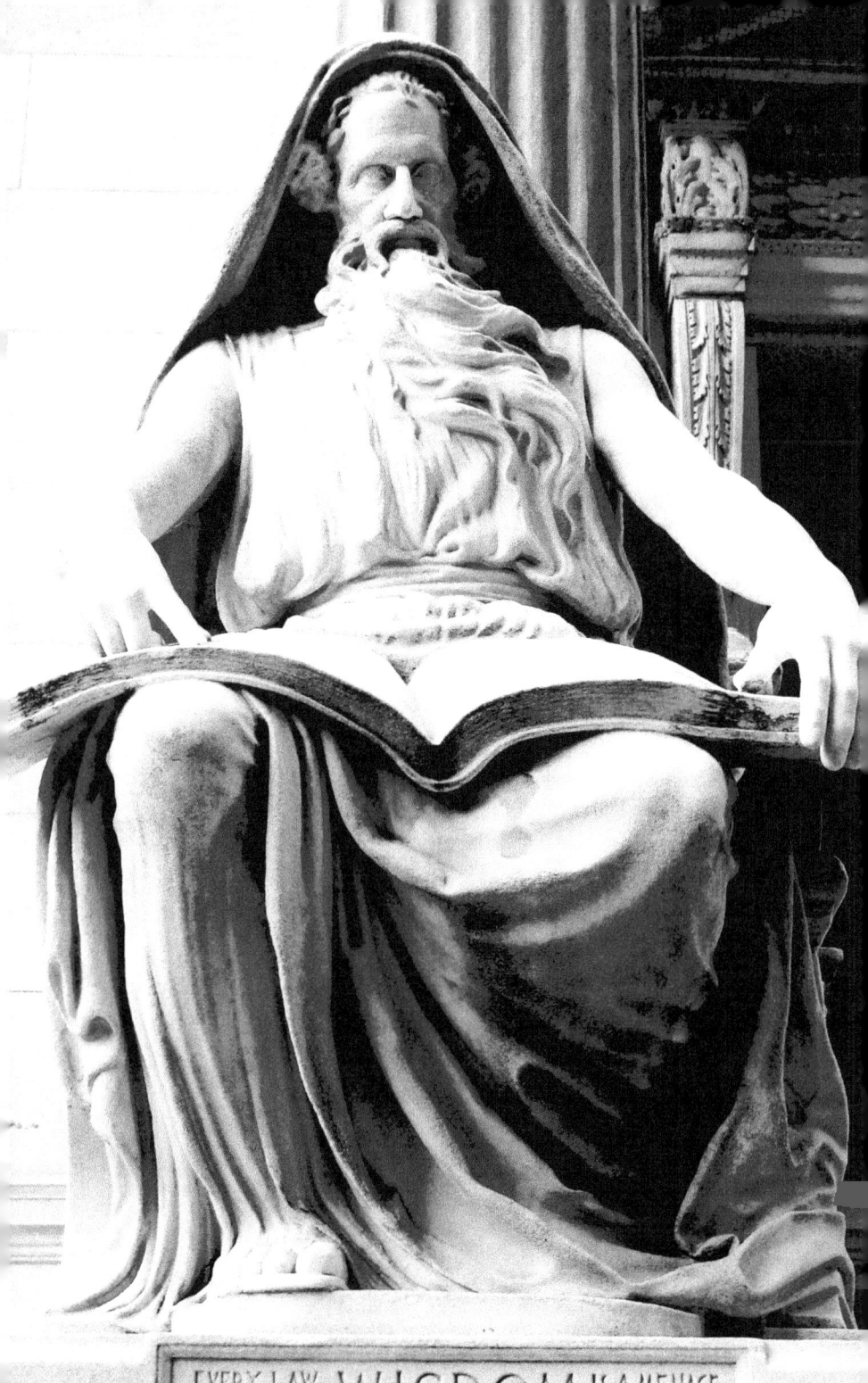

EVERY LAW
NOT BASED ON WISDOM IS A MENACE
TO THE STATE

REALIZE

Understanding a fate that is our being
We come to realize our existence
The feeling of losing everything has come
We learn to free our acceptance from reality
Birth of a supernova is upon us
Shards of glass that reflect the inner soul
As beads of sand fall through clenched fingers
Flooding over debris from a broken hour glass
When time will never be able to stop
Roots from our veins will grow deep into the earth
Binding us to this world through our imperfections
Storms of mass destruction seem to calm the land
Beautiful rays of light grab us from ourselves
Choking us with the darkness from the glow
We begin to feel purity of the unseen
Acceptance will be the gift given to our creatures
Like a tattoo placed upon you to remember
Trying to forgive the people we deceive
Pity will be the demise of our kingdom
Armies of devastation will clear the fields
A path will be made to keep us all safe
The screech of hawks cry above us
Sounds of evil make the ears bleed with pain
Smiles of blissful days we once had warm us again
Hope glows in a great ball beyond white clouds
Raining on our feet warmth to go forward
Winds blowing on our back the breath of life
Horns sound over the mountain's snow peak
Our mouths water for a taste of peace
Hiding in the perpetual motion of life
For our existence will never be taken
It is hidden deep in our souls strive for life
Our sacred lives will always be preserved.

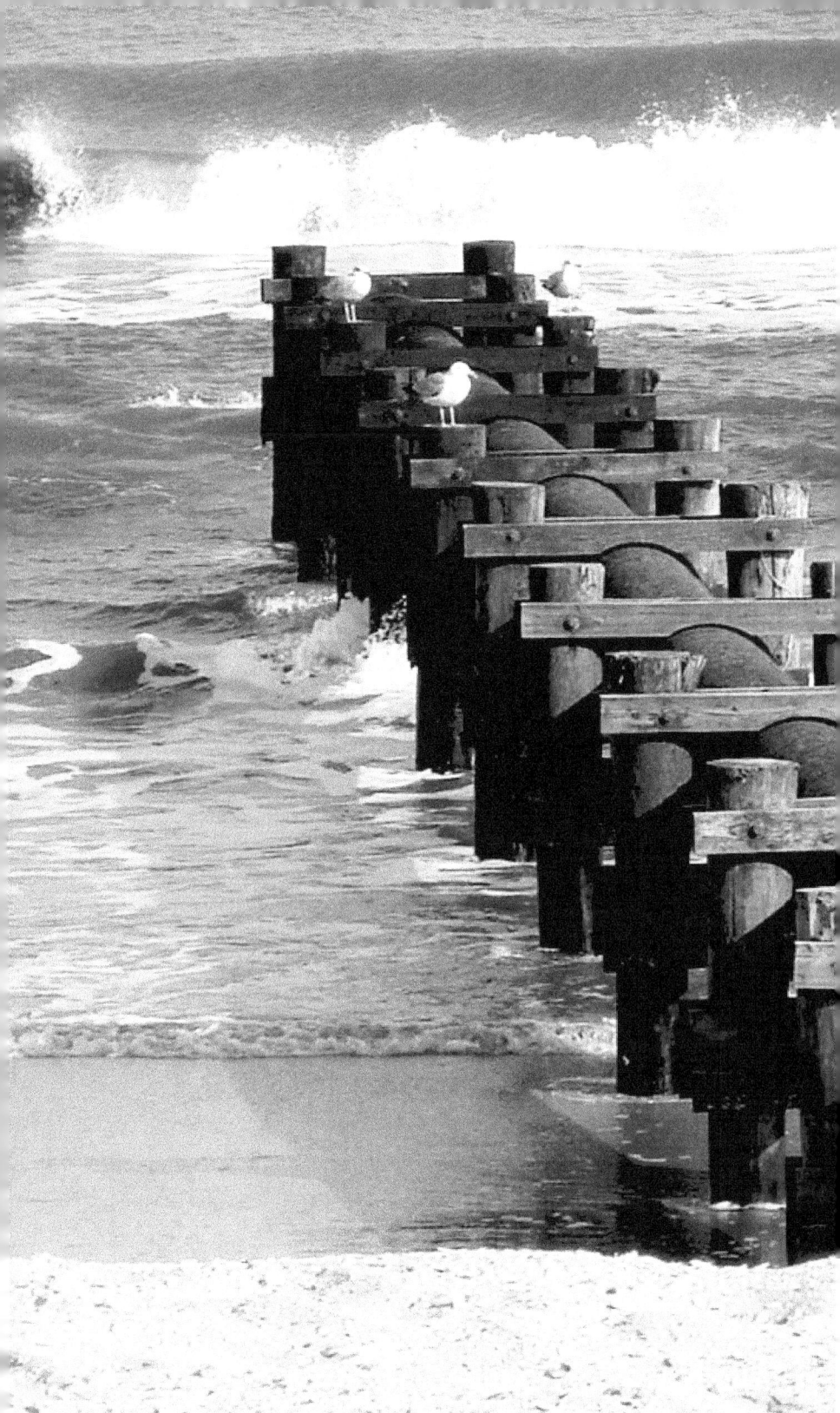

THE DRUMS

The soft beating drum of a once forgotten tribe
Making music sound as if it is the only thing alive
The rhythm helps to sooth the everlasting pain of a past
Warm vibrations fill a body with incredible pleasure
Masking the harsh reality that we are not pure
Hoping to one day realize a truth that has been hidden
Like stars without their own place among the galaxy
Spinning black holes use their gravity to pull you
Chains of cloth bind you to your true figure of life
Hopeless dreams fill a mind which never seems to stop
Love which fills a heart that would never love again
Caressing time as it passes by ever so slowly with grace
Winds blow the scent of happiness through the air
Smiles appear on the faces of frowns in the midst
Minds are eased once again by the beauty of the drums
Soft kisses heat the cheeks of the mighty dancers
For the skill is possessed like ghosts of another kind
The mystery of drums has baffled men since time began
Creating ancient stories of when the first drum was heard
Truth be told our God was the first drummer of the land
Telling the earth in which direction he wanted his creation
For he knew the power of the drum and could play it's vibration
See the vibrations.

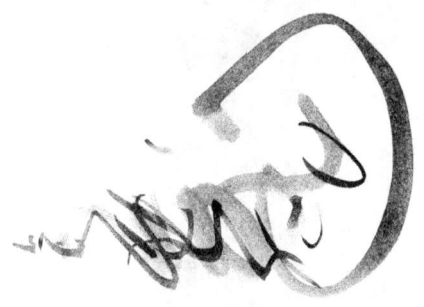

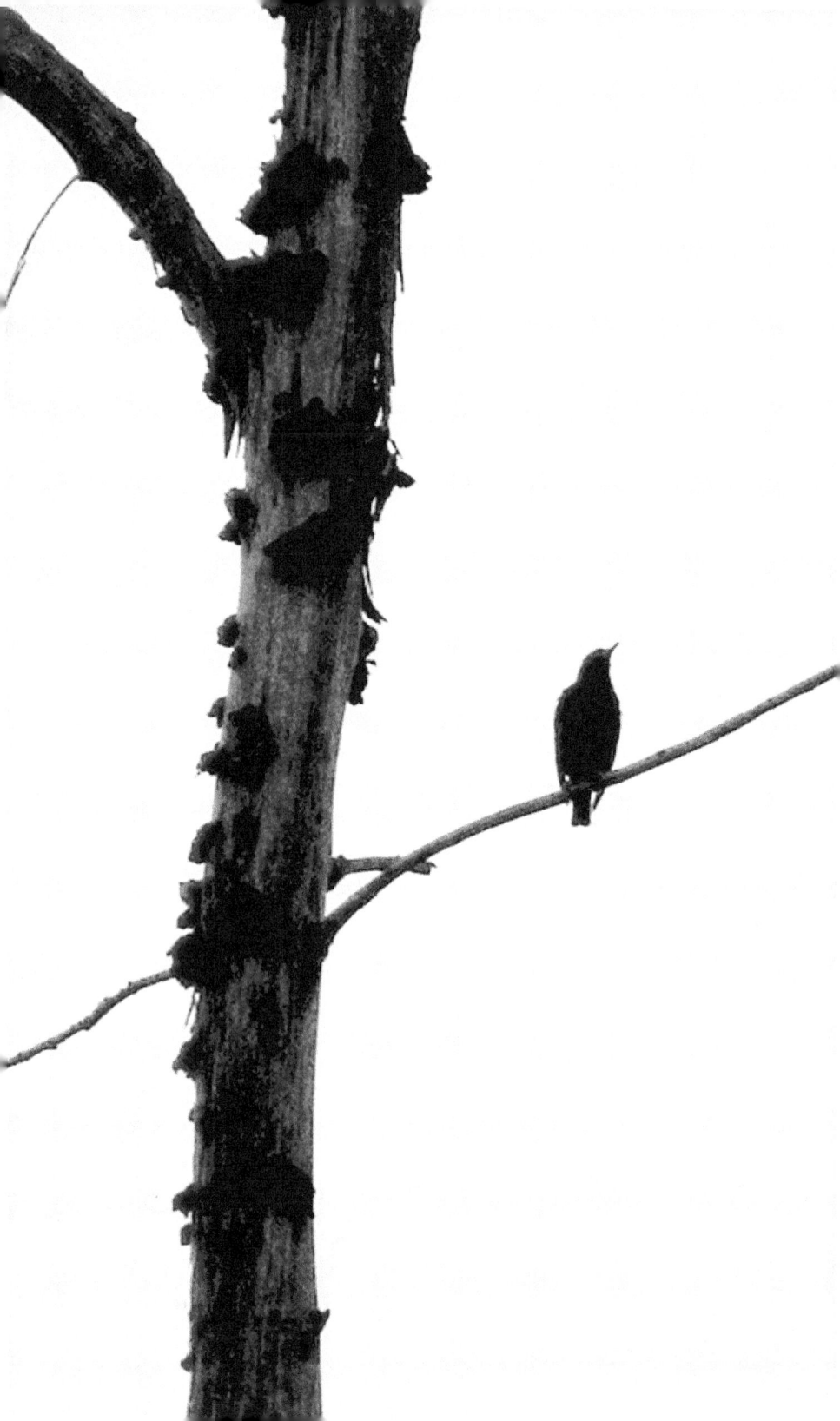

GODDESS

Golden light shines off the crystal blue waterfall
Cascading shadows upon a goddess of true nature
Her hair like soft silk blowing amongst the fairies
Eyes which have seen true love in heavens
Effortless in her stillness with radiance of beauty

Lying motionless amongst green blowing grass of thy lake
Elegance of falling petals gliding to earth
Birds melodies touch the soul of her innocence
Dense forests surround her virgin body
Masking the harsh realities of this world
In soft hands she holds creation of thy light

Eyes are set on great efforts against thy struggle
Truth be told by thy lips of a goddess
For time lingers amongst shadows of thy light
Shadows which do not live without thy glow from heavens

A soft breeze blows a wild red rose upon thee
True love is expressed to a soul never touched
Intensity hidden becomes fire burning deep inside
An explosion of passion is set forth
Earthly secrets are made to be known
Meant for lovers to share in thy divine light

Sunsets revealing a song magnificent to thy heart
Golden rays which sooth thy soul with pure love
Embraced, two lovers become one under God
The tale completed with a love combining spirit
This praise is given to thy goddess of true nature.

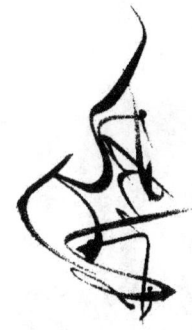

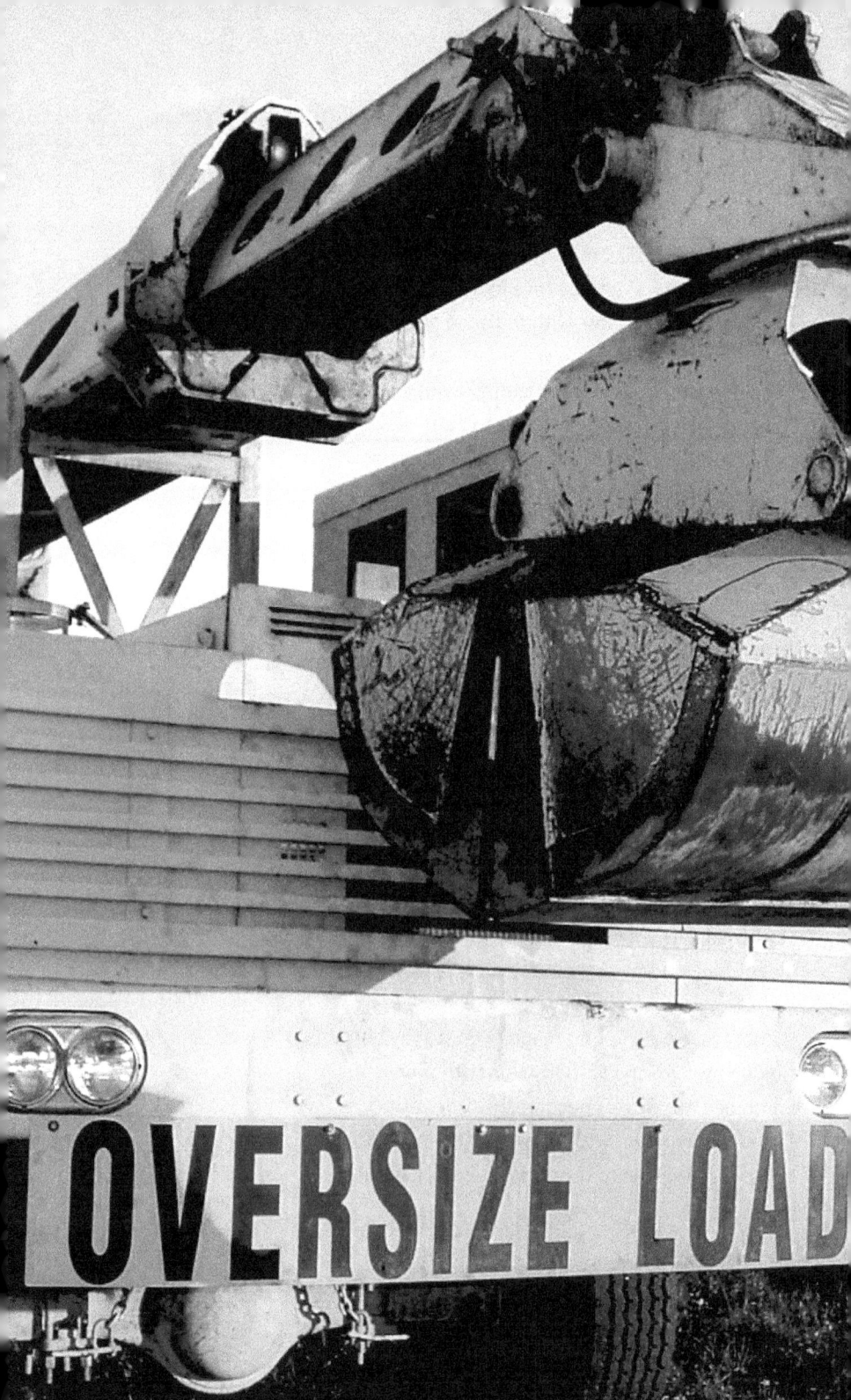

TOLERANT

Winter death makes cold blood boil
Fiery heat makes blue veins freeze in place
Horny dragonflies try to win the race
Mass confusion sets wild elk into motion
Toxicity of the lion waits in molten rock
Sacred beings walk a vast land of mythology
While two great stone hands hold our world
Galaxies spin about trying to maximize life
It's inevitable what is to come to be
Falling planets trace our skies with icy fire
Actions that may dismay our only belief
Like wax dripping from the chins of hornets
Descending upon a fly that's not paying attention
Inter missing a once deceitful variety of affection
Basking in the flavor of our forgiving existence
To one day hold the saber of our Lord
Extinguishing dark enchantments which bind us
A monstrous roar from a blessed animal cries out
Layers that cover the reality of our souls
Ringing with music which glorifies the deaf
Blinding light which is seen by the unseeing
Almost devilish in all the ways of a beautiful angel
Rays that break through soft clouds of anger
Reflection of a deceitful myth upon us
Masters of a mistress in a domain which hides us
At the breaking point of an eternal voice
Making the unseen a mythical reality
All the while a black widow spins her web of funk
Giving an insect a reason to live among them
Beauty will deceive even the strongest of minds
Making the cutting edge a dull line of fate
Exempt from the fears of our being
Tolerant to the world as it bleeds to us.

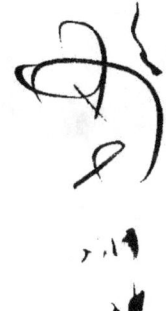

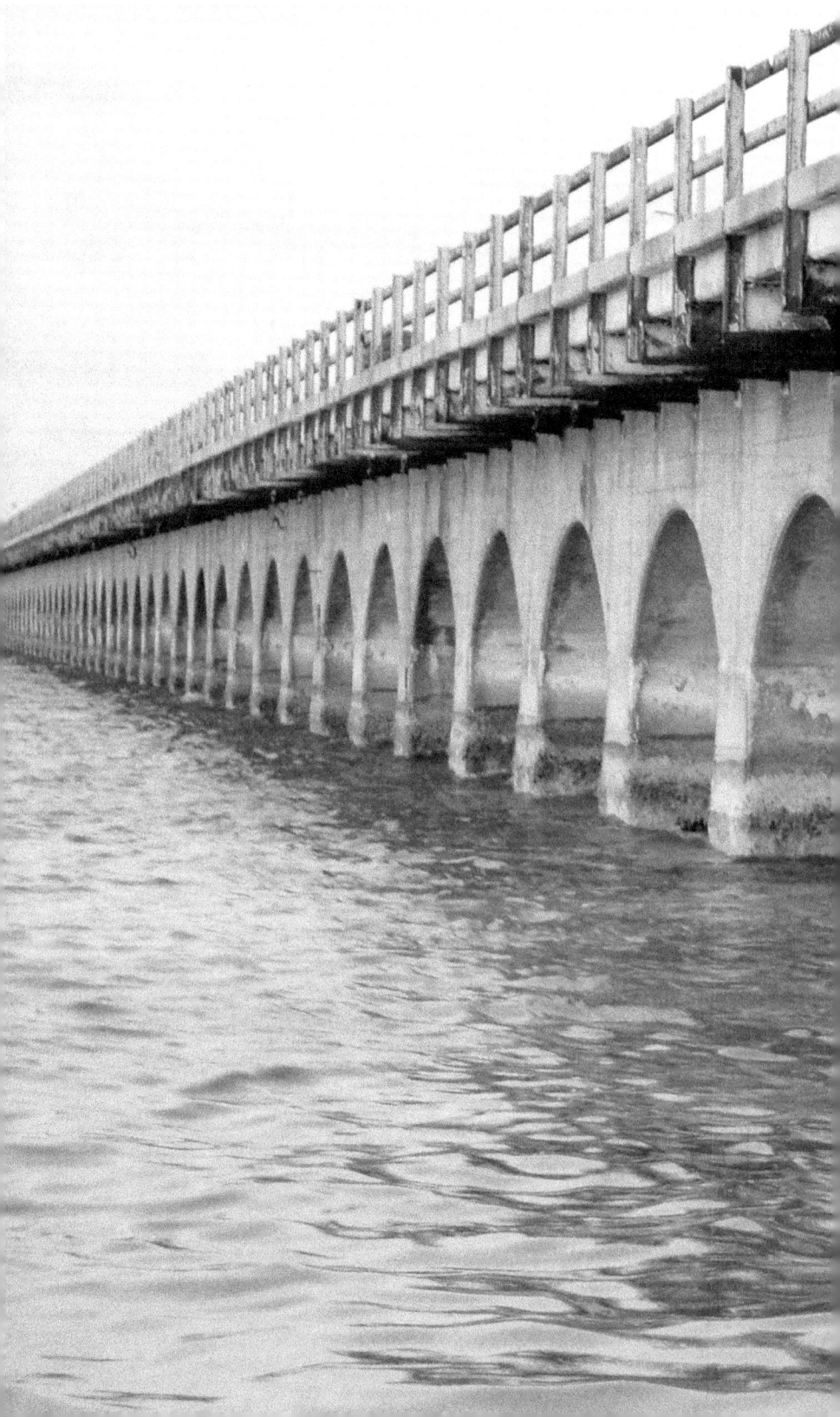

A CONCRETE JUNGLE

Like cannibals running through a dense forest
Junkies savage our streets for a fix of life
The vampires devour their blood to get high
Little creatures of darkness pick up their remains
Zeus rains down his precious powers for relief
As Aphrodite caresses us with her everlasting love
Only to the sacred sphinx does this seem natural
As the heavenly fairies release their only desire
The mighty centaur keeps guard of the beings
These friends of the amazing concrete jungle
Are the makers of this world who turn it the way it doesOnly they have
seen the beginning of our existence
These wondrous creatures know our truth
The jungle is beautifully filled with vines of constriction
It once harbored the most powerful cities
Now thick luscious arms entangle the mighty buildings
Huge flesh eating birds nest upon these castles
The one creature who is almost extinct among them
The fantastic mechanical potent powerful Man
To the wonders that were once magnificent feats
That now stand motionless against the great sands
Volcanoes which once stood docile in nature
Have begun to spread their inner spewing
Of a liquid of history of a past that was
Which will never be known amongst mortals
Now a new breed of creatures roam the fields
Maybe this time a civilization will last
If so, maybe the end won't be so vast
So when lying motionless in your existence of life
Do not have any emotion of fear
For you will have enjoyed the journey of truth
When you reach that moment thank him
He will be happy to see his child.

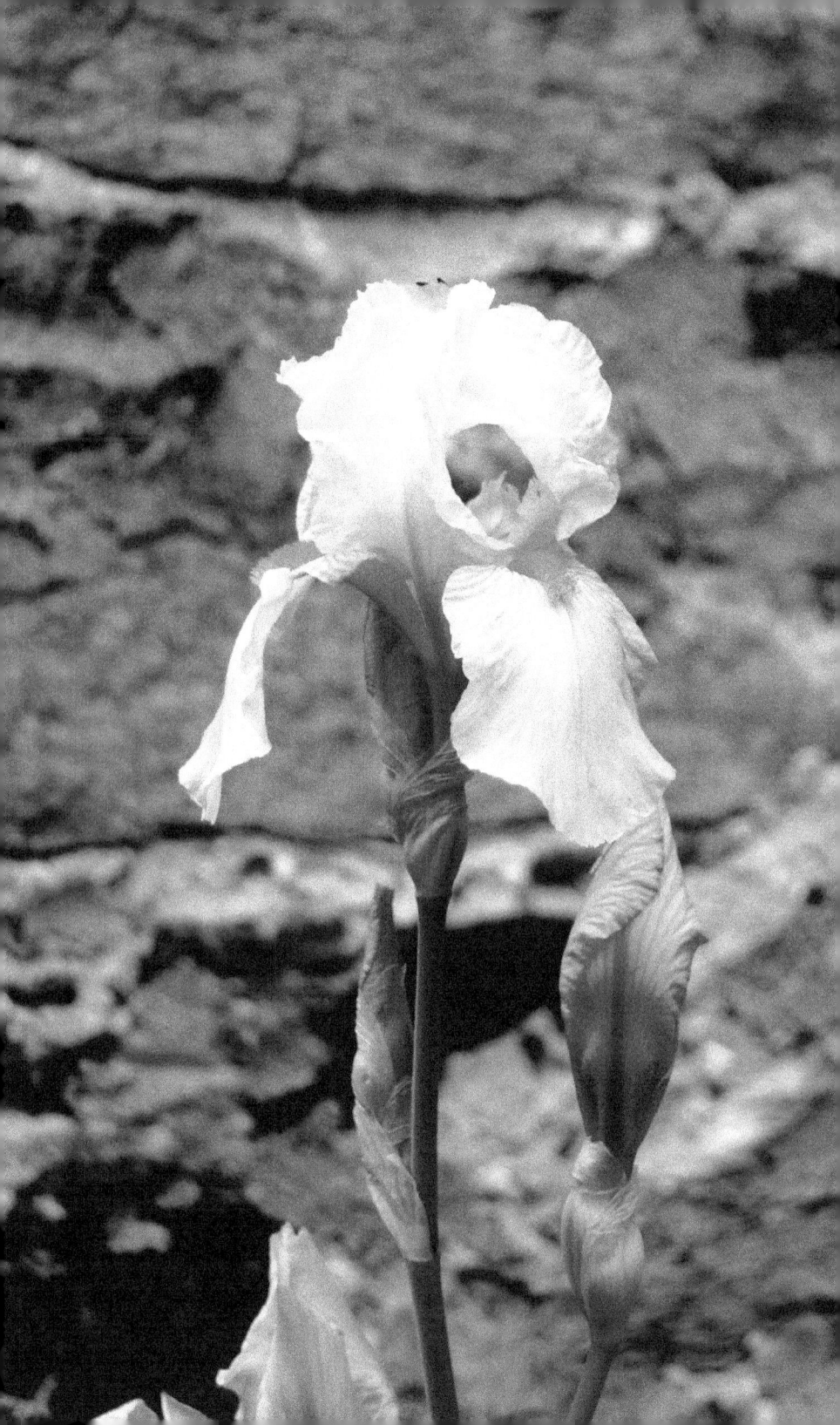

AMONGST THE CHAOS

Touched by the gracious hands of the gods
As a Spaniard passes with a flavor of the past
Teaching of a land once forgotten in an ocean
Telling of the secret remedies to help calm nerves
As a circus of elephants pass by waving flags
The Lion squad is entangled in green ribbons
Claws rip away as a roar is released from fire
Exploding into a celebration of the creator
As metals of tiffany hang in their dangling way
Trolls wait in haste in the shadows of the beautiful
Vast tribes of children flood the streets of Avalon
Showing to the world that they are to be
Masks of animals parade by scaring the tribes
Musical mayhem breaks through the crowd
Mass confusion ruptures out of the pandemonium
An angel sits motionless amongst all the chaos
Has she spotted the god who watches her
Standing from afar one eye is kept on the goddess
Elegant in the nature of her beauty she waits
Like a heaven sent rose amongst the thorns
She stands out in the eyes of the God to see
To far to ever be engaged by the sounds of her voice
Only soft glances will be exchanged back and forth
A smile breaks from both their faces of sadness
They turn away as if the first time they have ever blushed
Strangers for now but hope of a day to which will fade
Like the color fades off the leaves of a spring time
Now gone from sight the people begin to leave
Nothing here but the left over remains of filth
As if mirrored reflections don't show the truth
Anticipated by the next move of our being
To maybe for one second understand the harsh reality
Hoping that there is a force tending the tunnel of light.

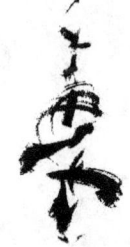

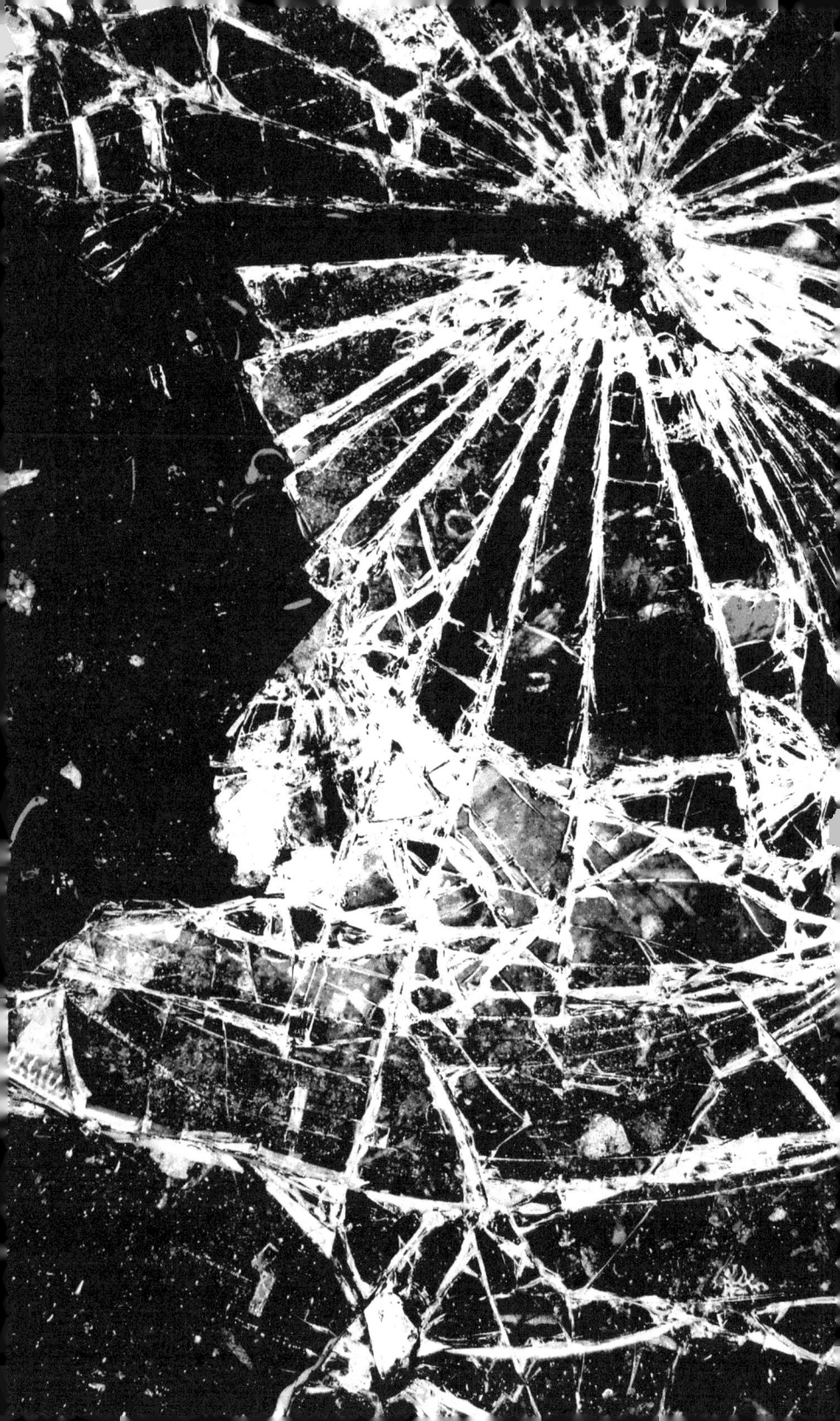

BEETLES OF FIRE

Vibrations waking an eternal soul from somber
Crippled beetles of fire limp in unbearable agony
A drop of poisonous rain falls from cliffs above
There seems to be a meeting of tribes again
Ladders lead to the heavens for the gathering
Kings and Pharaohs from across the land come
Sharing their wealth with the people as they pass
Journeys through a vast range of mountains
Glowing skies split to help show the way forward
Talks of war come over the waves of communication
An evil has come to show itself amongst the holy
Warriors of the tribes come to fight this battle
Indestructible suites protect from the darkness
Swords of light penetrate the hidden shadows
Leaving scars for eternity to dwell upon
The rain from above is now above once again
Drops of piercing precision break through
Revealing a weakness to which will be used
Cries of mercy sweep across the land of death
Making the impossible a truth which will be seen
Exposing to the world a darkness that hides in light
An eruption from afar shakes the ground
Leaving puzzled faces which never seem to leave
Lost in a dark vision of a reality to once be
Only the ruler of light can defend all
For he and his knights of light can defeat them
Something in the distance glows with power
An explosion is let out across the fields of a dessert
All is wiped clean of its impurities to the evil
The great light helped those to understand
Peace for a time has healed the black hole
Till the two are bored and decide to play again
Mercy for the beetles of fire who drink acid rain.

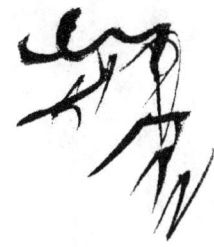

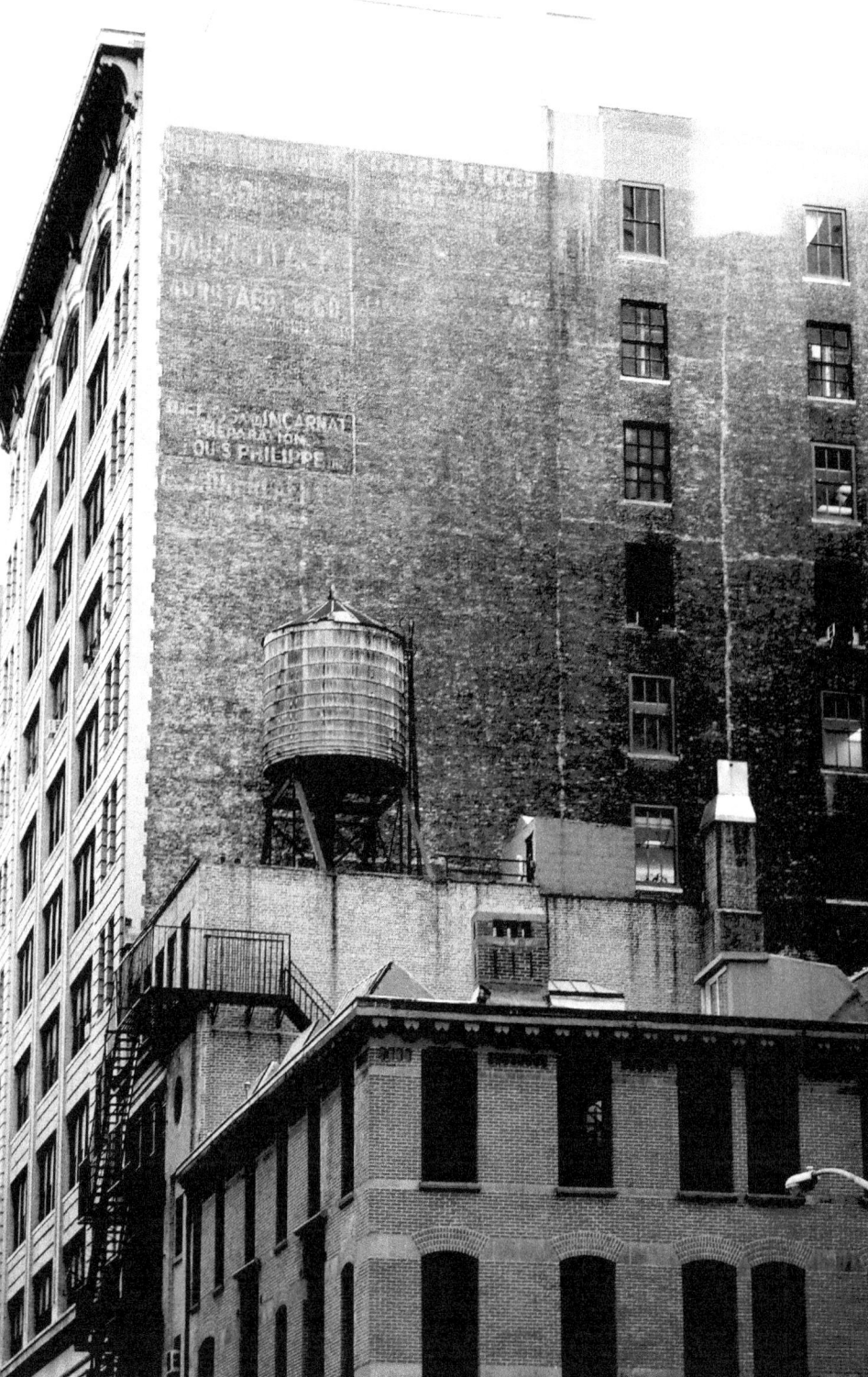

DAY IN THE JUNGLE

Tired as eyes held open by toothpicks of steel
Metal which binds the hands of a leader
Guiding indestructible forces of nature
As if hemp is a rope not used for anything else
Self-medication is the way people help themselves
Chewing on wild ginger for a taste of a special spice
Little child fire fighters scream their siren for all to hear
As African queens yell in excitement of old friends
Mothers carry the children of forgotten child fathers
Bags of heritage pulling their arms to the floor
Daughters of kings who act as if they are queens
Lost gazer of a time that was once known
Belly rings that dangle in the absence of a touch
Bubblers which help pass the days with clouds
Peace pipes that help to calm the rage of tribes
Making the fallen seem as champions to all
Birthday friends who make the day brighter
Yellow glare as it shines through the plated glass
Pink angels stroll past in light blue shades
Giving everlasting smiles to the Gods she passes
Good dandelions wait in fair warning of them
The sweet Goddess makes her self-known
Waiting in boredom for a spark to ease the pain
Lighting the internal flame which burns us
No such water can cool the intensity of its heat
Our angels scope out the land for their God
Approving that which is to follow the aftermath
Words of disaster fog the brain, unable to speak
Half sentences come out in the form of gibberish
Confusing the listener in to leaving for bad
Only now do we understand the reason
It's dust blowing in the long lasting wind
Drifting around till we meet another day.

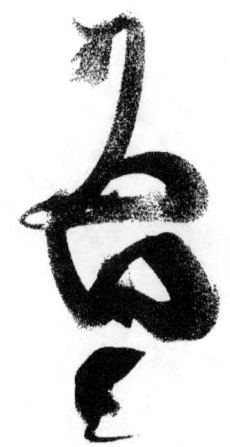

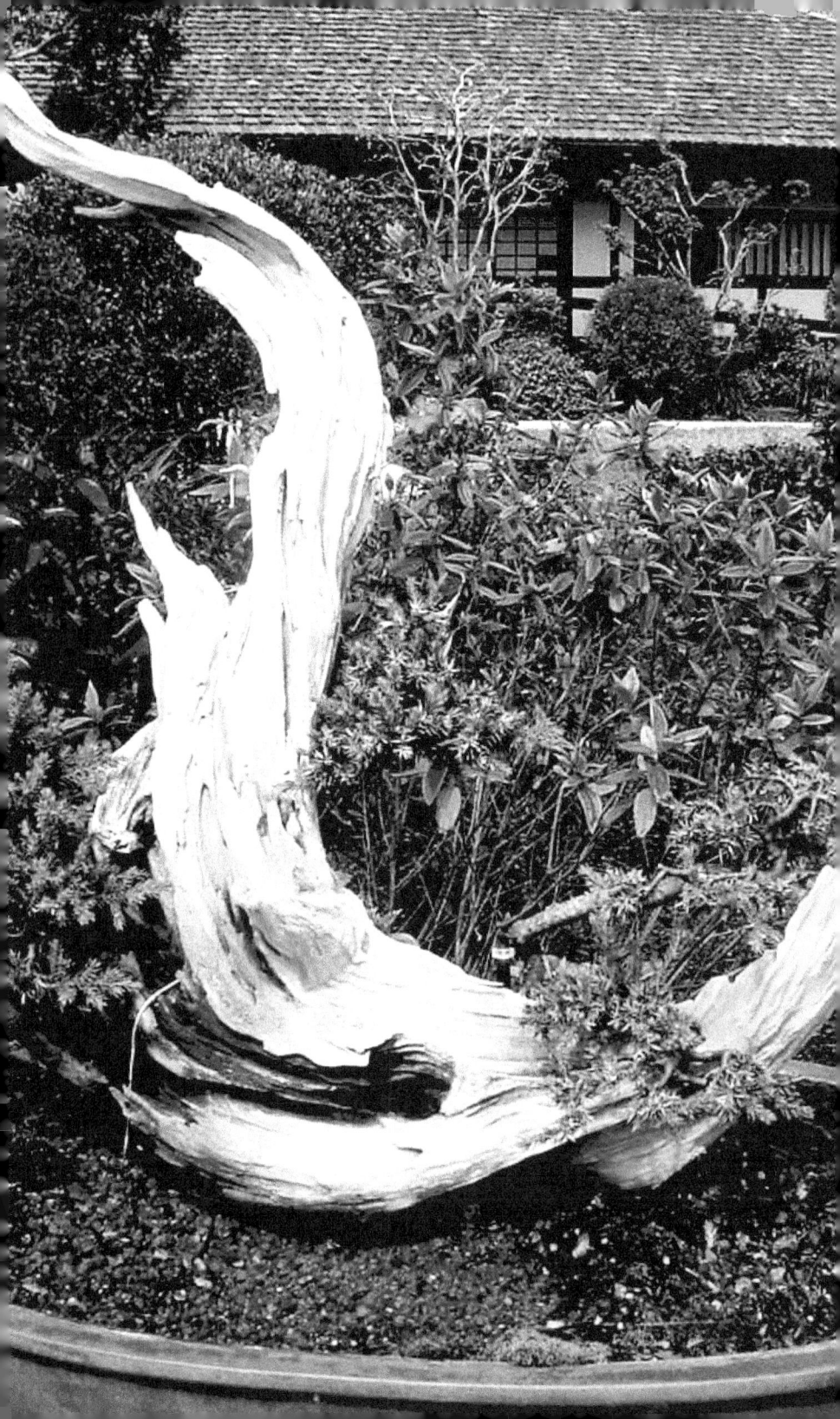

EXCEPT

The gentle bang of cricket legs pound
Making the silence beat in virgin ears
Hearing the soft melodies playing to soothe
Relaxing the intense reality of the day
A soft breeze blows a secret scent throughout
Filling the room with moonbeams from the sun
Casting mangled shadows for the unforgiving
Hopeless dreams of lost days once seen
Looking to the future to remember a past
Which shows us a fold in our great history
Fallen soldiers of war lie motionless in space
The dark cold nothing brings light to the surface
Skimming the top of a corrosion of mass confusion
Not knowing that we are, what is to come to be
Showing vanished memories which plague us
Revealing concealed tombs of ancient Gods
Exposing a deceptive truth made of fables
Scriptures which lead the masses in their ways
Creating an artificial truth, which acts to know
Like a tender hand holding up our society
A way of life which leads people into falsehood
Lied to from the beginning of their existence
Rapid eye movement might have the key for us
Explaining what may be the reason of our survival
Immense generations passing down their genes
Confinement, which will be, kept no more
The Lion God will one day understand all
Making the Bull God jealous in his way
While the eye of Ra will keep a look out for us
Seeing all that there is ever to see which is hidden
So new beginnings will be made once again
Keeping the true blood lines pure of knowledge
A secret that will be told to no one, except.

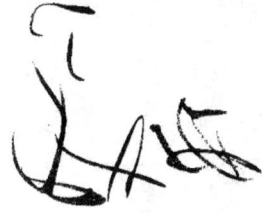

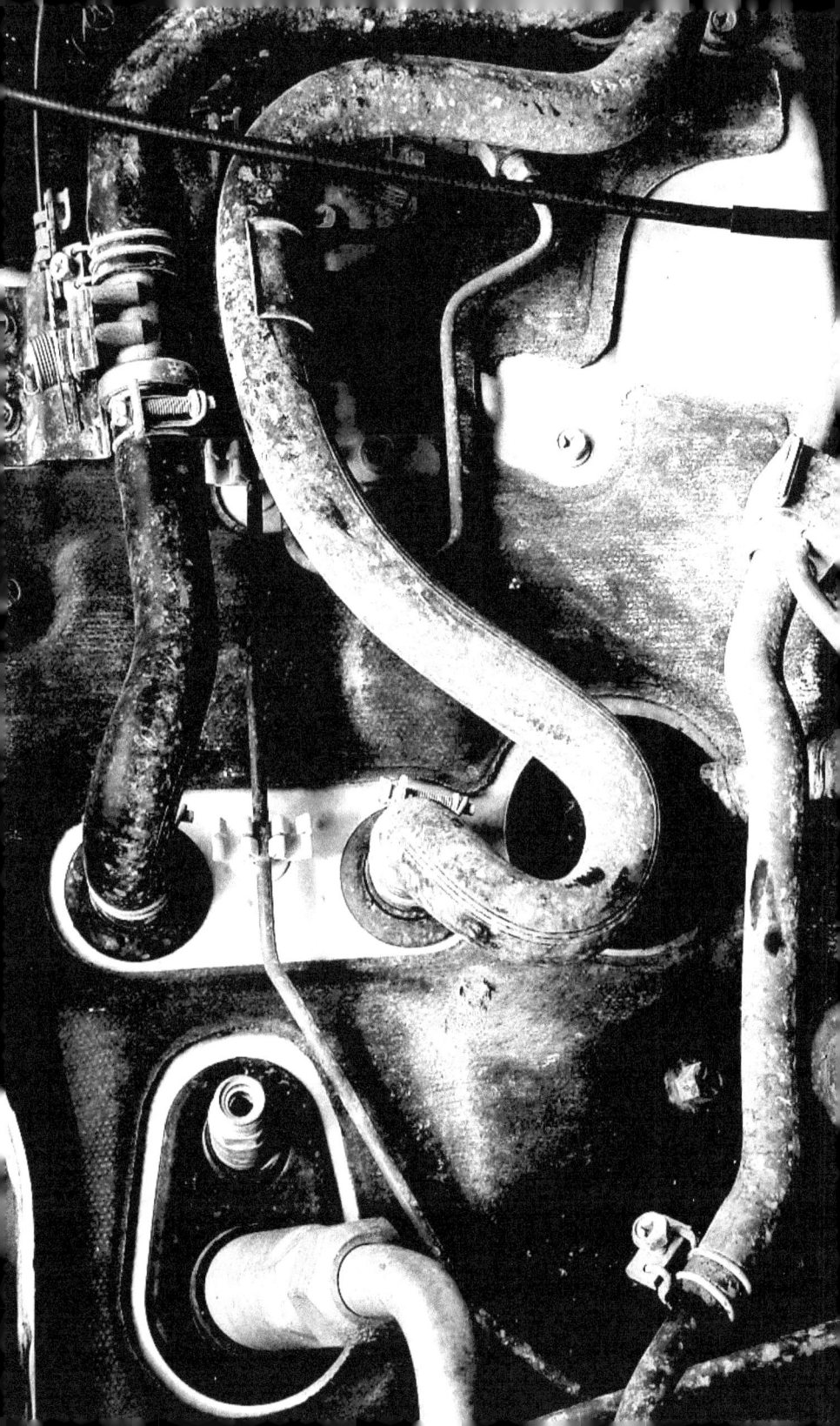

IN AND BACK OUT

Deep rooted cracks in our time which has been taken
A drop of rain pours out of the sky like a lost child
Crashing about the land hoping to one day be pure
A great river of life flows to the abyss of a molten core
Extinguishing the instinct that leads us into another
Which path will be chosen resides in the dragon
For the neon bird holds the key to the dragons decision
Only she can open the crushed pearly white gates
Which are incased by a moat made of dying flesh
Sores that rip the skin of a once beautiful frog
Breathing the toxic air makes the inside become one
Paths of flowers open the air to the Mayan spirits
Seeping from within the dense forest which hides them
Steam rises from them filling the air with toxins
Dribbling through dense clouds, the flowers begin to turn
Paths which even the Mayan spirits do not take
For if taken outside will become in, and back out
Breathing toxic fumes from open sores of ripped toads
As we drink the sludge of a moat floating with flesh
Will this open a gate of pearls which has been crusted
A pile of feathers glow with neon as a bird grins
For she points the way in which life is ready to take
As smoke rises from the instinct that's been extinguished
Molten lava from the core flows into the river of life
The crashes will start to leave scars which help to be pure
A lost child is covered by the drops of rain which poured
Cracks of deep roots begin to fill with water of the unspoiled
Time is taken when the Gods begin to drink the taste within
Their hunger is what fuels the engine which runs them
Filling the air with the fumes that choke our society deep
Revealing the mask which hides us from all wrong doing.

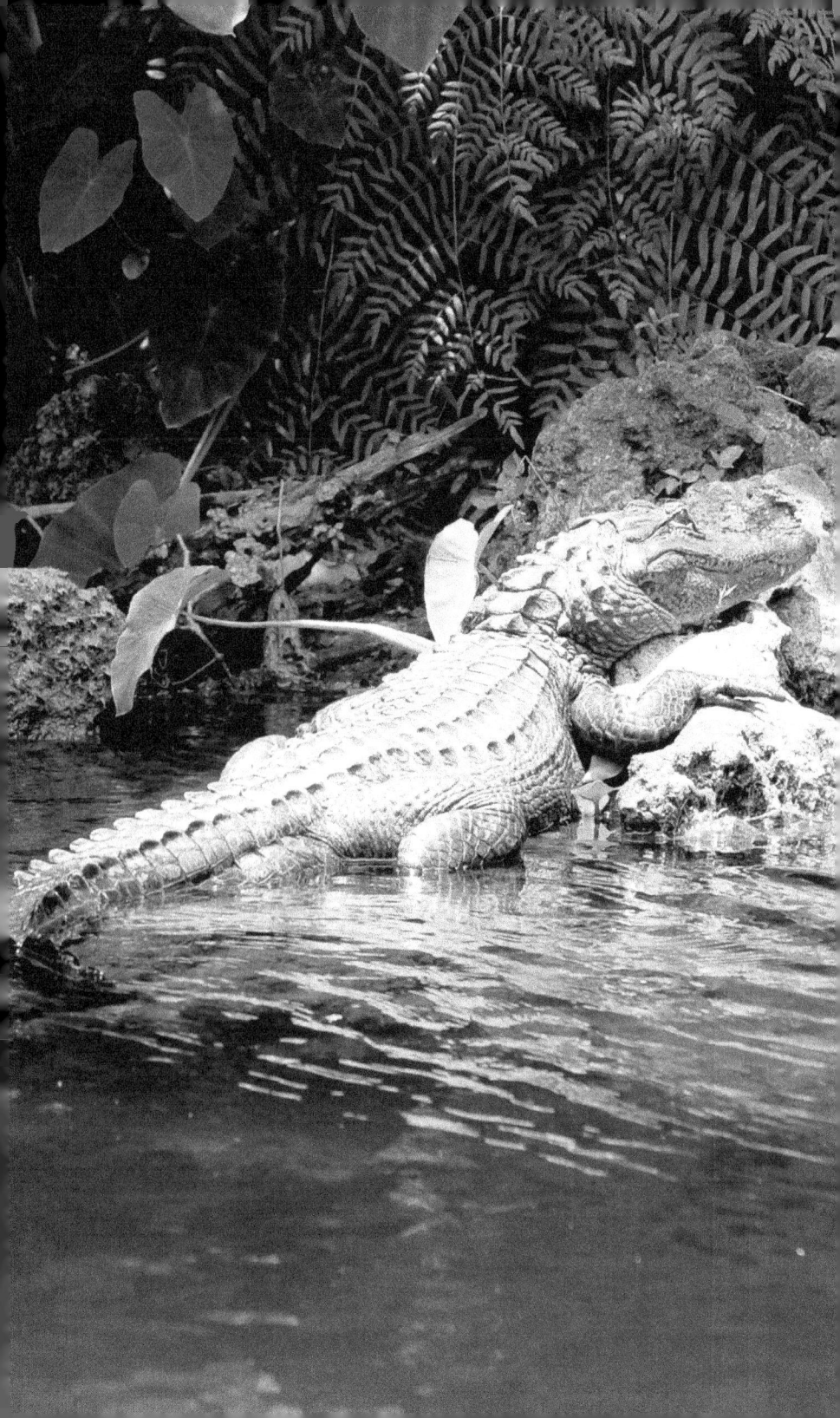

JUST A DANCE

Pillars hold the substance of a massive brain
Goo drips to the floor to splatter its green gel
Creatures scurry in fear of being washed away
The fuzzy hippo runs to the glowing source
Tripping the alligator as it passes with smooth skin
The two ambient creatures fall into their graces
Worlds stop in place as the two share a moment
Rose petals fall from the pink clouds above
Covering the ground with its sweet freshness
The two new lovers rise together, eyes locked
No words need to be spoken, only expression
Horns of great power play in the heavens
Violins play as the wind pushes the lakes current
Low soft drums rise from the surrounding forest
Their dance begins with a step and a brush of the cheek
To their surprise, they hear a loud massive crash
The brain has fallen to the floor of glowing goo
They must have bumped the pillar in all the excitement
A loud crash of heavenly lighting startles them
Hail replaces the rose petals from the heavens
Soft music is replaced with a horrible roar
The lovers world has been crushed in an instant
They thought their love would overcome all
The poor hippo dropping to her knees in disgust
As the alligator saw this, he had an epiphany
What if he placed the brain back upon the pillar
Then maybe chaos would be restored among them
And with that he heaved the mass up over his head
With a loud plop the brain was given it's existence
Order was bestowed upon the creatures of myth
The alligator was declared king among the many
And happiness was given back to the lovers
Who danced in eternity to the heavenly music.

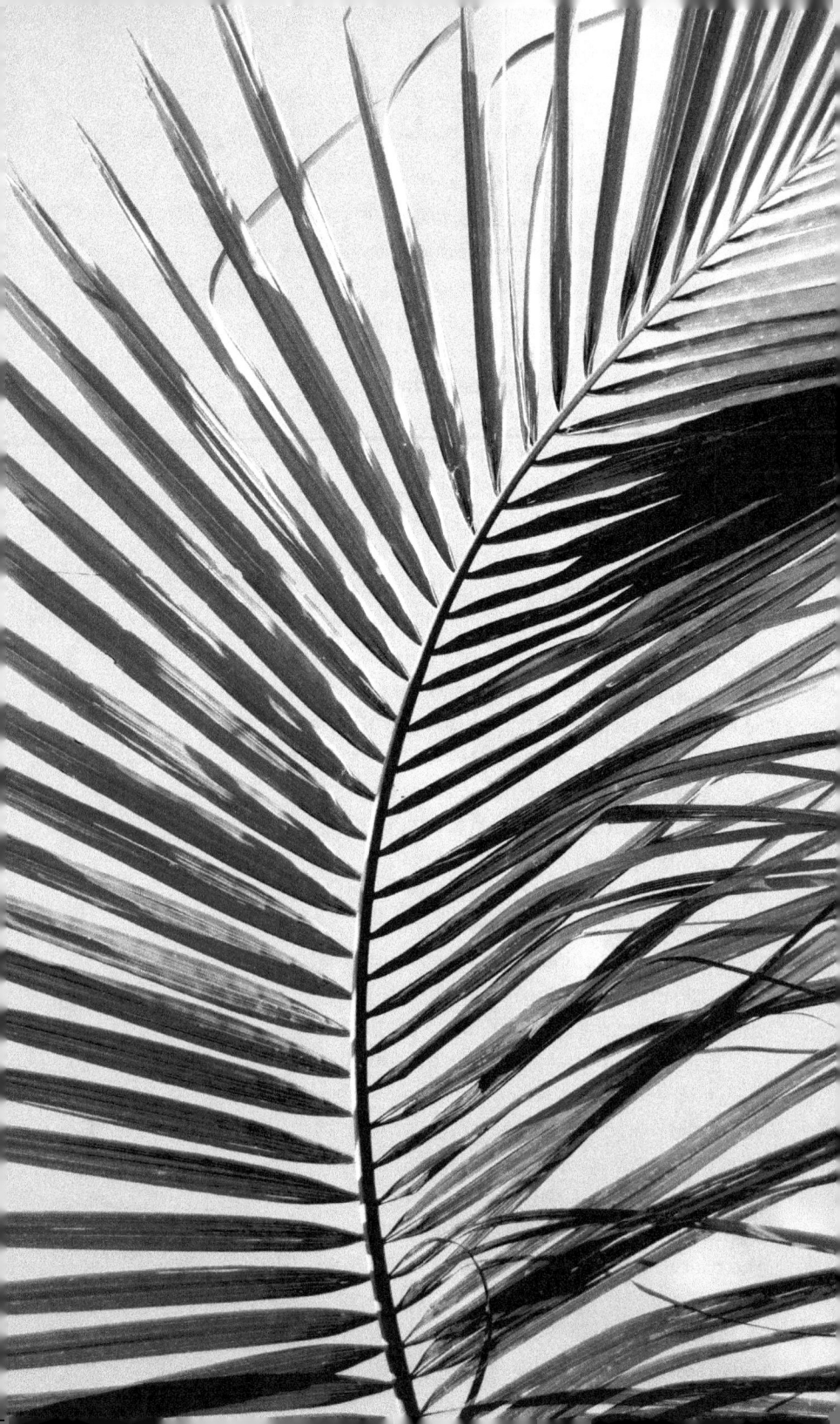

JUST FOR US

Elastic resisting against every sudden movement
Snapping back the grotesque reality of the womb
Birthing an image of a once metallic supreme
Gods of silver demanding the innocent lie guilty
Realizing the truth of a lie once told in secret
Walking on crutches being held up by the world
Spinning about lost in glaciers of a galaxy once seen
Sight which blinds the massive stone forest people
Humans froze in time amongst trees of the tropics
Rain forests, which harbor the cures of great illness
Sickness that plagues the mortals of a forgotten planet
Orbiting around asteroids carrying a song of a bird
Singing warning signals to ward off the unwanted
Like outlaws sitting next to a pool of reflections
Bound by mirrors which show the world nothing
An emptiness filled with light and undying love
As two beings collide leaving nothing but a wild child
Growing up to realize the truth of our living
People going from day to day running in the race
But who will be the one to make it the greatest
Like a speeding train headed for the rails at end
The end will only show us the truth of man
Only then will we use our minds to understand
The knowledge which will set our minds free
Free like the birds, which grace us with their song
Singing wondrous melodies for the masses to hear
Like a soft moving wind chime blowing in the breeze
Cooling the dense land with a smile of joy
A happiness that spreads across the horizon
As the sun creeps up to greet the moon
Glowing in haste to show off its light
Warming our cool skin as we watch
Seeing that this was made just for us.

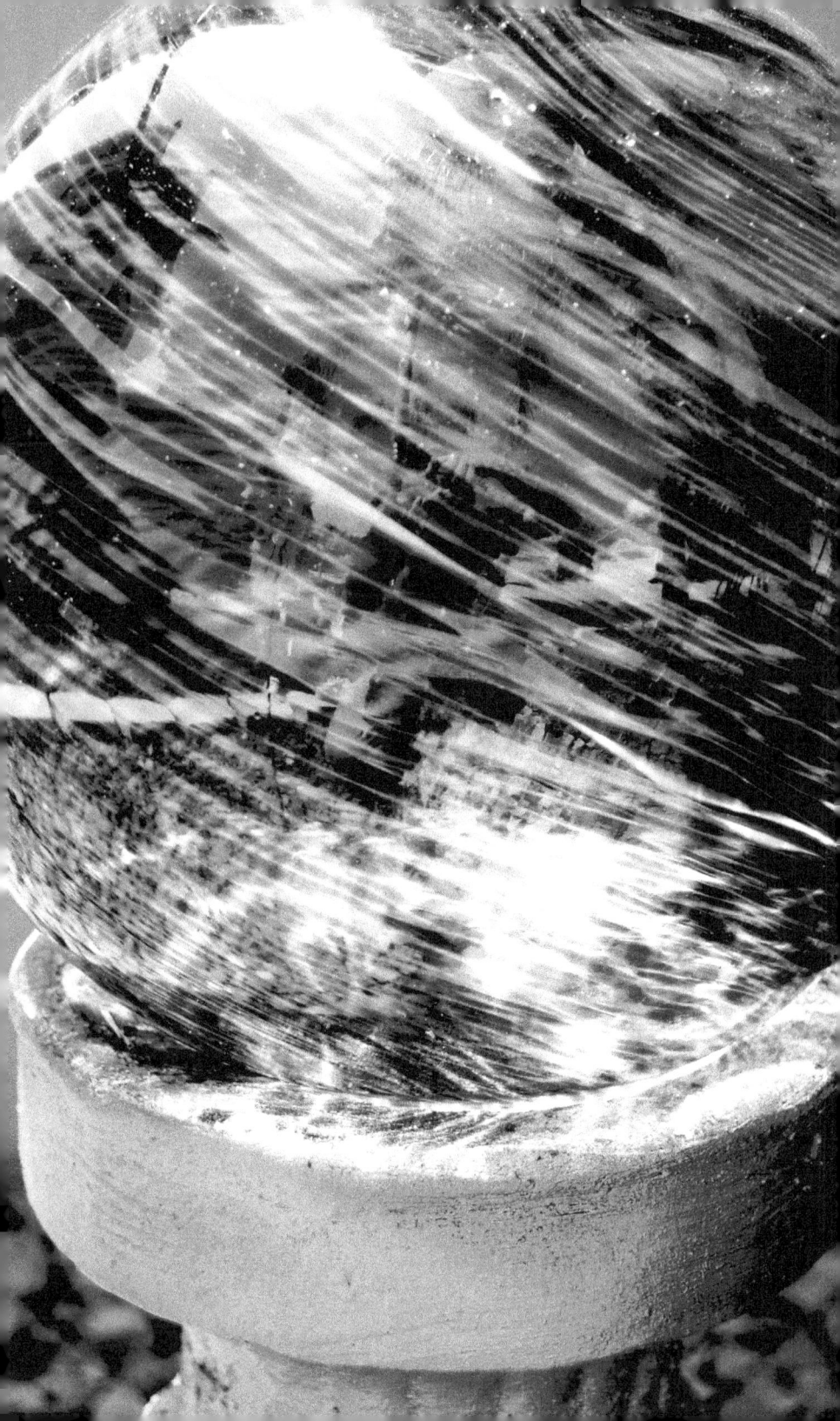

LIGHT RAIN

The rain is starting to seep through the cracks
Filling bottomless waste at the top of a whole
When will it begin to overflow causing disease
Famine will be the death of all nations united
Only then will the truth be set free to know
An angel shares her song to help understand
Her smile helps to soothe the chaos not known
Questions of anger confuse the threatened
Making a false reality come to know the truth
Holding a ball of flames in sleeved covered arms
Igniting the idea that we are what we make
The waters level is rising as we wait in haste
Packages bringing gifts of devastation of faith
Keeping the winning team ahead of the game
Once lost, kept in a secret book of knowledge
Hidden in the sunken city of beauty and grace
Pushed to the limits of a scene gone to far
Mass destruction is the fatal blow of any army
Like a pain in your chest, which aches to death
A princess and a queen gallop by waving to the God
Cries of a child whose world has been crushed
Causing forgotten mothers to express their anger
Suffering is the human nature of a soul, which bleeds
The blood now flows between the mighty cracks
Overflowing waste of disease fills the bottomless
Death of a flame is spread across the nation
The truth is now set free letting all know it
Songs of angels begin to fade, leaving silence
Her beautiful smile is lost amongst the darkness
Answers are giving to a false reality, yes the truth
The ball of fire has gone out with the idea
Water has now risen to the level of fate
A new gift of showing love to which only light will be born.

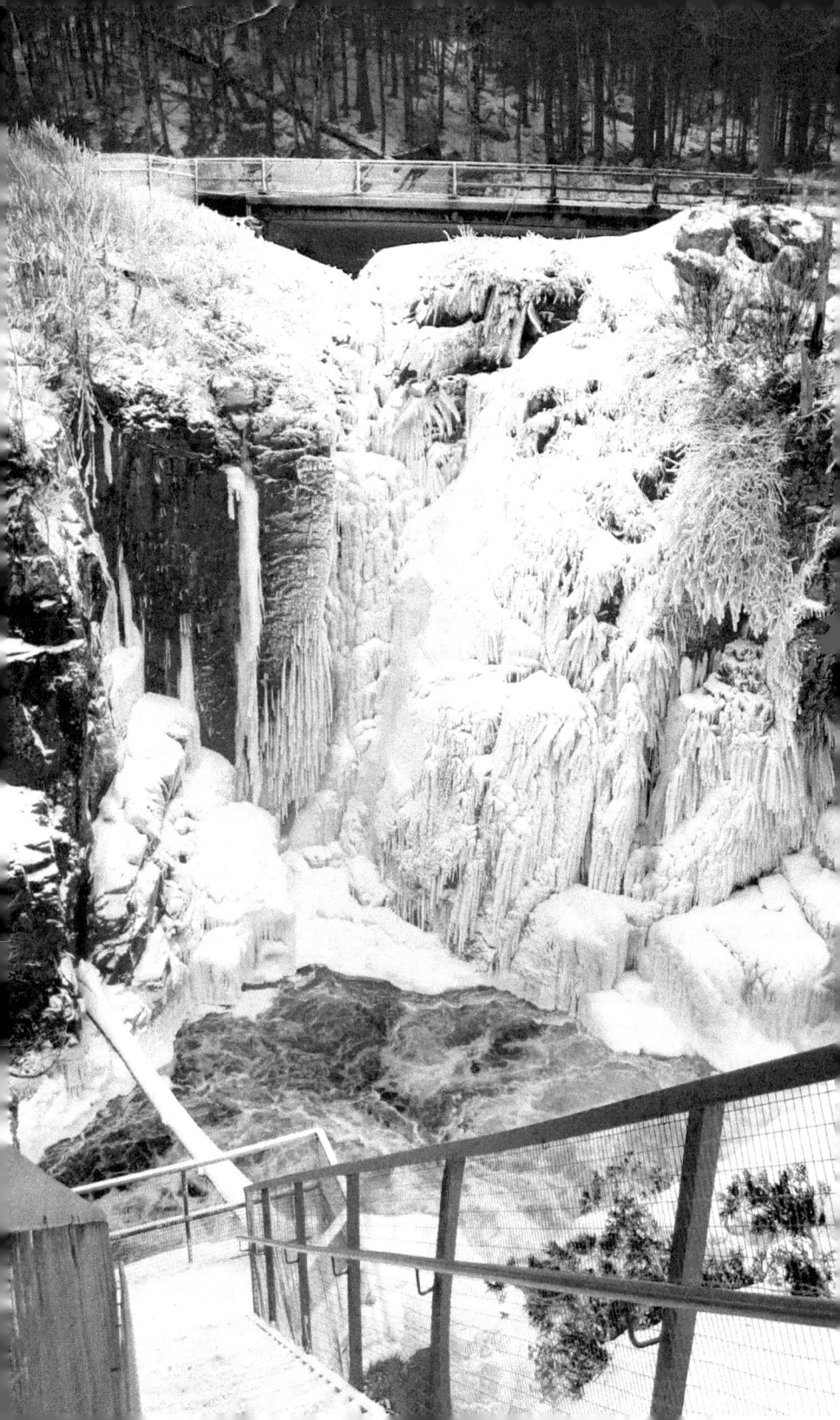

POOL OF GEMS

Angel of beauty in blue so soft and pure
Sitting by pools of gems on an island once lost
Surrounded by luscious trees which protect her
Vast arrangements of orchids sit on both sides
Gazing at her book of knowledge she reads
The calm wind blows her sweet scent through heavens
Carried like the chariots of Gods that once ruled
Looking for the rays to darken her soft skin
The gems of the pool dance on her glowing body
Catching the attention of Gods who watch
Flowers bend not knowing which way to turn
For the angels glow is brighter than the sun
Drinking the orange nectar of a forgotten fruit
She stands now to say good bye to the pool
Gems which glow so intensely off the horizon
A grace which exceeds the minds of mortal men
The breeze helps her tender stride as she passes
As if to be floating on the clouds drifting above
The angel's remembrance is left by a simple note
Hoping to cross paths on a journey of faith
Now sitting amongst the dense forest she writes
Witnessing one of the fables once told today
A myth of the goddess Bethel, who sat amongst the gems
Only by true coincidence did eyes ever meet
A path followed not knowing the true end
Statues of huge mortals marked the entrance
A gate of white ivory surrounded the gem pool
The light of the heavens shines to the source
Reflections that cast a sparkle of light
Glowing around the beautiful goddess as she laid
So if ever you come across the angel in blue
Do not approach, for she is to gentle
Just wait in graces to admire her presence.

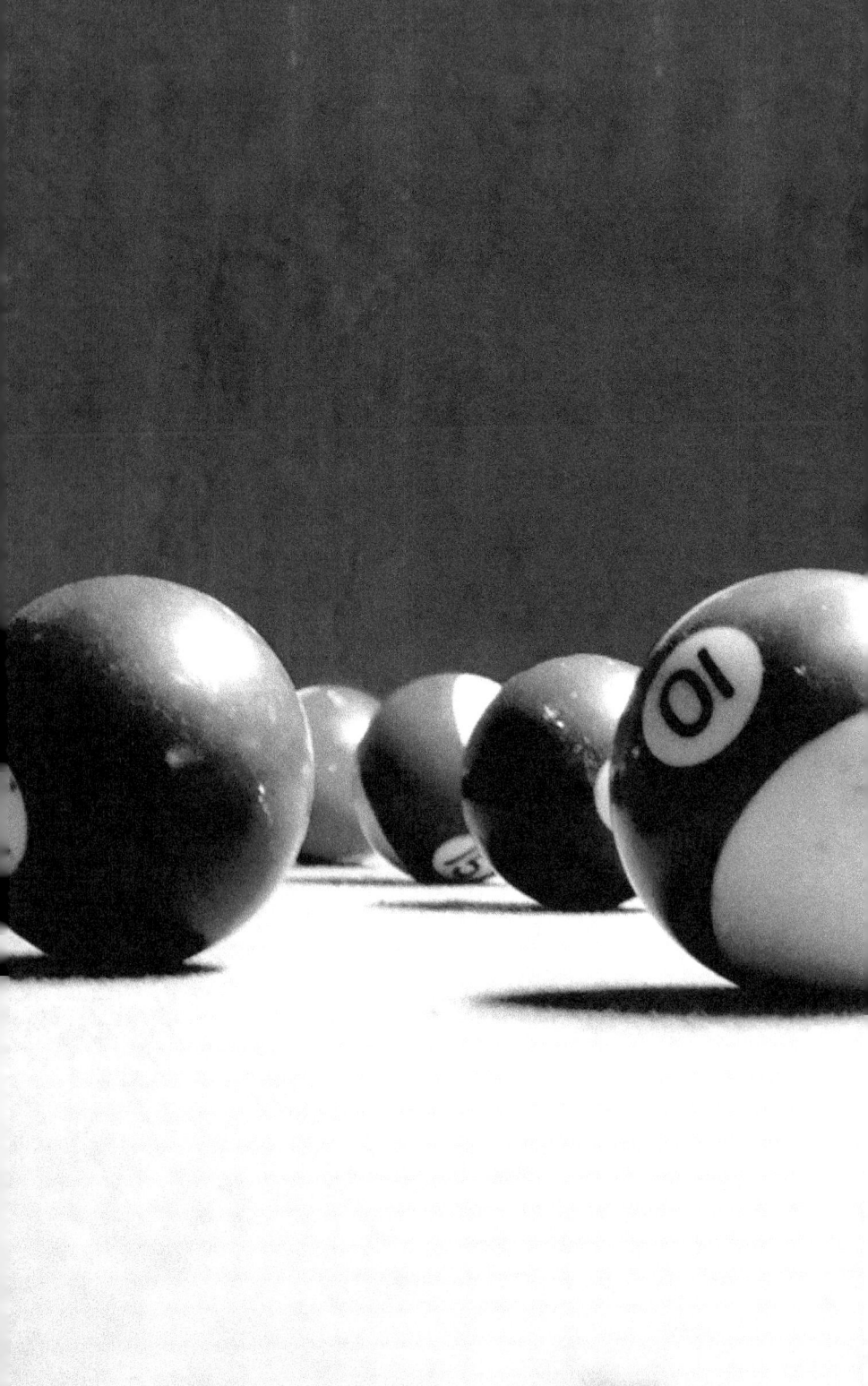

SAME OL FRIEND

The waking hour is like an illusion
There has been a beautiful conclusion
When you hear the birds in the morning sun
It's time to say the night is done
It was one of those late nights again
Must have run into that same ol friend.

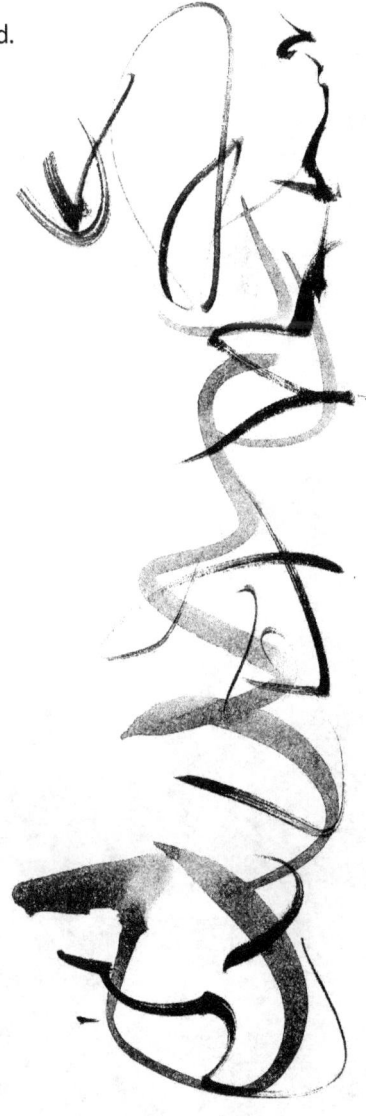

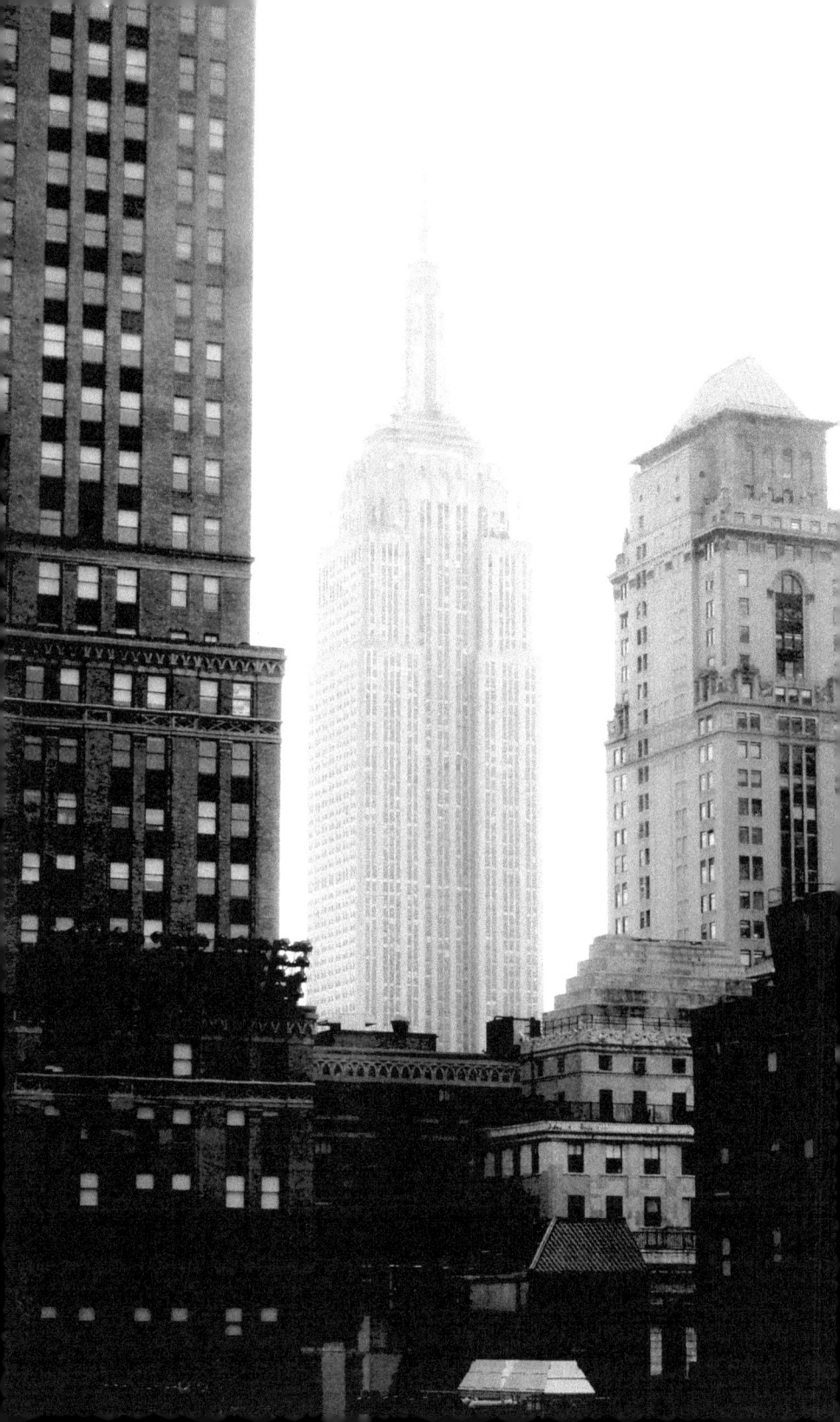

TO BE FILLED AGAIN

The abyss of a shallow dark glowing puddle
Thunder shakes the leaves from their holders
Crashing to the ground they miss the puddle of glow
Star cut diamonds fall to the earth with confusion
They ripple the glow of the puddle in endless just
Seconds pass by letting reality know its about to stop
A strange light reflects its sparkle in the distance
The tree sees the light coming, leaves turned out
Hoping to shelter the glowing puddle from demise
Diamonds help to fill the puddle before the light
Growing in size like a flower looking for the sun
The shallow puddle gleams in the depth of its holder
Radiance from metal holders overhead begin to flicker out
Light begins to move closer, leaves are fully turned
The glowing puddle turns a different shade which to glow
Once star shaped now turning to a smoke of morning
Wandering about hoping to meet damp leaves
They drink the moisture as if it was their last sip
Hunger lies deep inside the thick of the holder
In the rings that wrap the past of our lives
The light moves closer as if time never stopped
A sweet dew is spread across the land of darkness
For light has showed us the face of warmth
Bringing with it the sacred desire for life
Fresh beginning has arrived in this time of dawn
Showing the world a new start is around the corner
Glistening off the water which glows so bright
The heat begins to diminish the puddle of glow
A steam brings a mist of pleasure to the land
So calm in the silence of a brand new day
The many creatures sing their song of delight
Happiness fills our souls with love and respect
We have been given another beautiful day
To be filled again.

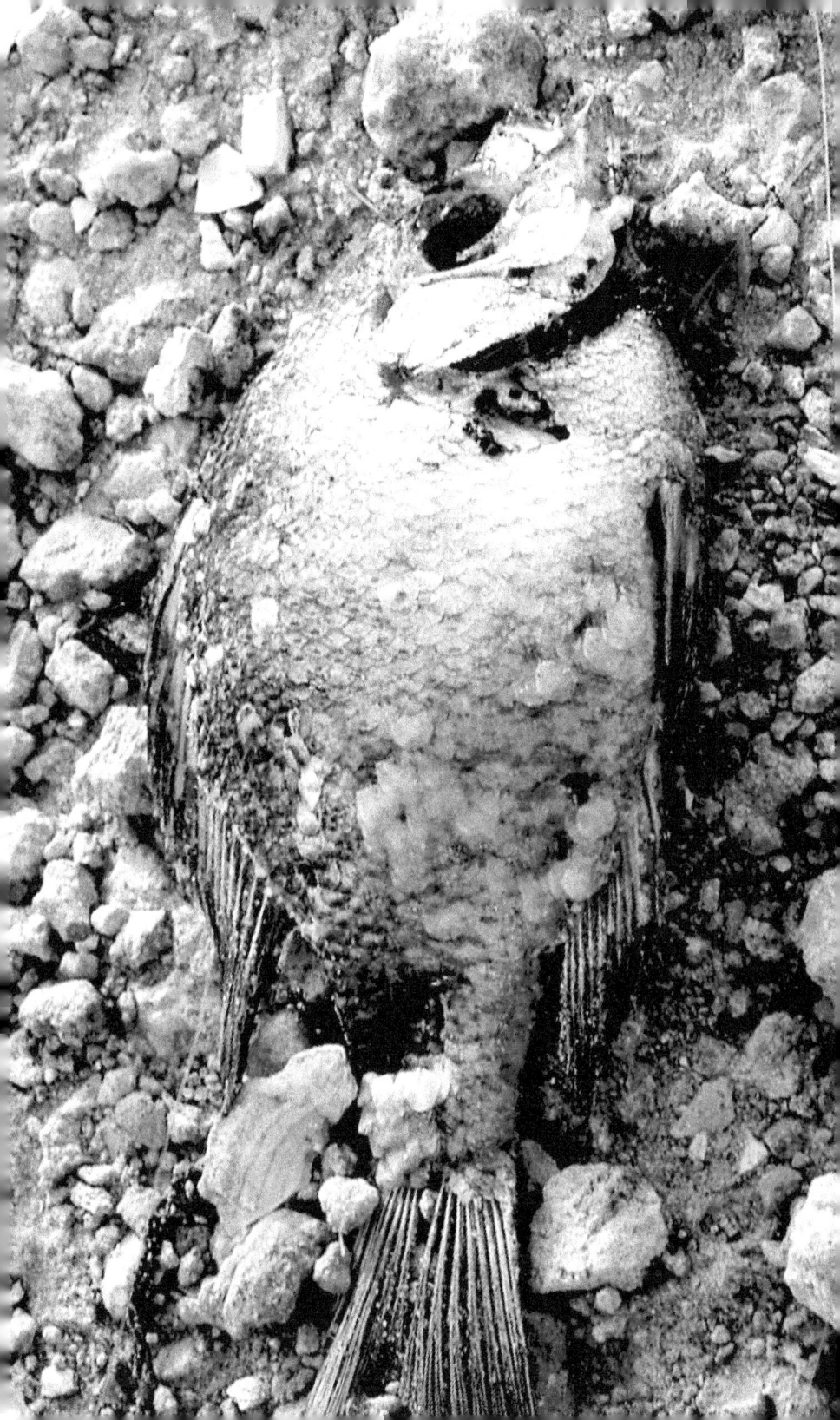

UNAU BEGINNING

Unau, the singled cell amoeba
Drifting in the tides of time that make us
Organisms collide making sparks of life
Like a sweet breeze pushes the flowers
Bits of existence are blown to the next destination
An instance of life has begun its journey
The knights of shining light spread their love
Through the chemical reaction a beauty is born
Making death seem as if it would never be
Scents of powerful nectar fill the air
Overwhelming the senses we poses
Almost setting the world into an endless motion
Gestures of devotion scatter in the sky above
Hoping to pacify the land of this great siphon
We become skeptic in the fables told
Is the eye of Ra really watching over us
The sphinx seems to point in the right direction
Shadows make up the birth of Venus by dust
The twinkle of the reflection off the great stones
Gems reveal their beauty only to be hidden
Lovely smiles are marked by their lies
Cupid still seems to be shooting his arrows
Changing the way people seem to understand
Trying to except the impurities of our being
Hoping not to erupt the ozone of emotion
Amplified by the silence which keeps all open
The trauma of our soul is a great travesty
Where the valediction of us and creator is made
Volcanoes begin to emit a new beginning
The ground is covered with molten heaven
A yellow flower emerges from the dark rock
A new era of life has arrived to start again
Nothing with which we have, will ever end.

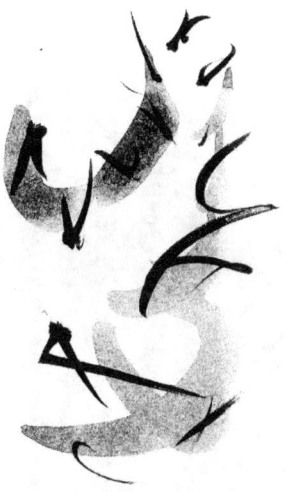

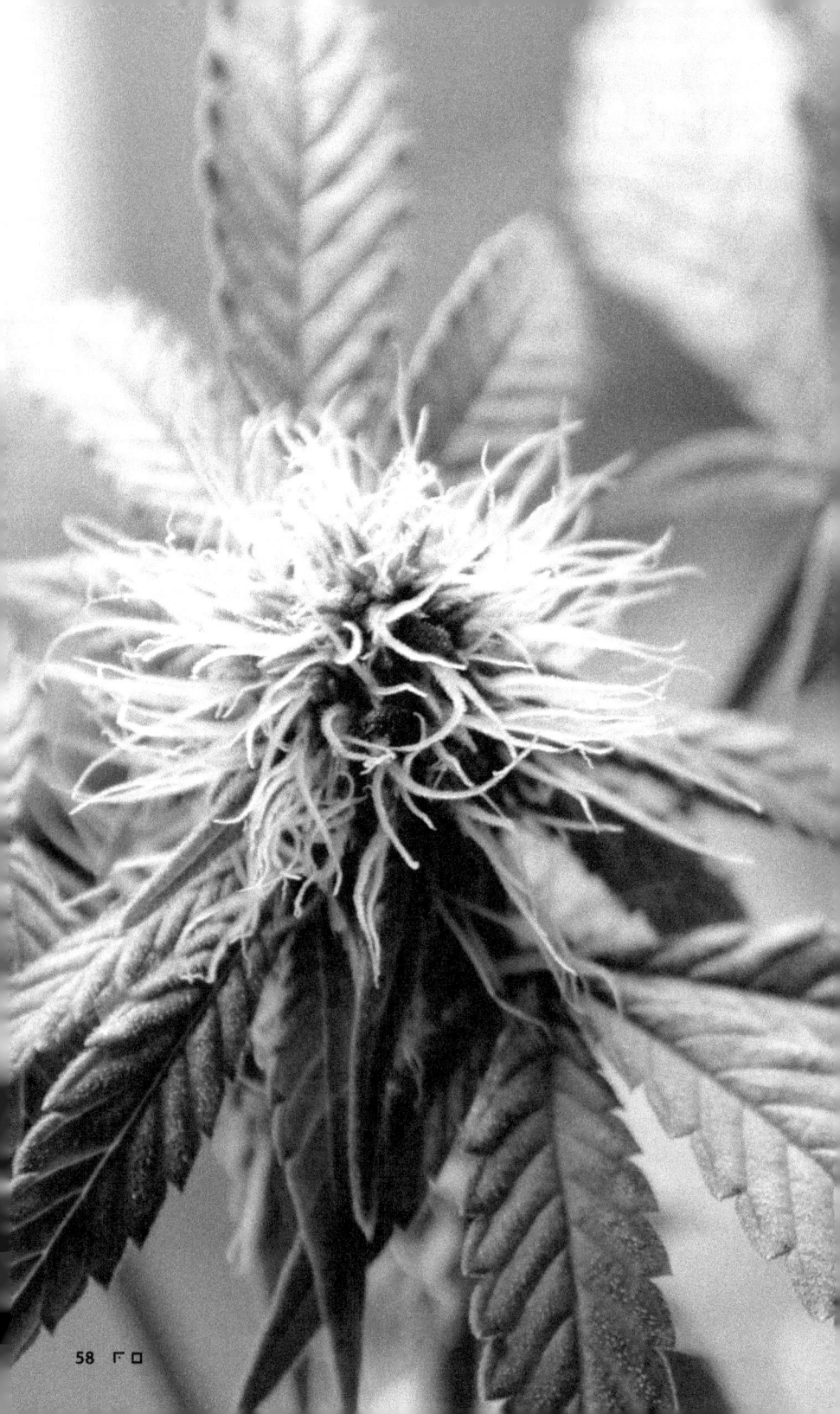

THE BLACK BOOK
THE FIRST WRITINGS EVER MADE

Dwayne M. Adams

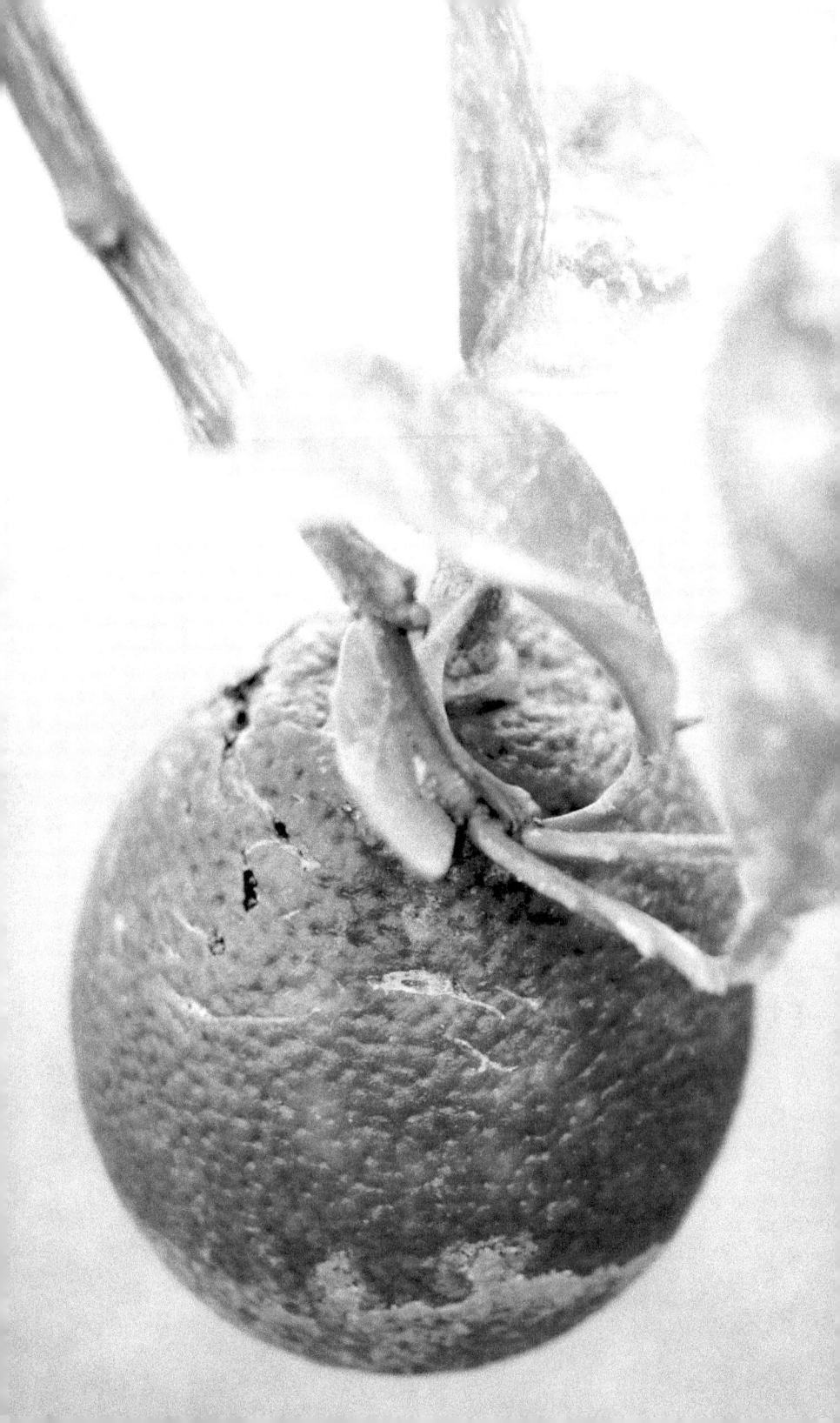

EXCHANGED AMONGST

Exchanged like the north wind that has no dream
Brought about like stars that will never fall without a touch
Plucked like the endless leaves from the tree of life
Reflecting in the shade as to know what the warmth is
Showered by the resistance of a ill stricken society
Masked like the stories that help to explain
As if a darkness will ever understand how much the light means
Pushed away like the child who was never wanted
Banished to a land of men to expose his only ability
Is one ever lead in such a way to know where to go
Yet each is made to know the wrong path like no other
Asking is there ever such a reason one could have been
Slaved amongst men who know his truth but deny all
Changed are they as the breaking point is never made
As light explodes from a body of light to blind all watching
Making a thunder to shake the earth of movement
Pouring on rain of lost angels who cry without regret
Cooling the skin of a son to be made endless with love
An immense heat has risen to show its true nature of being
To baffle the minds of the weak to make sense
Yet still as a child who lies motionless like a lost puddle
This one makes an exchange of glances asking to say hello
For one will have his day to lead a path to our father
For meaningless rants have no place amongst them
Insight is the understanding that most will never posses
This is the truth of exchanges, making all except a fate held.

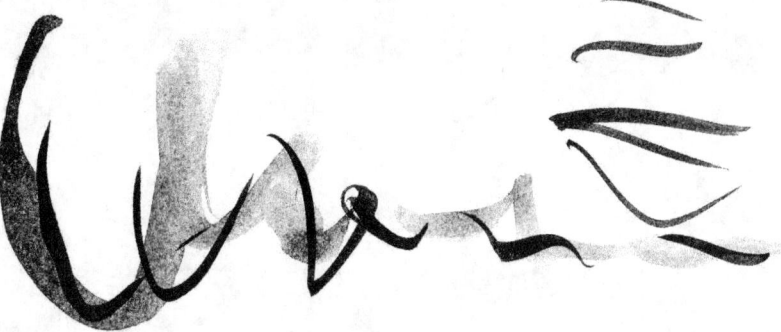

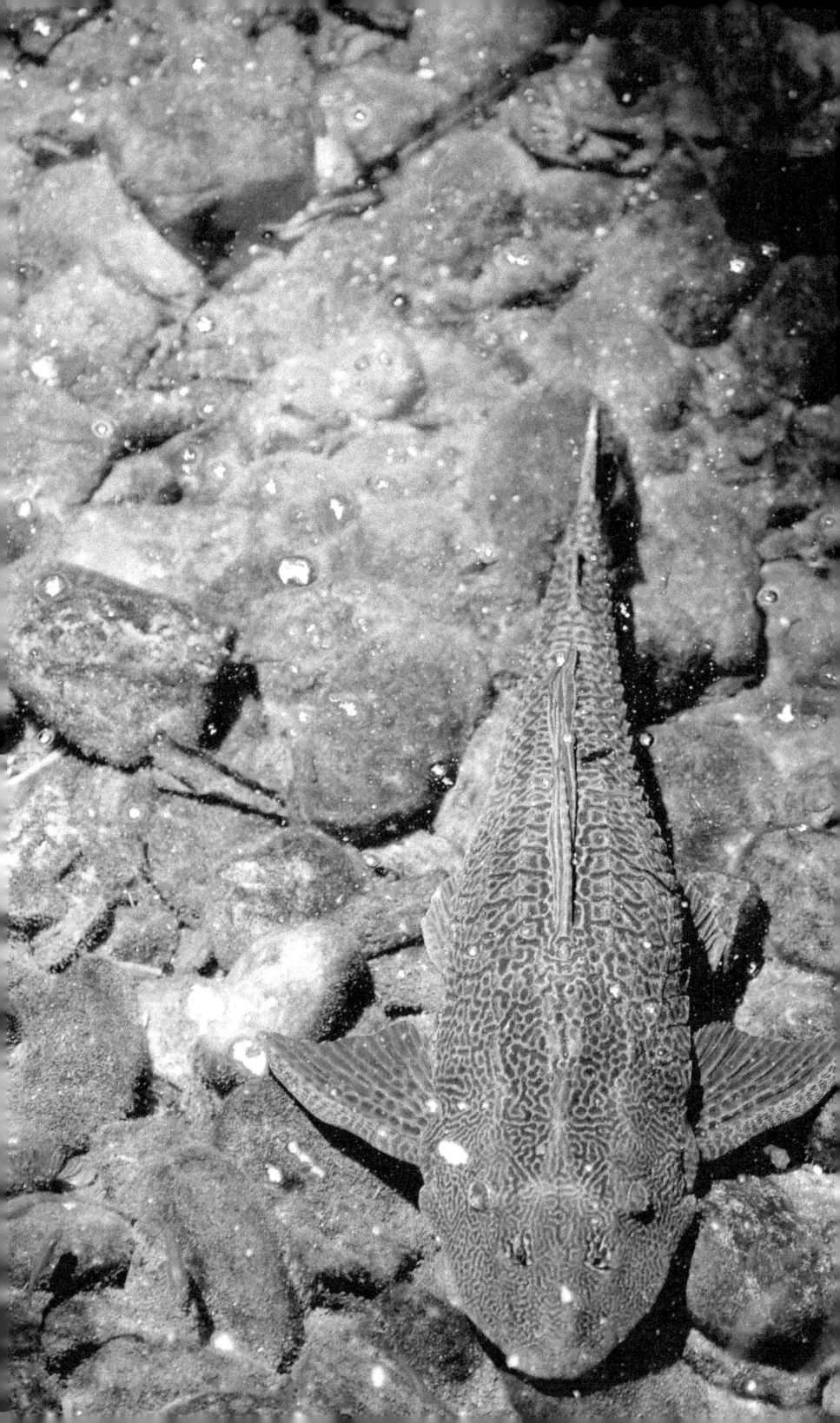

SQUARE CORNERS

Why does one ever even try
Like once lost in these dreams of know
As if tomorrow there is going to be some kind of change
There is only this dust with wind and no place to go
Do they not see this as they pass like birds in flight
Smiles which never seem to fade in a darkness like it has no hope
Only fighting to be an existence like no other has ever had
Arms crossed in this walk as to know which way to turn
Amongst it all is one who's hands never seem to slow
An endless mind that never seems to end
Sleeping is only the beginning of something we will never realize
Like sand which seems to slide through fingers of truth
Drums which beat in a distance can only bring light
Banging like the skins blood once did in their own life
Does one not understand the screams which are so loud
Does it sink with out ever even touching the surface
Has one been chased like the food of hungry mouths
Names which ring through these drums of an ear exposed
Lead like a stray animal only looking for comfort and warmth
Confused like an idiot which has never known anything else
Sitting in places which have no meaning to each other
Like lost memories of a blood stained hand reaching for life
As if to be a shovel filling these thoughts with moist dirt
Again the endless chase begins only to follow in the same circle
Like a square without any corners made of light.

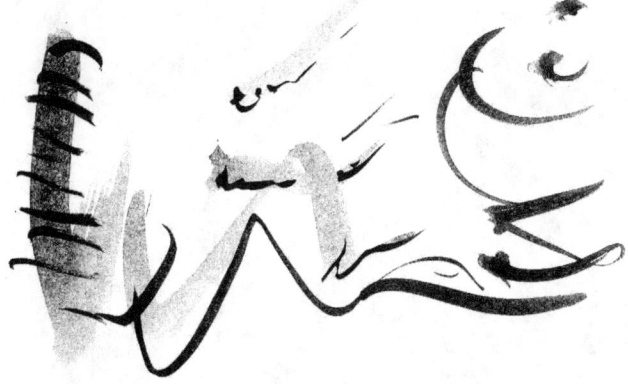

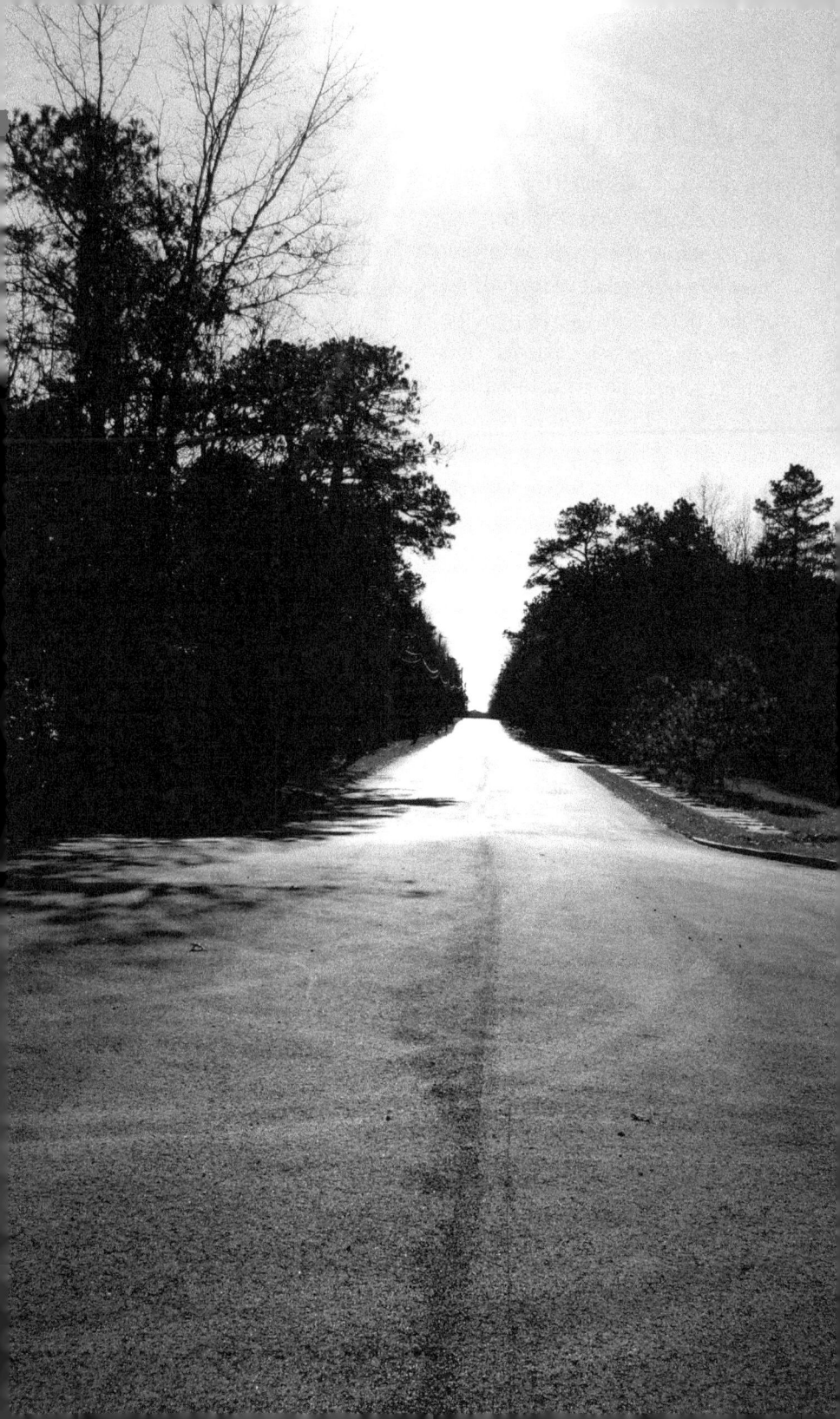

THE TRAVELS

The travels of a new comer are never with ease
The trails which lead to magnificent caves can move a city
Like a blind women who stops in an energy made still
Or a screaming man making sense for those who don't listen
Do these adventures lead to a knowing of existence
Does seeing one man times three in a week made of one count
This is the reason as to which most people pursue them
Asking to be placed amongst these undesired dreams
One sleeps as to bear the thoughts of looking through a window
Notice the reflections which cast shadows upon true studies
Writing as if to explain the truth of some unknown belief
Smooth as if to never say it will be rough without pain
Why do they fall with such anger as only they repress
Linger away do they who will not look beneath these layers
These rides are what makes them understand which way to go
They stay in undenied motion only to never see the real pleasure
Middle like there is no top with in a reach for most pullers
Like a string which seems to always slip away when wrapped
Explain this they say to them with no regard for their own lives.

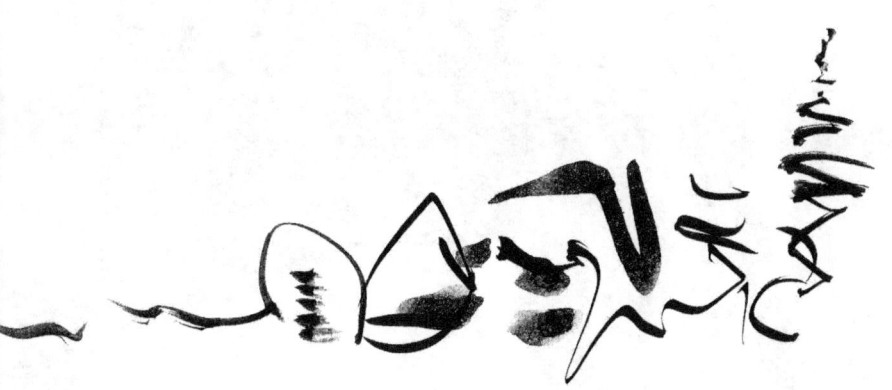

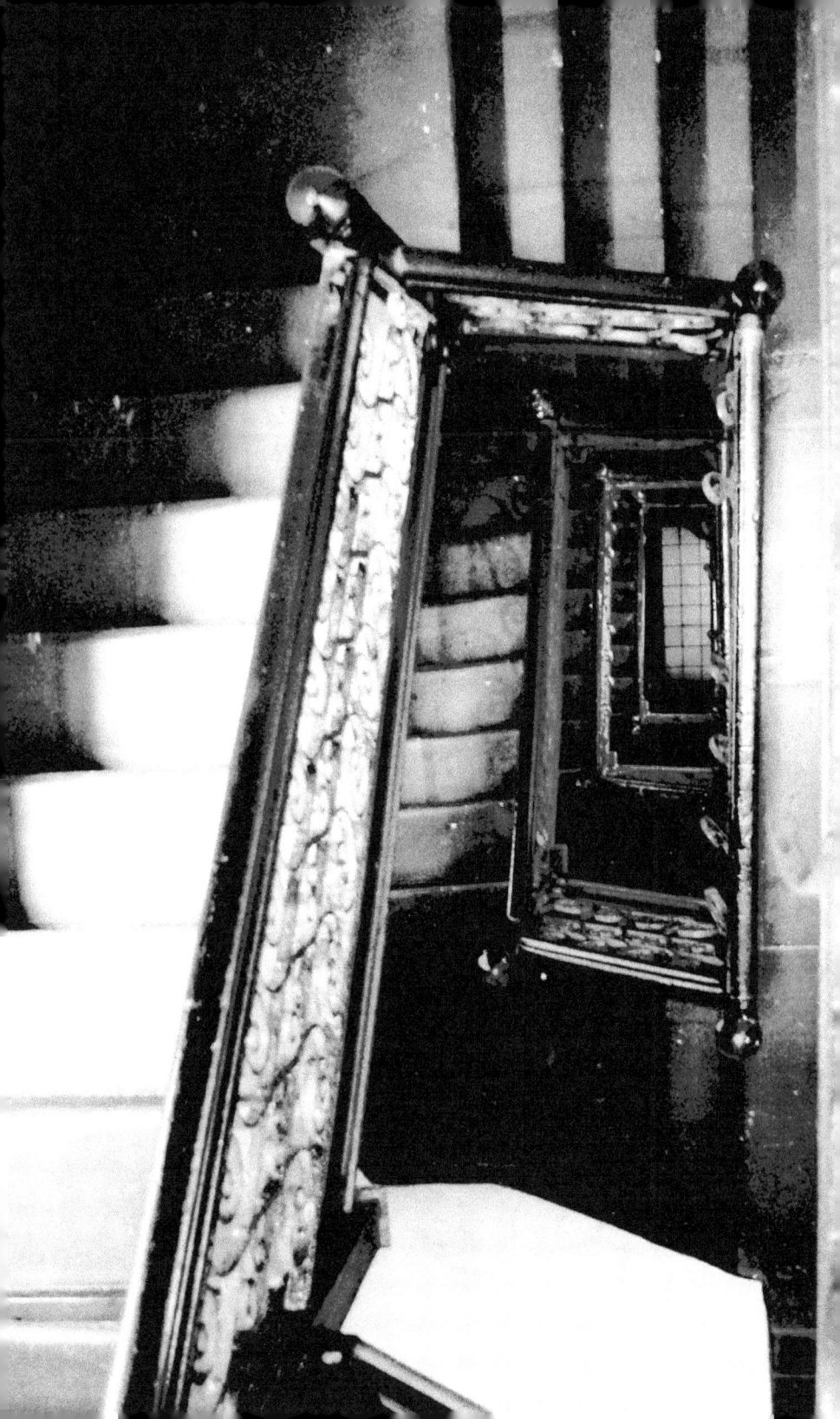

WHISPERS OF NIGHT

Bound by gravity which expels life
Kept in untouched air for all to see
Like a germ which is never meant to die
Voices which have no help against them
Asked to stay strapped only to feel pain
Secrets read amongst these tales of love
Reflections smashed against these thoughts
Angels give pose to those unseen meanings
Gliding over lights which seem so far
As if to cut air like its something we see
Does one feel anxiety of their moisture
Knowing only soft scents to make anew
Like a dream to be made only a reality
Stories of old ask to say no difference
Making unreal questions a past existence
Filled with passion are most never to feel
An anger as a blood can spill a truth
Feelings touched by motionless fingers
Checked only with a wind made of breath
Falling further are these whispers of night
Plagued by delicious sounds of love made
As if there was no pain to ever feel life
When does an extreme motion become seen
Darkness which can fill these eye of light
Precise as a rolling ball with no path
This is the truth of nonexistent reality made anew.

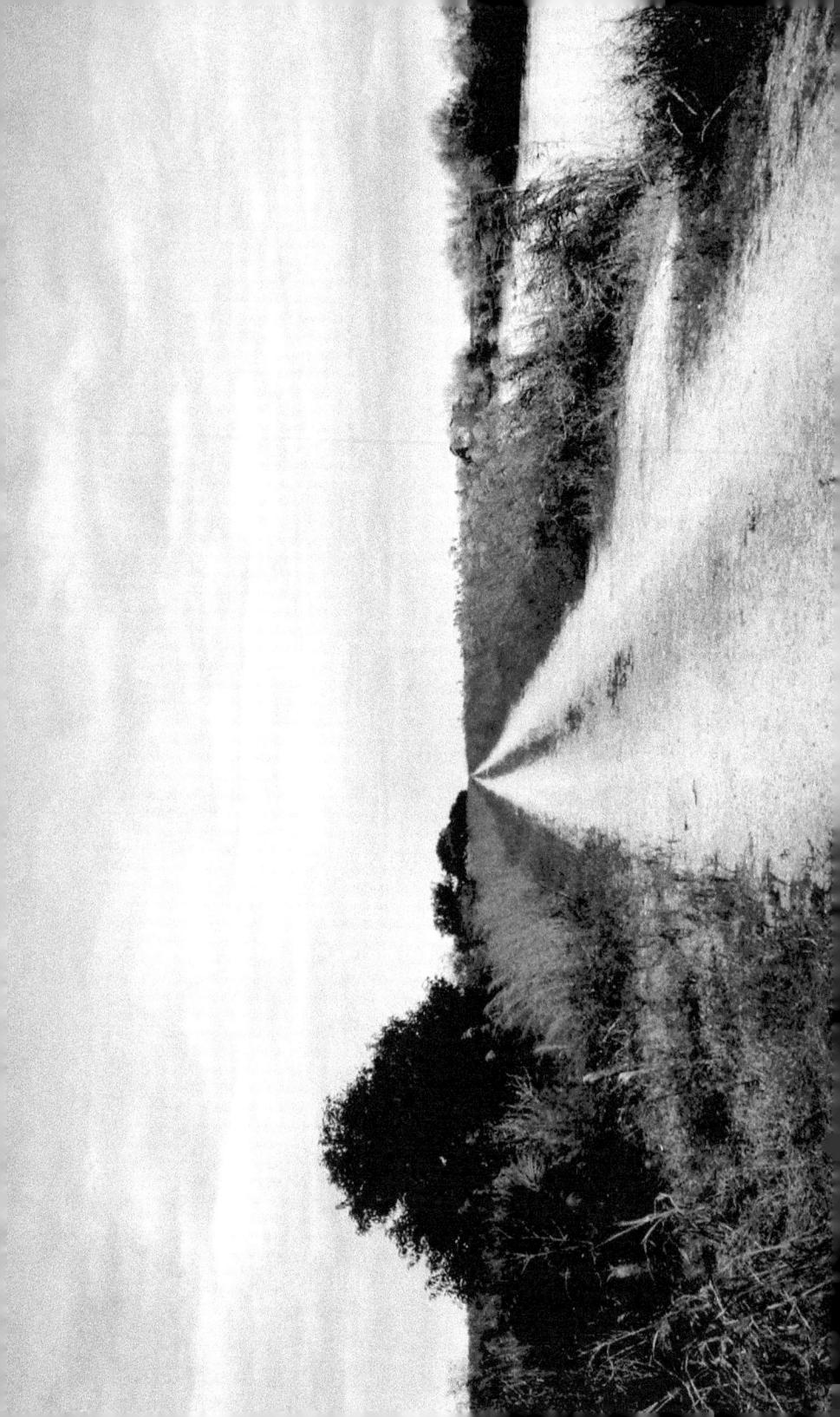

PATHS ARE MADE

Red velvet sand creeps up the stairs
A white crown molding enchants the glass
Held like a black tar which binds life
Smoke filled rooms which choke the flies
Like a sea of waves that move with the wind
Do the doors of humanity creek with pleasure
Or do lights show a way to villages on the D
Explained like broken splinters stabbing them
Blocked in killing most that enter wrong
Blazed like fires which only exist below
Released are the stains made to windows
Casting gruesome shadows upon the night
Does one not seek an angel amongst
Lost out in a world which has no regret
Making all knowing scared to know itself
Traced like the wind which pushes above
Cracks in an earth to never be sturdy
Dirt which fills the years of time
No comfort is to be expected for this
Only speed which was made to want
Send one upon this path to a truth
For an existence will be made known
Nothing is without loss to this day
Paths are made paths are taken again
Putting a trust before any that never ends
Making each journey that much more
For ease is something to never know.

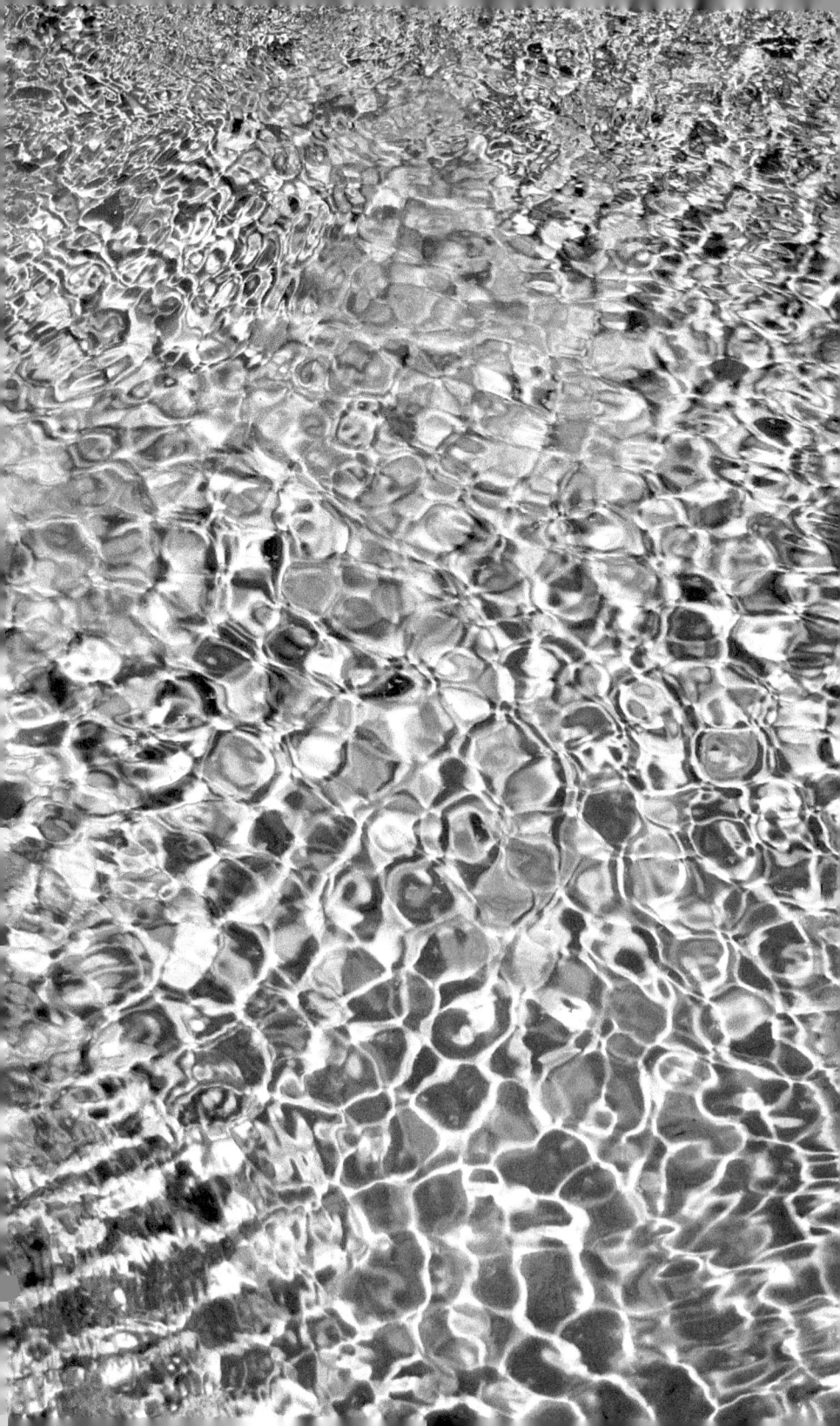

SWIMMING AGAINST

A peace has been made like a breeze
Lifting spirits as if to never worry
This makes dreams to know a truth
False ways pass like a stranger of old
Bags which are carried like lost whispers
Making a weight as if to have a back strong
To the arts these payments have been made
Only to hear that choices must be seen
A blindness which expels such a darkness
Like stones that bind these stolen fountains
Dreaming to only ever run in the sand
Lost escapes only used to confuse these
As if a leaf could ever push its own way
Using grounding force to challenge them
This helping to realize the travels of masses
Like a root that peaks through the cracks
Does this explain why stories are told
Desires which help never to understand
Releasing only scratches made in the clouds
As if a tiny traveler makes too big of steps
Swimming against headless fish to breathe
Shadows which move without notice again
Like orange trails which show patterns
Only to express the loss of begotten noises
Held like a brick that delivers its gates
Strong like the wings of a breath of stench
Clipped like the hair of a beauty of cities.

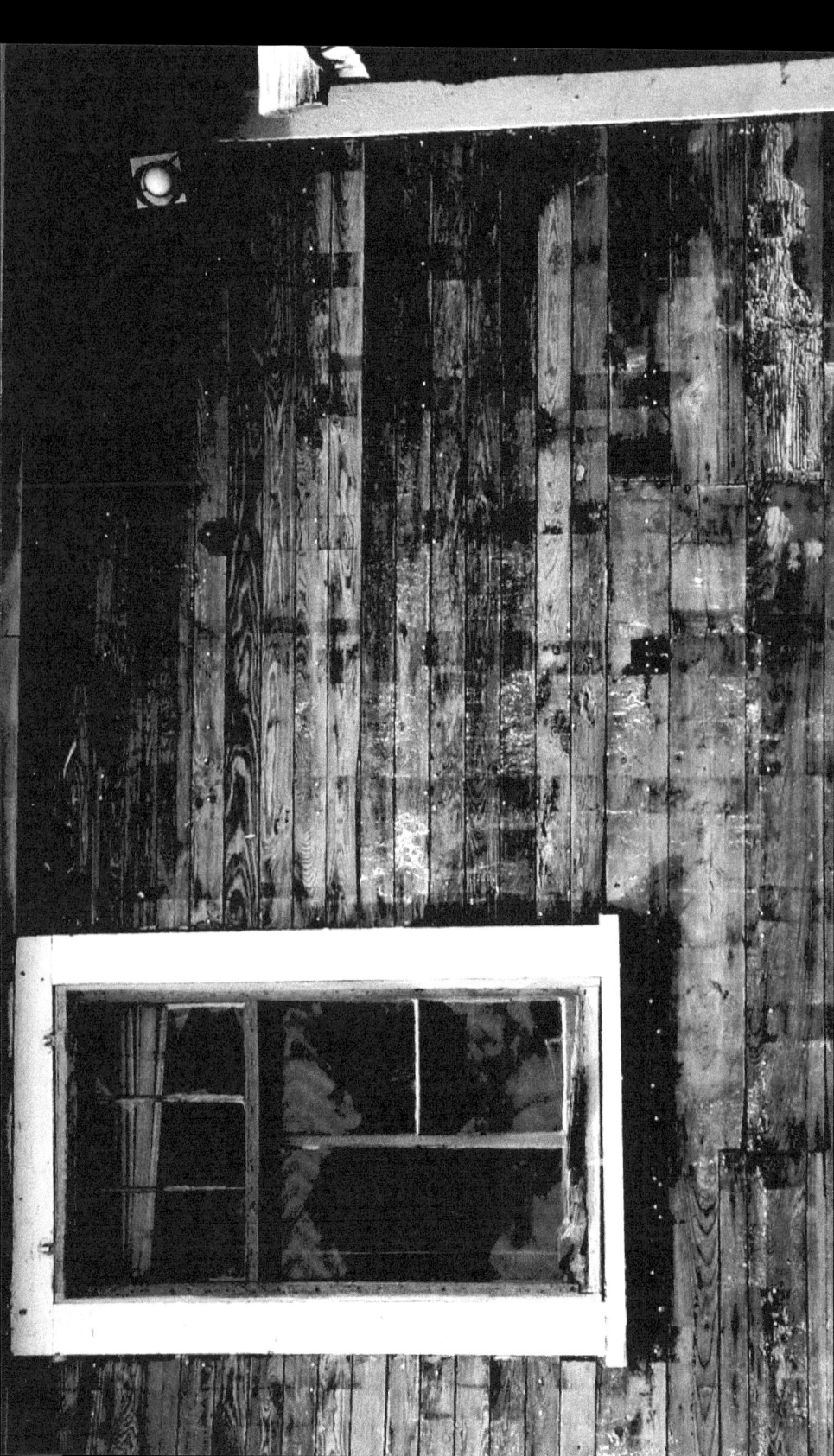

RAMBLE THAT FILLS

Once made a trick that helps to play games
Like a split shadow that has no end today
A sunshine flower that hides the water
Dreaming of an ant that plays against Asia
With these words that dance to strangers
Like a conversation that seems to quite
Exercising rights that were never theirs
Making green will help to explore
Like German tounges that speak to fast
Hung like a chain that binds the necks
With staring glances that shift to slow
Changing directions seem to know the way
Book of yellow with that direction of this
Like an angel on a stoop that holds no meaning
Held like a door knob that keeps them out
Locked like dreams that have true meaning
Endless is the ramble that fills most minds
Keeping clamor to that which clicks to hard
Like a skating ice that seems to hot
Pulled in between that which is made anew
Timeless clocks that seem to never travel
Like a restless rhino that steams into life
Or the spider of life that has no web of hope
Blue like the sign that tells of a childless past
As if history tells that which is not true
Only to realize that a breeze never blows
Except when noises that help are ever made.

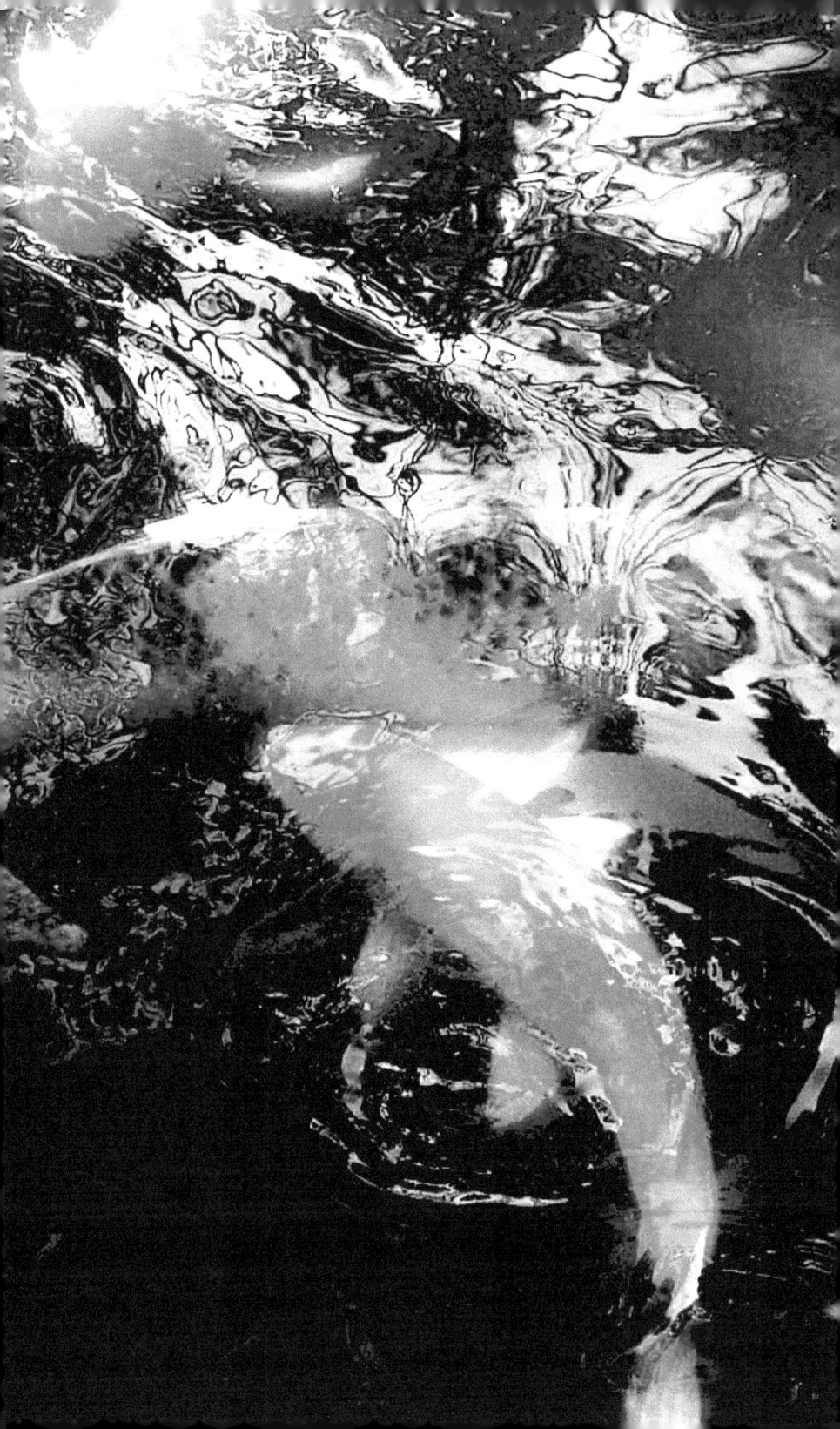

NO HEAT HEARD

A beginning to something that seemed no end
Banging walls like the headless that run
Taking away all that slowed endless spins
Released to make those ropes never held
Like a sleeping women that has no heat
With no responsibility except to live
Clutching to the skies for their guidance
As they rain down with the song of dance
Only to expose their true nature untold
Like the wind that pushes the leaves
Or the current that seems to know a puddle
Unlocked are they like the animals they are
Confused only to be lost of all imagination
Lost is what keeps all searching alone
To be made by a society masked by truth
Untold like the senses which become dull
Blamed only to make it worse by reality
This is what pulls forces into the unknown
A theory which has no excuse to tell
Held tight like the rest of life which is made
Only those inside will never have to know
Like that which makes rocks turn to sand
Or the rain which cleans, then turns to ice
These are what makes life seems so real
When does all seem to fake to play
As the motion that crackles in your ears.

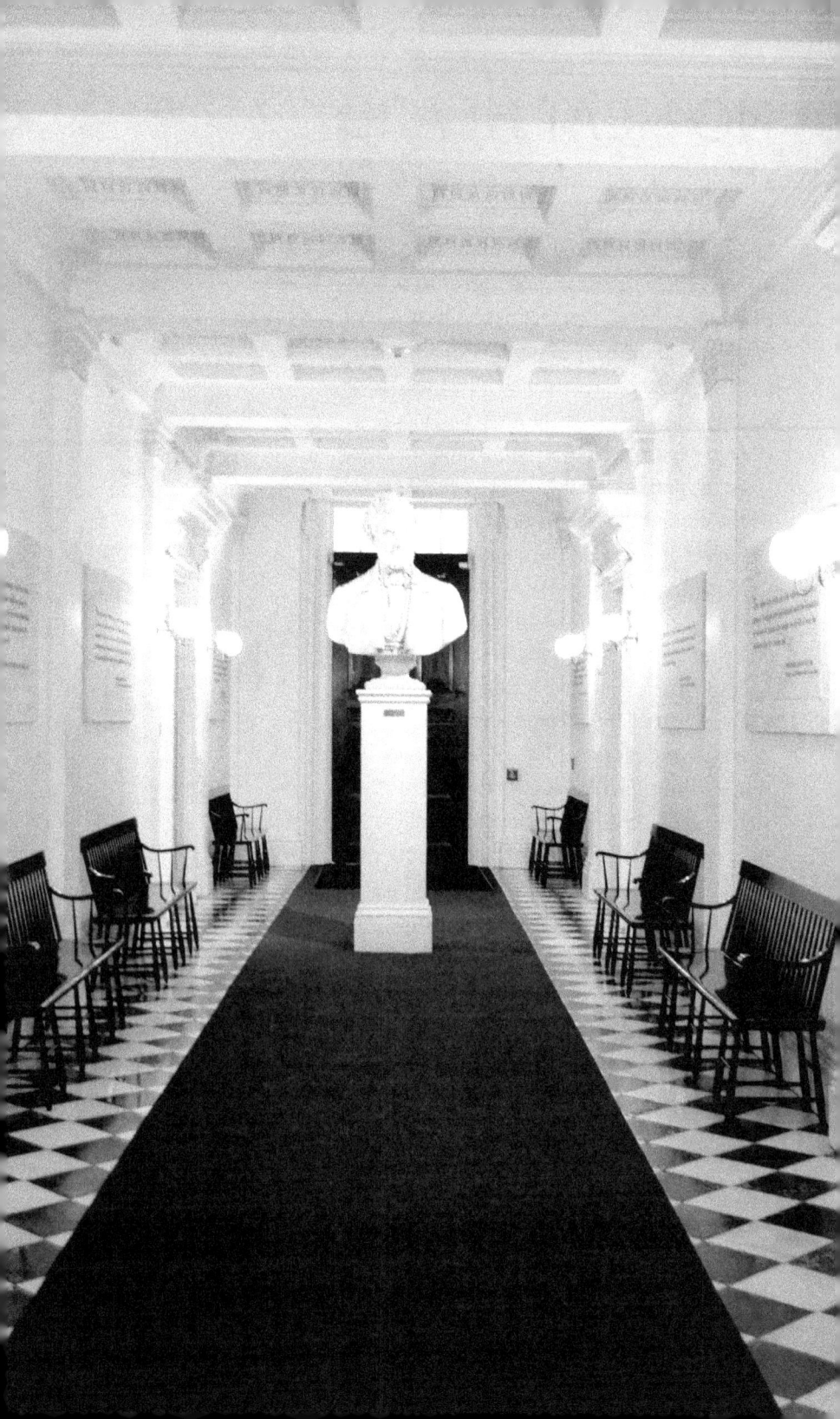

ESTRANGED EYES

Trips on lines with endless rails of confusion
Asking ways of hidden angels to tell a way
Like the cold which has no direction to know
Held tight with the soldiers who lead a stray
Only windows show such a truth of existence
Industrial like the shadows of clouds to play
Like a made table only to hold mistaken dreams
Each saying the words of another to express
So is each as to take a drag of the smart
Punching tickets to tell a time as to never pay
As a bell rings to let all now see that transit
Only the left behind will be able to canter
Like the passing bricks of a wall never cleaned
As the time of an hour seems to never end
Trapped like moving mice to be feed to the rats
These are what moves estranged eyes of life
Pulling at an existence of nothing but coldness
A freeze in filling life which exceeds no limit
Those are truths which act as streams of air
Embarking across cities with no excuse
As towers dot the skyline of beauty with brown
While an angel checks to make the time
A line which has been made by false hope
Only to realize the bounce can never stop
Like a city that has no way to go but down
Or a life that seems to make their dreams
As a truth only to be expelled by reality.

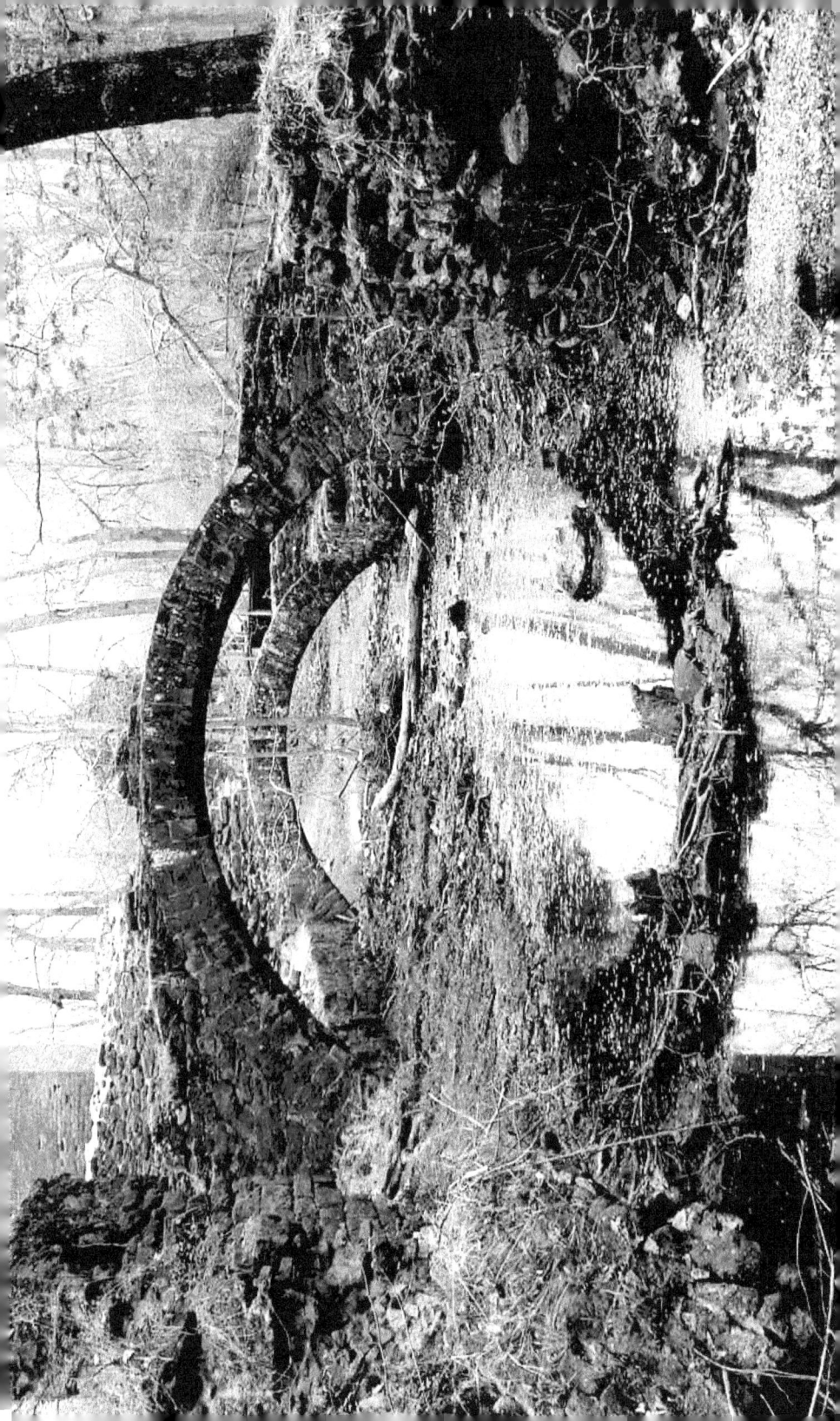

TO BUILD CHARACTER

Trapped in the unforgiving world of Lindenwold
Like the escaped steam of lost exhaust
Only to be sent within the hour of despair
Asking if such a journey needs to have life
Do these dreams make any sense as to know
Like the lost wondering amongst the streets
Or a bag that has no name can just be left
These stories are the songs that help to understand
As if a wonderer can excuse one to be lost
Which way do most travel to be as they are
Like an angel that gets lost making to be obscene
When does one end to push a coin for a ticket
Which can only lead one to the wrong path
Slipped in to be asked for the right way
Above all else does one stand by the rail
Not as a fear but yet an understanding
Asked directions to a place one will never know
Is it these journeys that help to build character
Only to sit and tell one of a time far away
This is to what most hear to be expelled
Pushed forward to ask if such a thing can happen
The destination is known but the pursuit is unreal
As if time will never move as fast as one thinks
Never thinking that the cold wet trees have a story
Like complaining the truth will make anyone care
These lies that seem to have no care as we see
Blinded by the existence that a society makes.

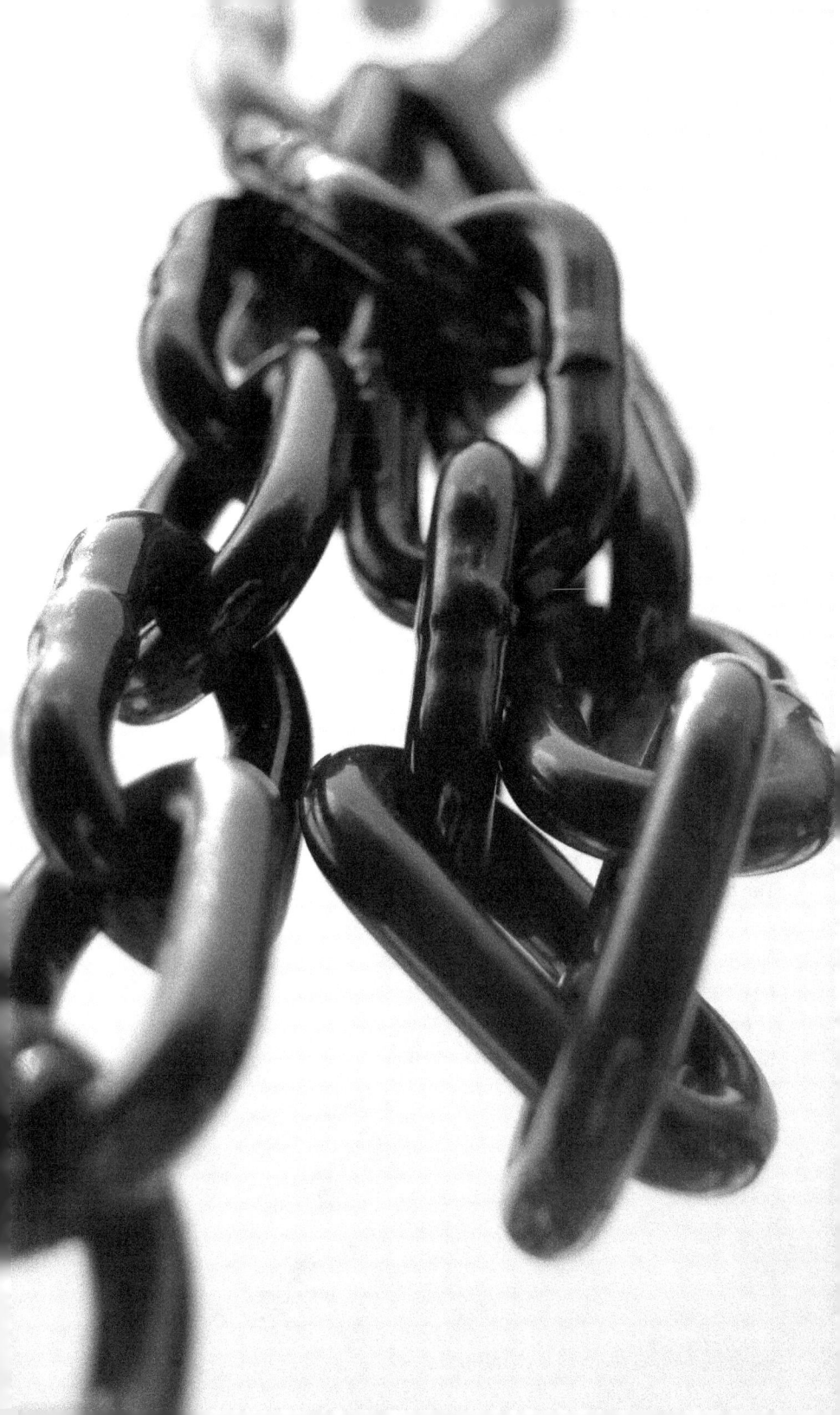

DULLING FABRICS

Drenched by the sound of soft thunder
Like a purr that never seems to be content
Orange like the leaves that scatter the moist
Explained to be not a wind but a motion
Pulling at each like a dust ball caught in a thought
While sitting in a room filled with soft light
Does a bird sit upon a branch only to wonder
Can life ever be sucked away from such a prey
Or do we ask why is there so many questions
As if a pinecone ever really has a reason to bloom
Scattered like rain drops without touching windows
Leafless branches that dot the endless sky
Like roads that pass through dead trees of life
This is the sand that holds such a feeling of truth
Shaken like the earth that spins in wrong directions
Or a flesh that is seared to make a meal of kings
Scratched by the nails of a dulling fabrics teeth
Like the green eyes that can see deep into a soul
Heating the soft touches that never seem to touch skin
Only to realize it is not what they see but who they know
As a reflection which has no source to make it be
Do they play such games to bounce light to know it
Or does it glisten just for the pure excitement of all
Even being held in soft blue backgrounds of thought
The dust will never settle as to make a pattern
Or be arranged by memories that have no beginning
Like the Absecon that holds kings to make a quest.

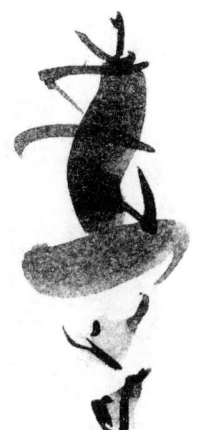

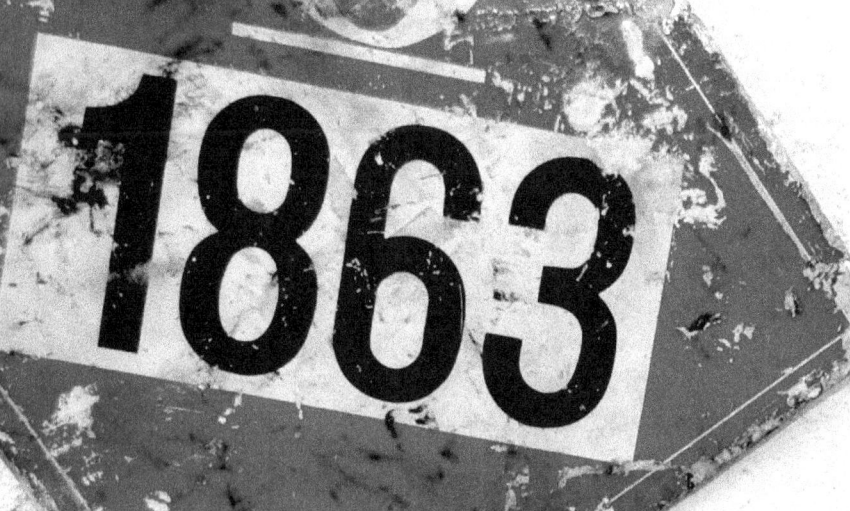

ONLY TRUTH

Undying emotions consume even the strongest
A pleasure of sand that cools beneath the feet
While drums of wind bash through soft ears
Or a spray to remind one is awake to this day
A year closing to give thanks for such a life
Like a bird that swoops to catch its meal
Burning like the cold salt of endless blue
Dotted horizons with slow moving bowls of jelly
Caught within the grains of time to be beaten
Like closing eyes that have seen to many frowns
Held like endless wings carried by the wind
With the elders watching over like blank viewers
These are what makes a pursuit seem to end
As the sounds release so much passion in it
Which has no explanation to be so true
Only those with a vision can move such thoughts
Pushing sent waves to an extreme will of touch
Asking to find things that have no meaning only truth
Yet settled with the signs that mean so much
Even being overwhelmed can not explain these things
As if so many things can be seen without touch
He who knows can be seen with glows of sight
Which will clarify the feeling onto which they play
This is the energy that rides with endless emotion
Holding such desires as to life will be known
Turning like evasions of ones world made true
Like the sweet winds which will always travel.

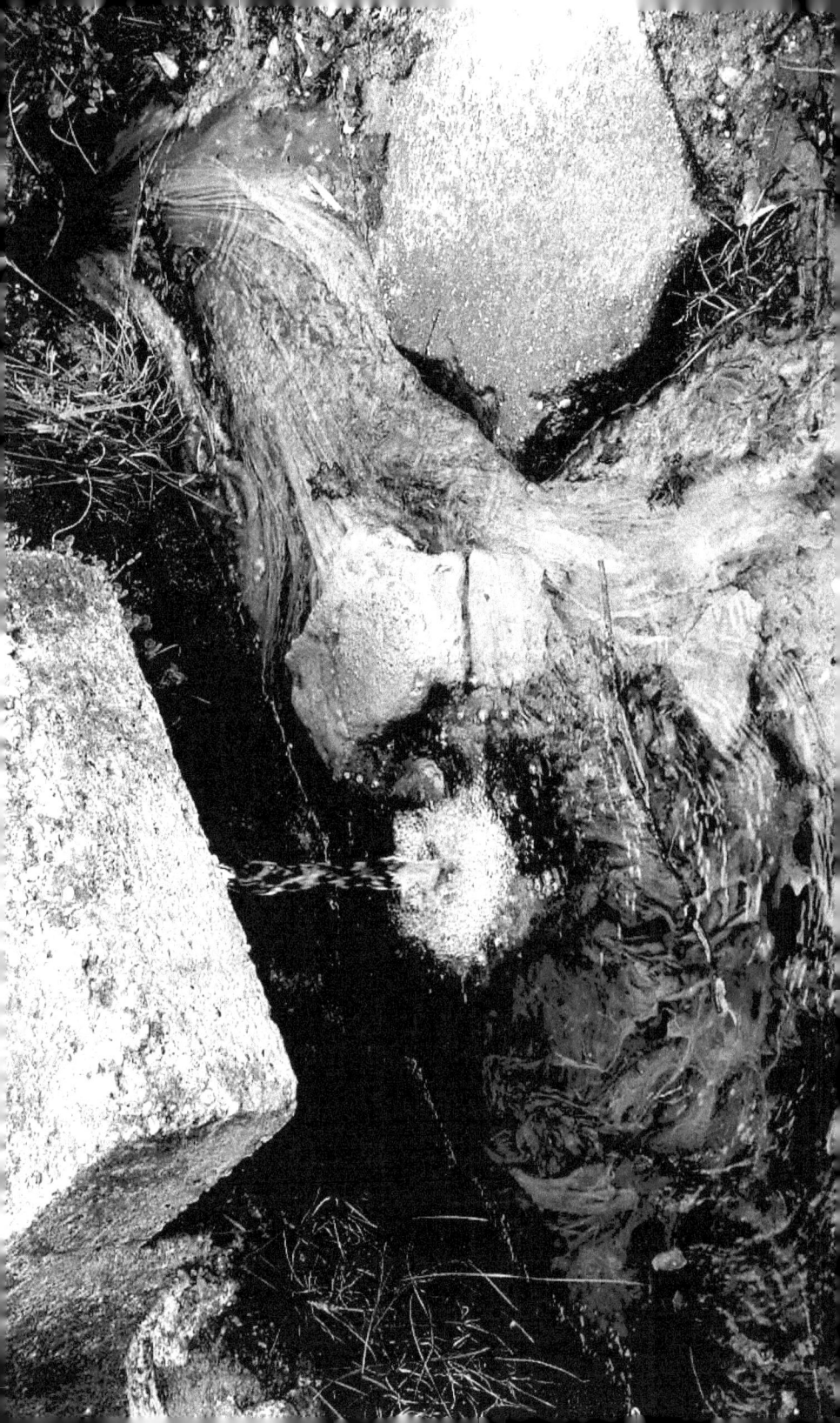

PLAGUES OF RATTLE

Shinning with silver as it blasts through the wind
Like there is nothing to hold it back from this
Speaking a tongue that acts as a trumpet played
Making the scab which is pushed among bushes
Rolled like the stones which bind the seas foam
Mixing the sand as if to have been a drink
Like the sweet that seems to engulf such pain
Pounded like the rhythm of a running man
Expelled from a temper of no such knowledge
As one can only sit upon stone walls of the sea
Walking along such paths as to be angels of hope
Riding with such speed as to break such realms
Like the wind that carries a kite to be ashamed
Entering the unspoken rustic plagues of rattle
Snapping are the sounds of laughter to make one
Confused like the endless curves of a women
Only to be posed as to run boundless with emotion
These are the remedies to such a life of storage
To be released to live amongst the unreal
Like a star being surrounded by too much space
As if chatter without noise will ever fill an ear
Pleading for a silence as if to know the sound
Riddled like the rumbles of children's hunger
Like a dog lead by a stranger with nowhere to go
As the beating sun makes a glow of life with ease
With the distant cry of a child's voice heard
The day makes dreams feel too real to ever explain.

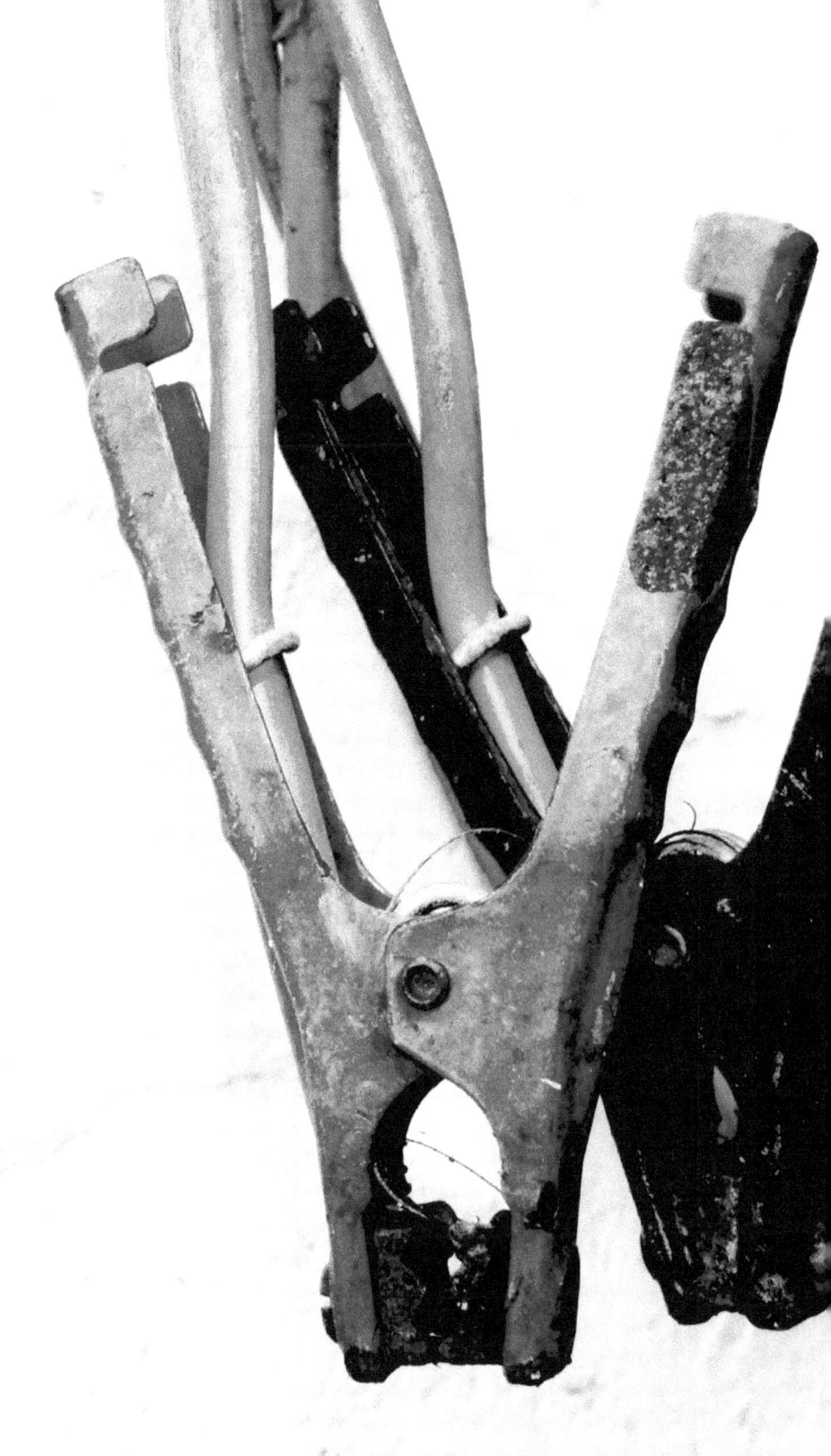

SOCIETY MADE

Watched like a sitting dove about to release
Motionless as the sound which makes life
Touched like the heat that binds the canals
Overgrown like the algae which chokes the water
Never will the Sun reach the bottom of deception
Only lost like the words which fill endless pages
Breathless are lungs that never seem to breathe
Pushed against wailing walls of devotion anew
Yet to still seem like a fight against the king himself
Justified to only be a different fascination
Like the floor which holds the balance of gravity
Exchanged like the emotions we hold so dear
Asking to be understood like the tales of never
Moons and stars tell us true meaning of it all
Making those who do not see, fools of nature
Ignorance will bind even the most savage beasts
Seen to never believe, like a society made of gates
Blocking everything only to fill with nonsense
Brought before us to explain the reason of
Drink wine as it is bestowed upon our life
Smoked like an earth with a body of hope
Eaten like the drum of hunger made to be energy
This will fill our being to know of true emotion
Held close to the living for our touch can be heard
Opened eyes held closed, tight to never hear
These words can never be seen to this day
For a truth is made with a spark of thought.

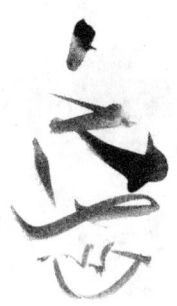

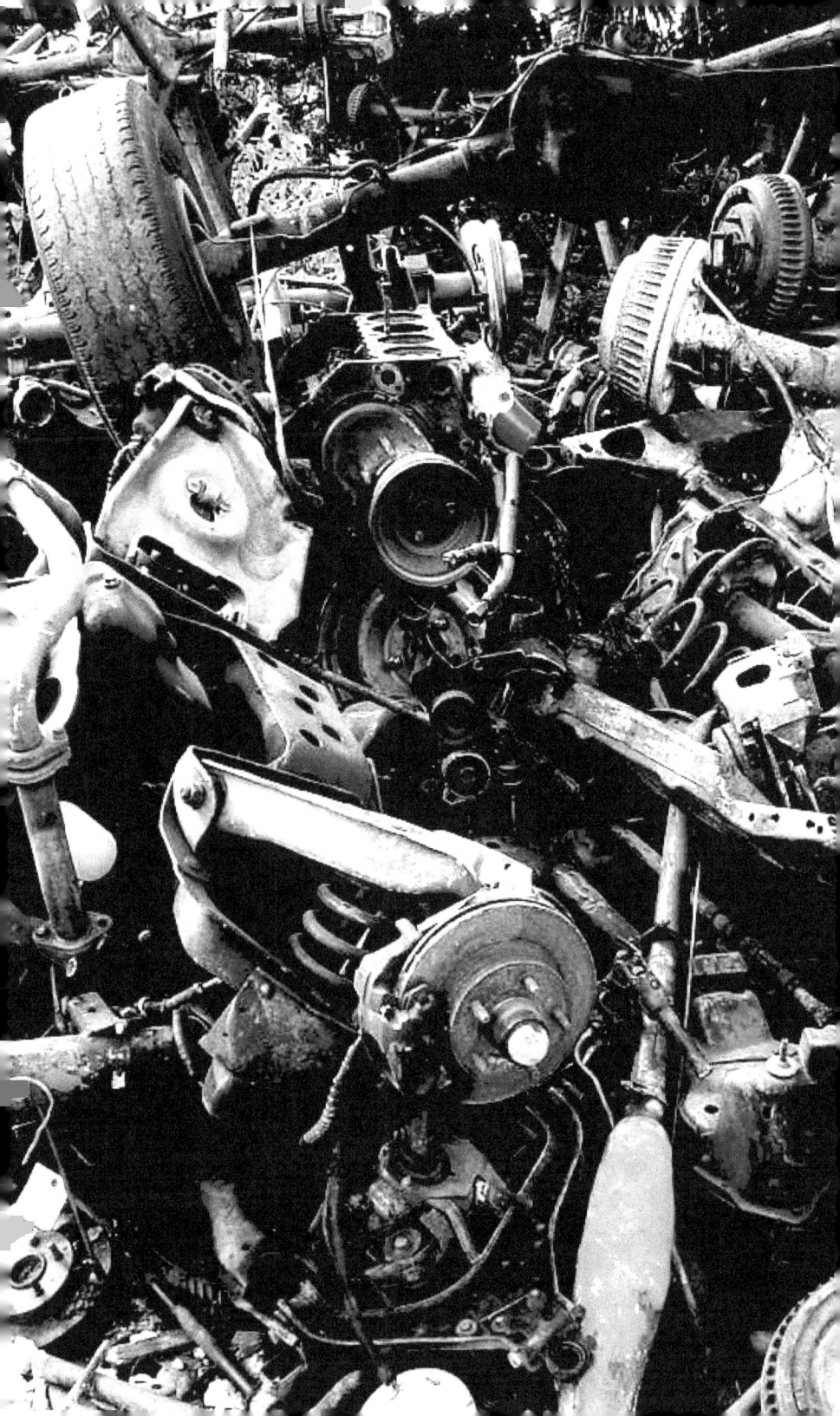

IN CLOSED CORNERS

Unusual is the feeling that makes men wonder
Like the wind that blows against their face
Yet the time short ago was filled with know
To reach a goal is what most will call success
Only a goal that has been reached can glance
Over lowered shoulders who hold the world
This they ask for dreams of times of slumber
Do we not see the touch that holds the truth
Like the soft whispering wings of a love bug
Who's beauty can lift a darkness to never be seen
As if the heavens opened to release the one true
Emotions are restless in their pursuit of freedom
They asked to be moved without fear of it
Only to be held in a richness of emotion
Money of this nature has no mass in a society
It's worshiped in closed corners to be dark
As if something this heavy would be weightless
Like a snowflake that falls to fast on the beach
Which makes them wonder if they ever can
Reach such a network to push them further
As if to be on the edge of a cliff only to be
Made bare by a decision to not know
Background has already been seen
The existing foreground seems so clear
Yet the bottom looks gray like hair
That never leaves your side and becomes
The only existence to ever understand.

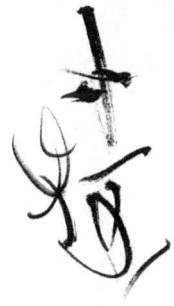

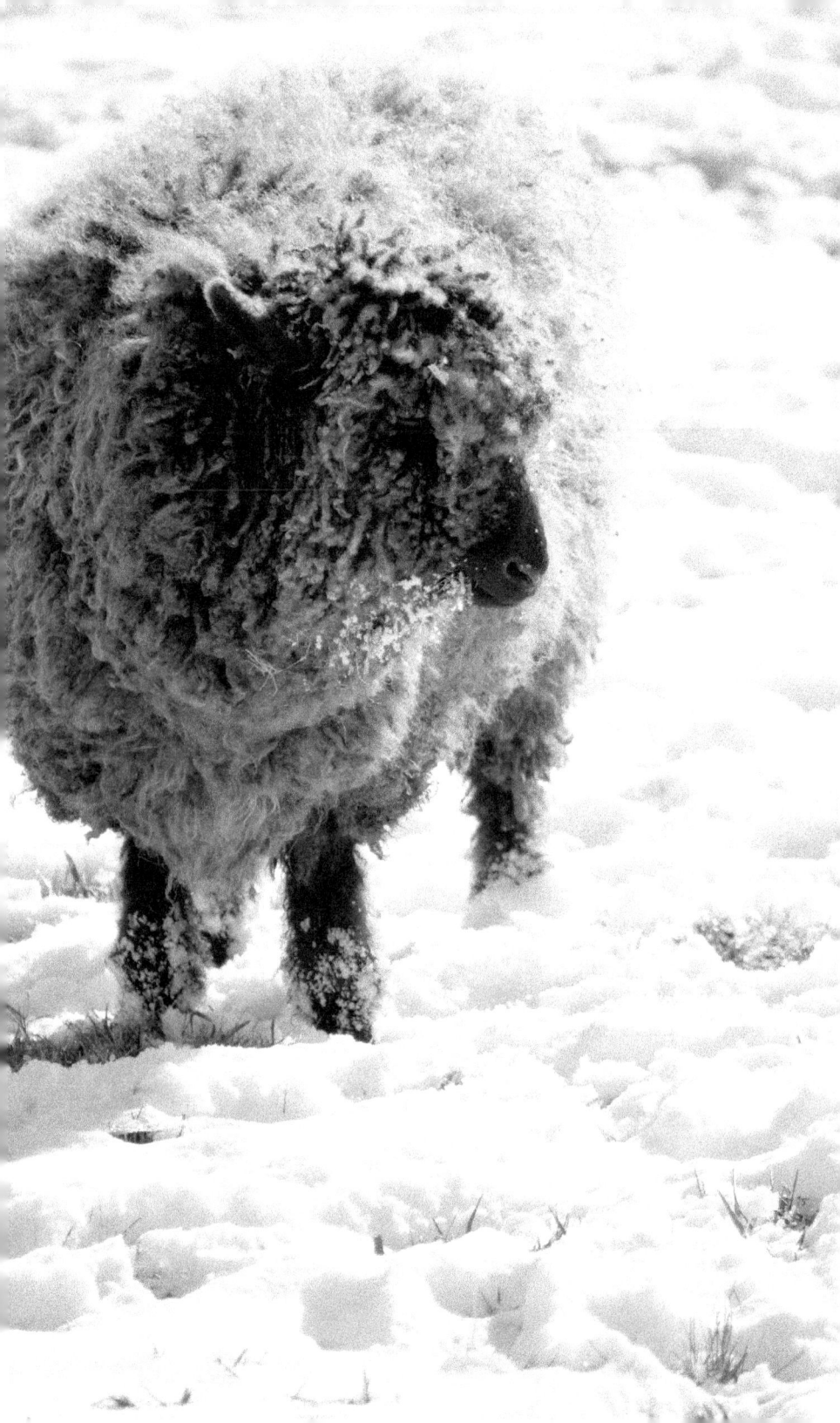

OUTLAWS OF NATURE

This pen is as it does nothing that matters
Like a soft bubble in the distance of air
Bringing a rumble of double to the sound
As if sight has no meaning if it does not tell
For a use is even made true if there is no thought
Like soft snowflakes on a hot day of spring
Truth be told as to never listen to explanation
Winds that push like songs of old with no tale
Asking to be made with stained eyes of truth
Only to whisper the knowledge as if to ever be
Like soft melodies that call upon birds of tune
They speak of a time when warmth filled
As if to join with rhythms of nature
Can it be said to make such a deal out of
If dirt can be made, so does the plant it consumes
Is this not what makes our being so pure
Expressed like an outlaw of nature only within
As if to be clean ever meant without justice
Like the rain that will wash sin as it is known
A word that has been spoken to you in belief
Held only by a grasp that tells of nothing
An existence that can only see so far
To lead further into something unknown
For the life of a story is made of true substance
That tells of a relief and of a struggle
This is the story of masters of men.

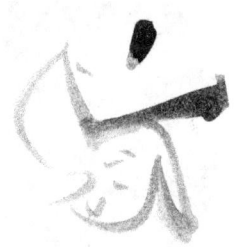

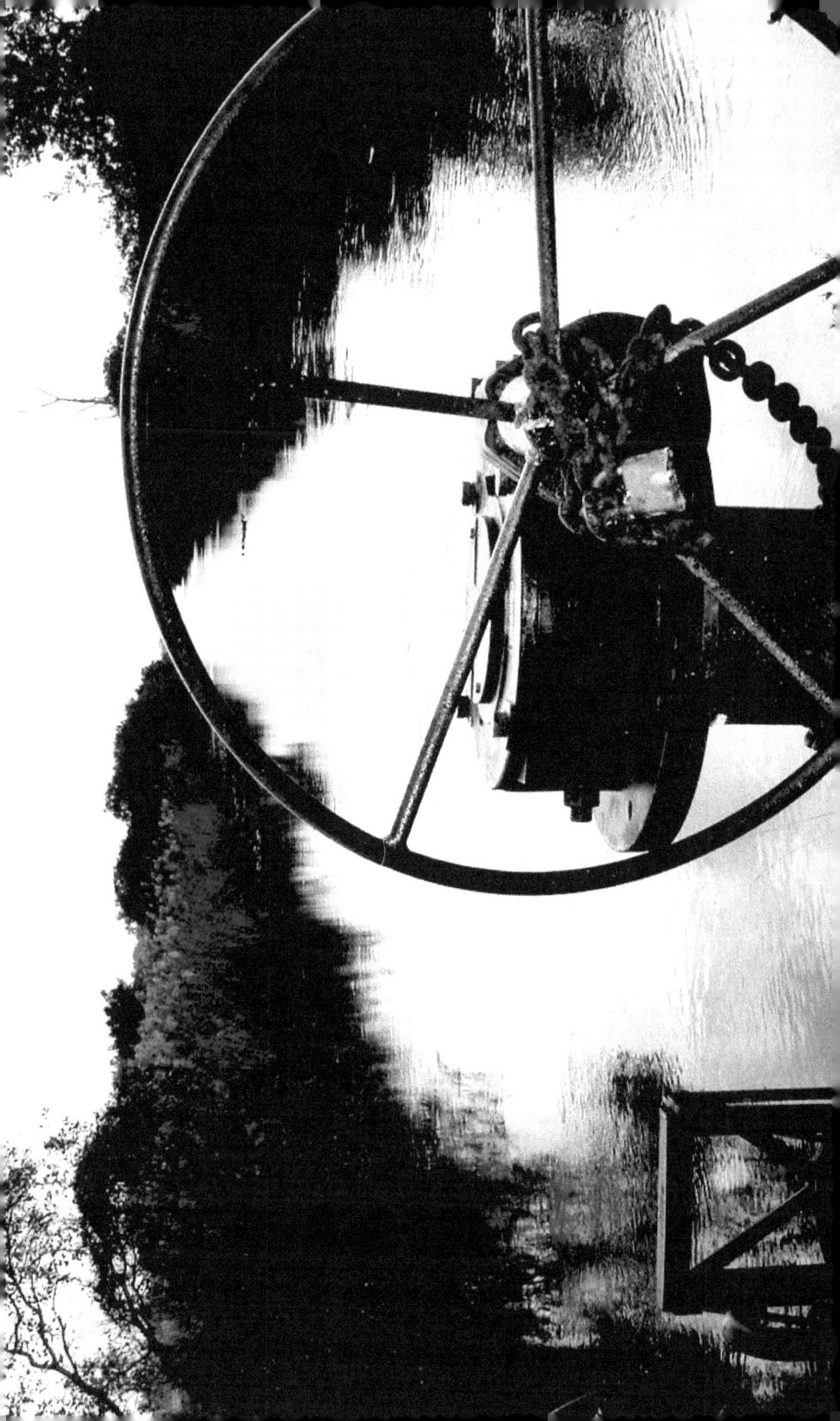

OF MIXED SANDS

Sitting in a daze of endless bounty to be
Naked like a sitting bolder amongst the tiles
Asked not to be made of water will drink
Yet to cleanse the change of a day
This is how one can write to deeply
Thought out like a plague of heart devotion
Made like kisses whispering unforgiving cheeks
But held close like the rain which makes life real
As if a dream will never tell the truth
Upon a ledge does one see the light of life
Held like an endless book of thoughts told
Each pieced with the shrouded aspect of time
Never embraced like the soft silk flowers
With a sensation a taste will be made
Touched like the sweat of the steam
To breathe only amazing lost thoughts of motion
Changed like the tides of mixed sands
Giving birth to generations of misinformed
Only to be left astray as to know a path
Open like the minds that teach our being
This gives an existence to never take back
On to which our thoughts will create our world
Like an energy we see only to never understand
This will be exchanged for belief of it
A sign will be asked of too never share
These secrets which we keep in ours
Will always have a true meaning of life.

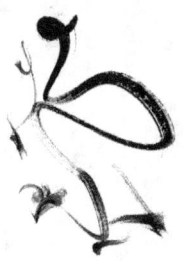

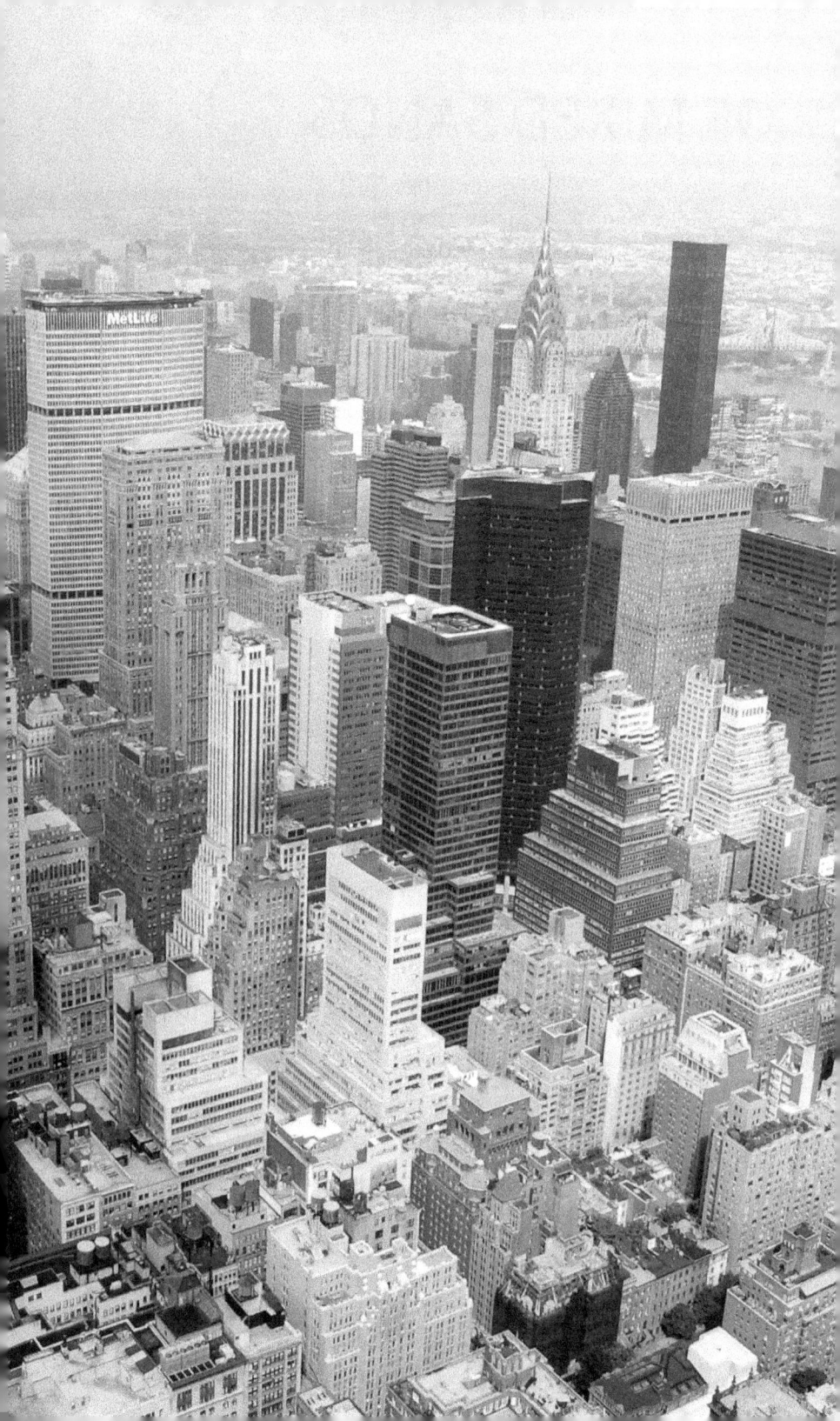

MOTION OF NUMBERS

Postmarked for days of endless confusion
As if stamps can change what is to come
Concerned with the uneasiness we create
Held by the sound of rumbling engines
Quick to make an escape does one without know
Like blank looks that expel deep into the dark glass
Shadows that burn too bright to make the sun see
Passing over like a plane carrying a message
To sail an open sea amongst such a storm of anger
There is no right for such a journey made anew
For these things can make useless seem unnatural
As a spider that can spin no web of pleasure
For it can not eat unspoken words of pain
Searing through broken cracks from pounding hands
Only to be left a drift to find an island made of power
This will create a purpose of unmatched emotion
To touch such a light as to please effortlessly
Letting turns of cranks subside to exist
Giving ease to an upset motion of numbers
Taking the test for them to be what's made
Like those who do not have what we make
A truth that all will be made to be lost
Without such a matter as to what we do
Will only prevail to survive such a creation
This disaster will have examined every angle
Only to be released to the masses as a doubt
For this is the only way for confusion to be embraced.

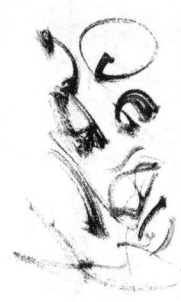

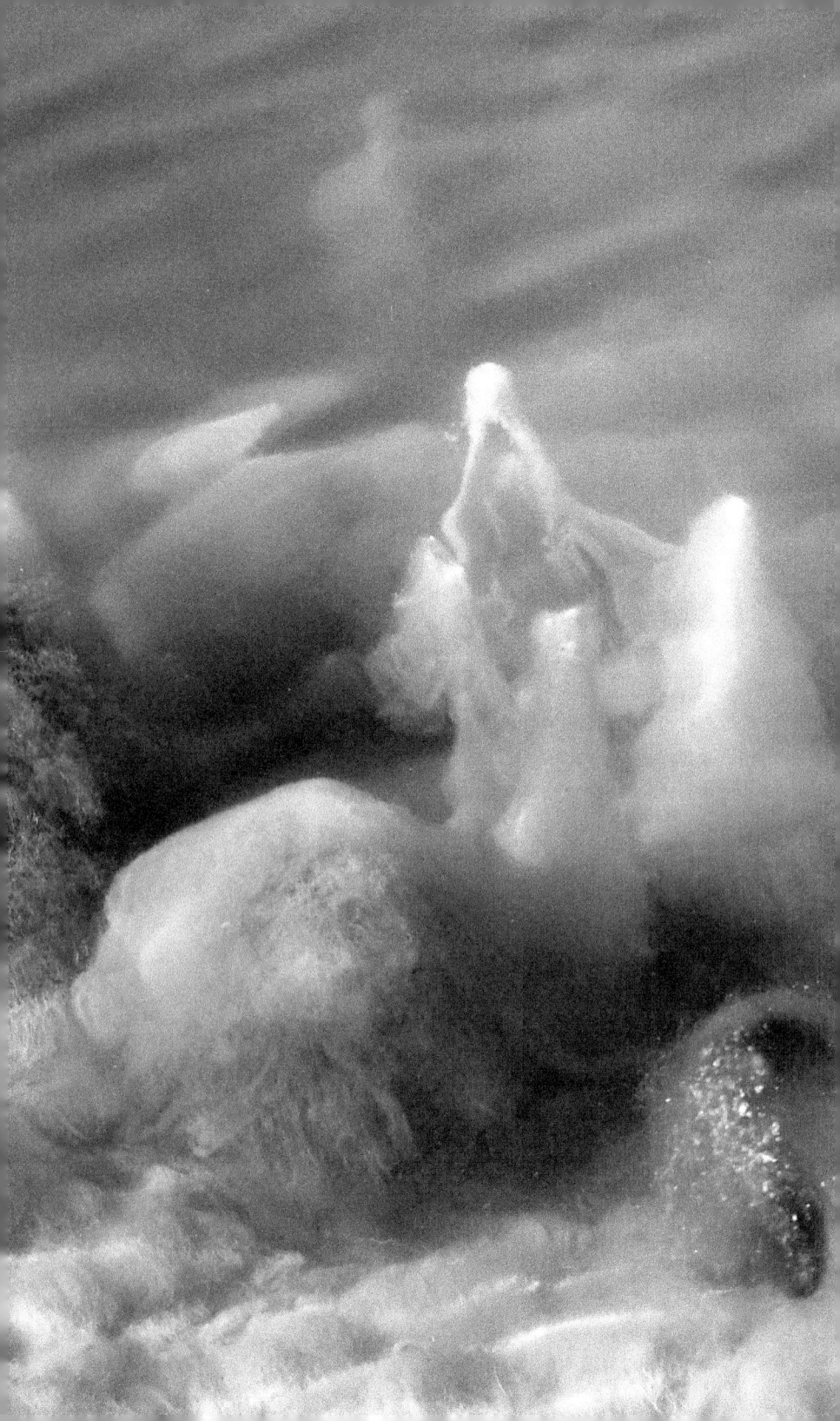

TOADS OF YESTERYEAR

Open like the true eye closed it sees
Not asking to sit amongst open rooms
Bangingaround like original beats
Touched by an exhaustion that pushes
To hard is the hand that guides this
Softer emotions which emit a flare
Unknowing of how real they become
Choking the only way one has ever known
Truth be told to those who do not listen
For anger of angels exhumes the delight
Of knowing if this truth can be told
As stories of old never seem to understand
Only repeating the whispers of a song
A rhythm that will always be played
Like a stone that sinks into the oils of pens
Drowned like a gasping fish not knowing how
Pushed to the end of the line like an edge
Looking over the stripes of double sided roads
Only to see the toads of yesteryear standing
Like hind legged beggars that only starred
Right of way do they not have their sight
Released are they as they stand and do this
Whisking the ever loving off feet of disbelief
Like the sands that fall through pained steps
Masked with undisguised tortures of why or how
What makes such a thing need to be made
Love is something most will never know.

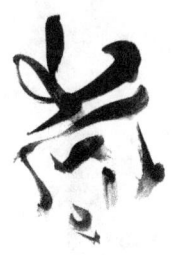

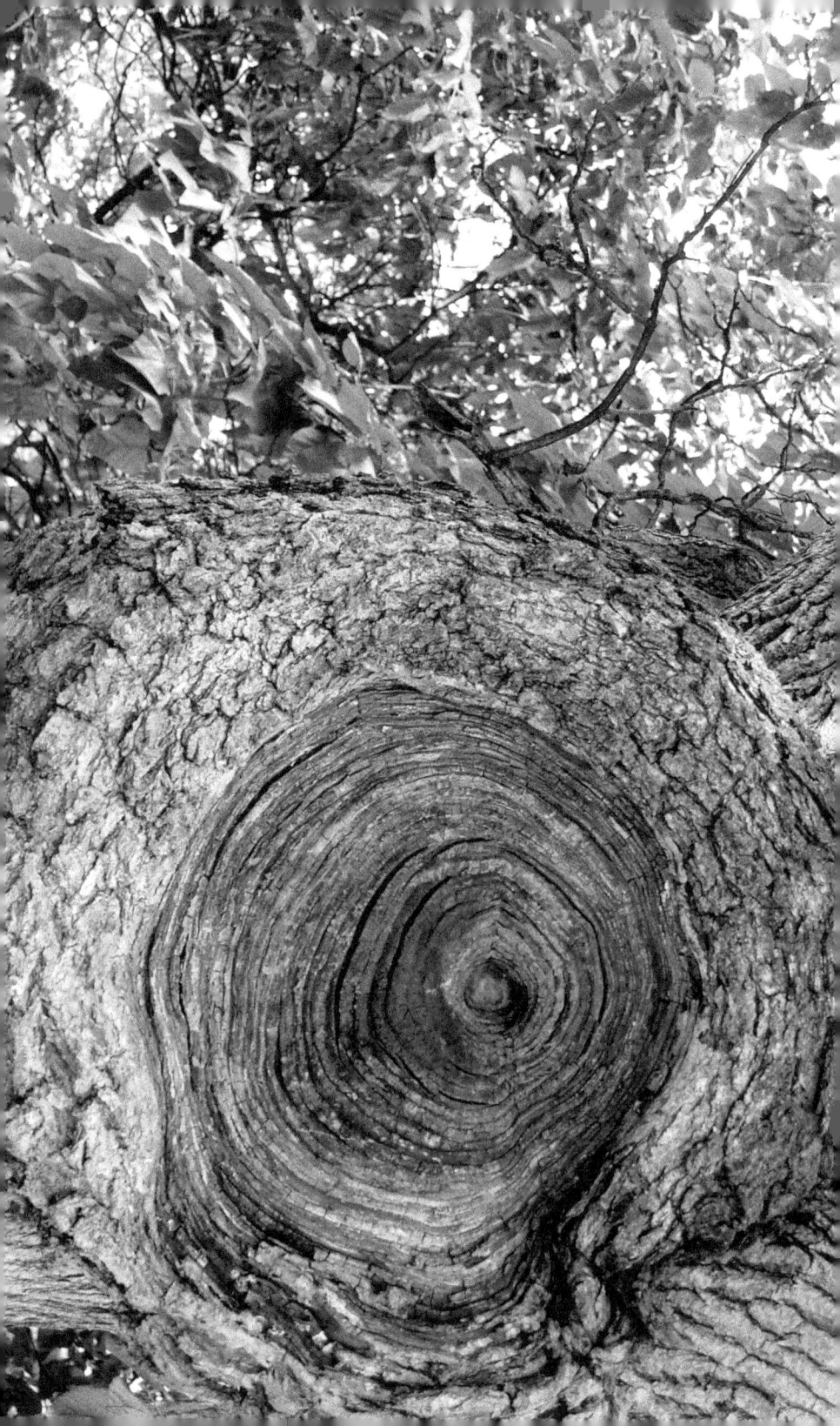

RELENTLESS BIRTH

Daffodils wings that dance on moonlit skies
Essence of these aromas makes one move
Lost in an exhausted world does one see this
Trust and truth most will ever know to utter
Stand like the trees of such a frosted place
The mountain that divides our most precious
Stones that never seem to move like a
Danger that seeks out the light to see
A day when most tragic tales come together
Like a distant second has no real reason just
A truth of unforgiving relentless birth
An experience always lived on two stars
Opened by nine moons made of seafood
Drifting like the slow tide never seen
Now alone for reasons never understood
Like a bull who has too much shit to be made
A first of not knowing what is real
Yet lost like a drifter who has no thumb
Roller coasters of emotions which fill
So deep as is the touch of being held
Only to be let go over nothing of fault
Back logged as to be given to the forefront
Like armies that have no respect for the truth
Just made up tales of how they always were
Never should such things be made true
Like delusions that have no spelling
Of eyes that shouldn't be seen.

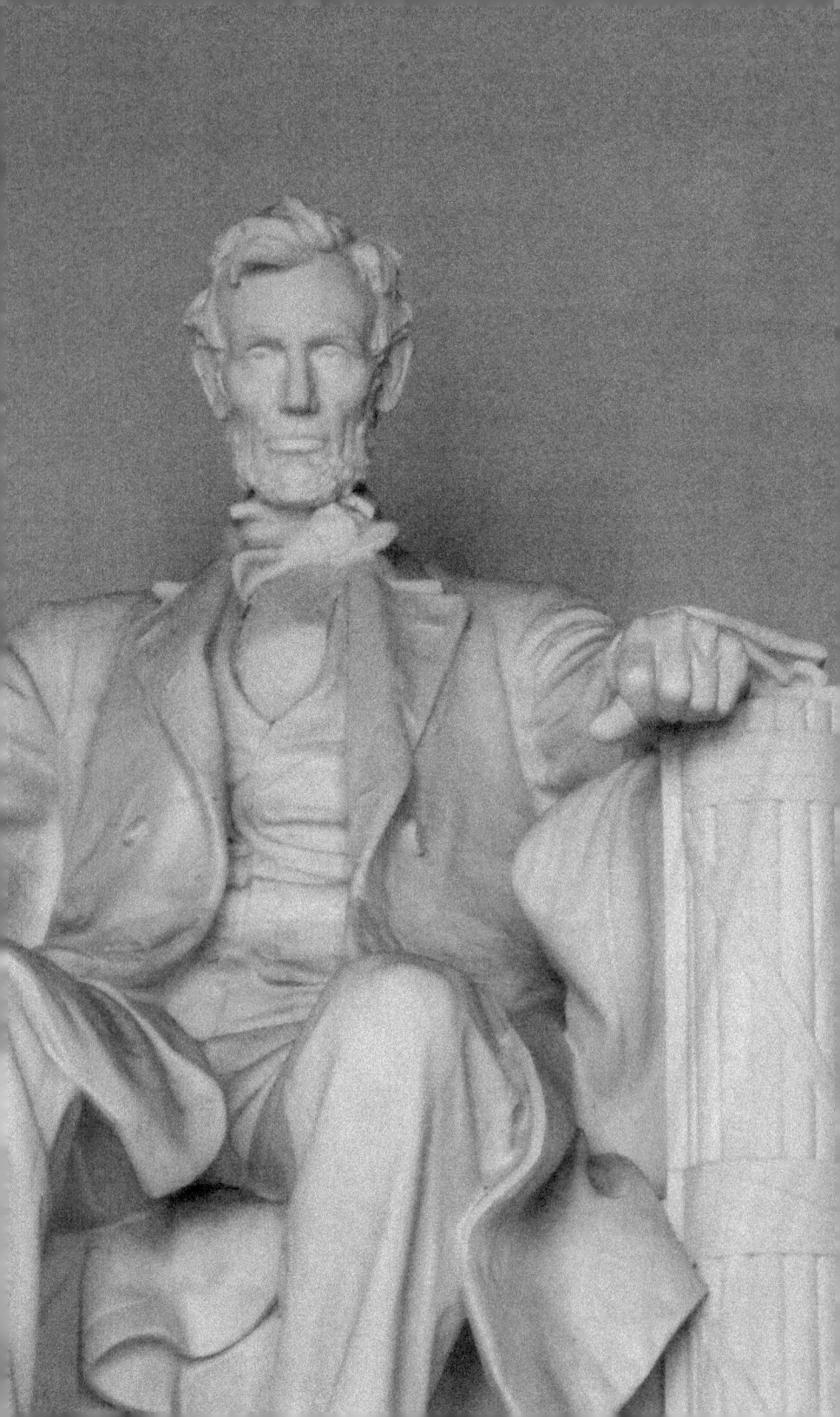

EXCHANGE OF BLOOD

A leader is to be chosen from nonsense
Debates that seem to make no reason
Second time around helps to choose
Only to understand a deeper sense of fear
A truth made to be false might make truth
Opening eyes that seem to have no matter
Making the stories of old come to life
This will agitate the reason of truth
Will a reason be made for such lies
Can one sit only to see life pass
Will the exchange of blood release anything
As if a constant ramble helps us to believe
They both speak of change yet to back
Can such a speech push a reason
Help anything towards our life
Repetition as we all know to deceive
Making believe they can change a word
When the choice has already been set
In hopes of a wrong to better this world
Stranded amongst a choice not wanted
To be made as if any of us know what is real
As if we have knowledge to make a just choice
Once told by an elder that this was all to happen
That the one with change to make sand green
Regardless of the desert that surrounds
Never to mislead the truth of life
They have decided we hope for change.

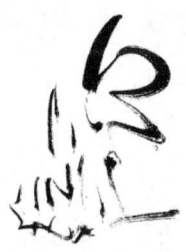

ONLY IGNORANCE

Set adrift amongst an endless sea of air
Again a journey to the city to explore anew
Left to dream the many ways a world can go
This only fills thoughtless dreams to see all
Watching only to feel the true life of most
Spoken on the whispers of untold lives
As if to make such a voice melt like wood
Stuck is the heat in the motion of know
Forces pushing the weight to feel a pull
Darkness expels the city lights for much
Asking only to express its truth to the unknown
Like a song that plays a disappearing melody
Drifting deeper into the realm of disbelief
Shadowing the writing which explains all
As if there was a site to make such a stand
Mistaken by stories which were always to come
Handling the written before such a note is made
With false hands will most hold such a tale
Entertaining the only ignorance one can hold
Alone will they stand to take in their self
Knowing there is a truth that's held to release
This light which is to bright to hold alone
Only with such a belief can this ever be true
Burnt like the day light that showers them
Held in the night in which they travel
For another adventure is to be lived
Letting the life of both grow together.

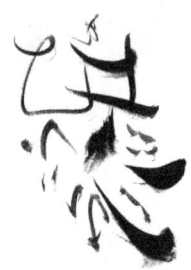

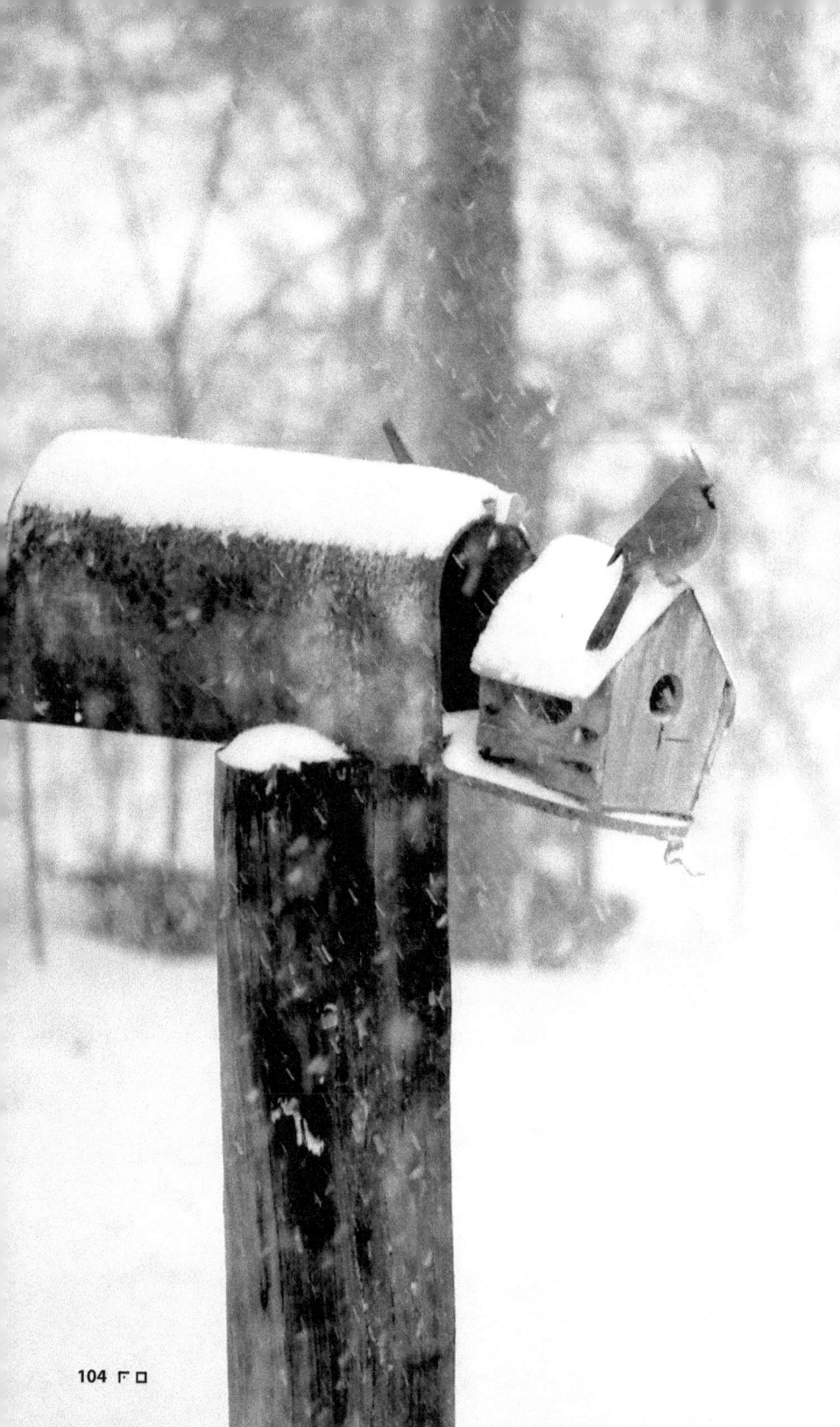

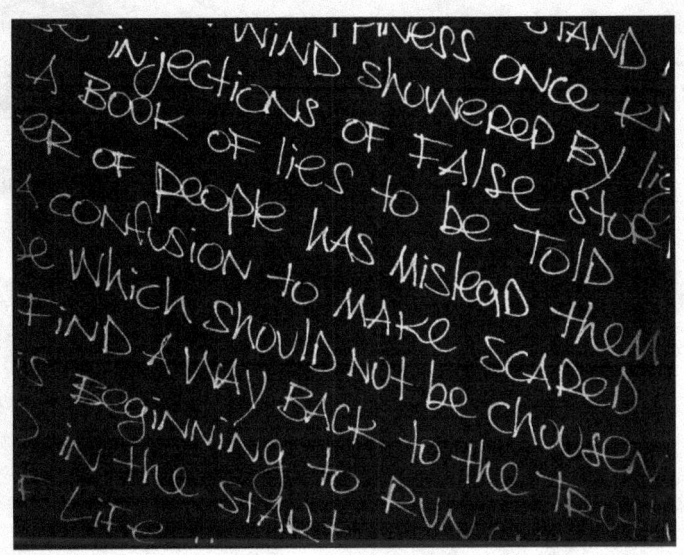

THE BLACK BOOK II
FILLING A BOOK OF WRITINGS TO BE TOLD

NEVER SEEMS

Water that never seems to dry
Heat that never seems to cool
Light which never seems to shine
Life which never seems to die
Love which never seems to stop
Rain which never seems to fall
Ice which never seems to melt
Darkness which never seems to fade
A path which never seems to end
Hunger which never seems real
Anger which never seems complete
A sun which never seems to hot
A painting which never seems finished
A mouth that never seems closed
Eyes which never seems to see
A thirst which never seems quenched
Sound which never seems heard
A heart which never seems filled
A brain which never seems right
A truth which never seems told
An experience which will always be great.

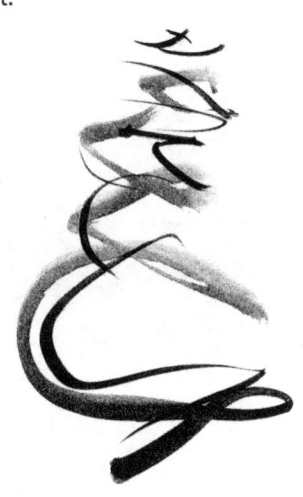

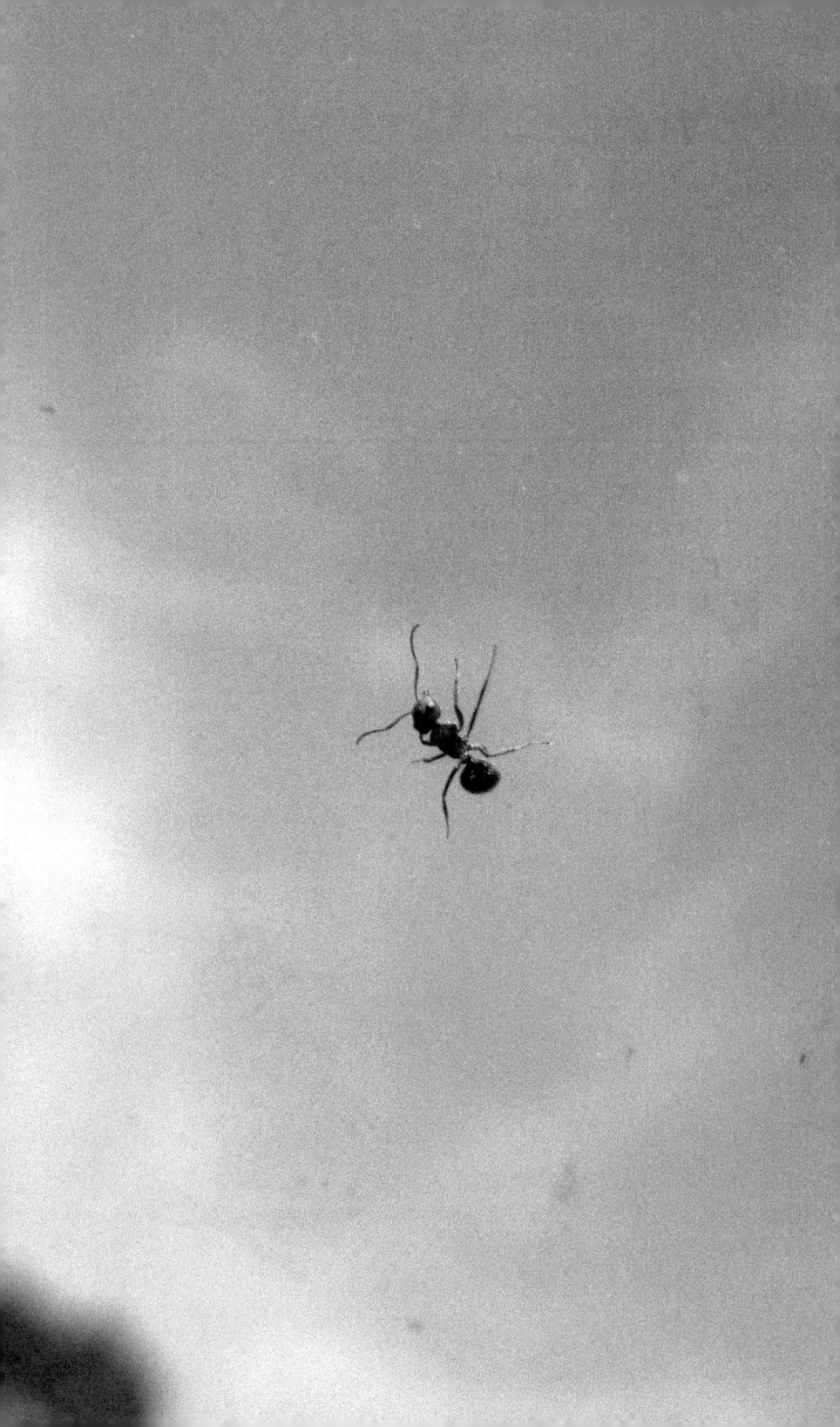

BEEN HERE ALL ALONG

Mountains falling making soft thunder
Sometimes you have to sit back and wonder
Did the sound come from the hunting horn
They have chosen him, he is the first born
He's been known to make people overdose
Sit and lie in their state of comatose
Forgetting the wondrous astronaut
Knowing he held the true free thought
That everything we write on a microchip
Will one day be turned into a battleship
For when a hand touches sacred tiger skin
You will begin to hear soft music of a violin
Look in the dark hidden lost places
To find the graces of these mistaken faces
Then there will be nothing to dispose
You will stand in beauty just like a rose
It will be like a glass of water you pour
Something you adore and will never ignore
It will be here for the day so long
You know he has been here all along.

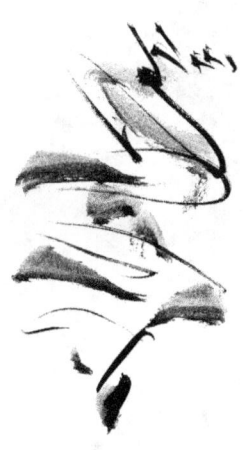

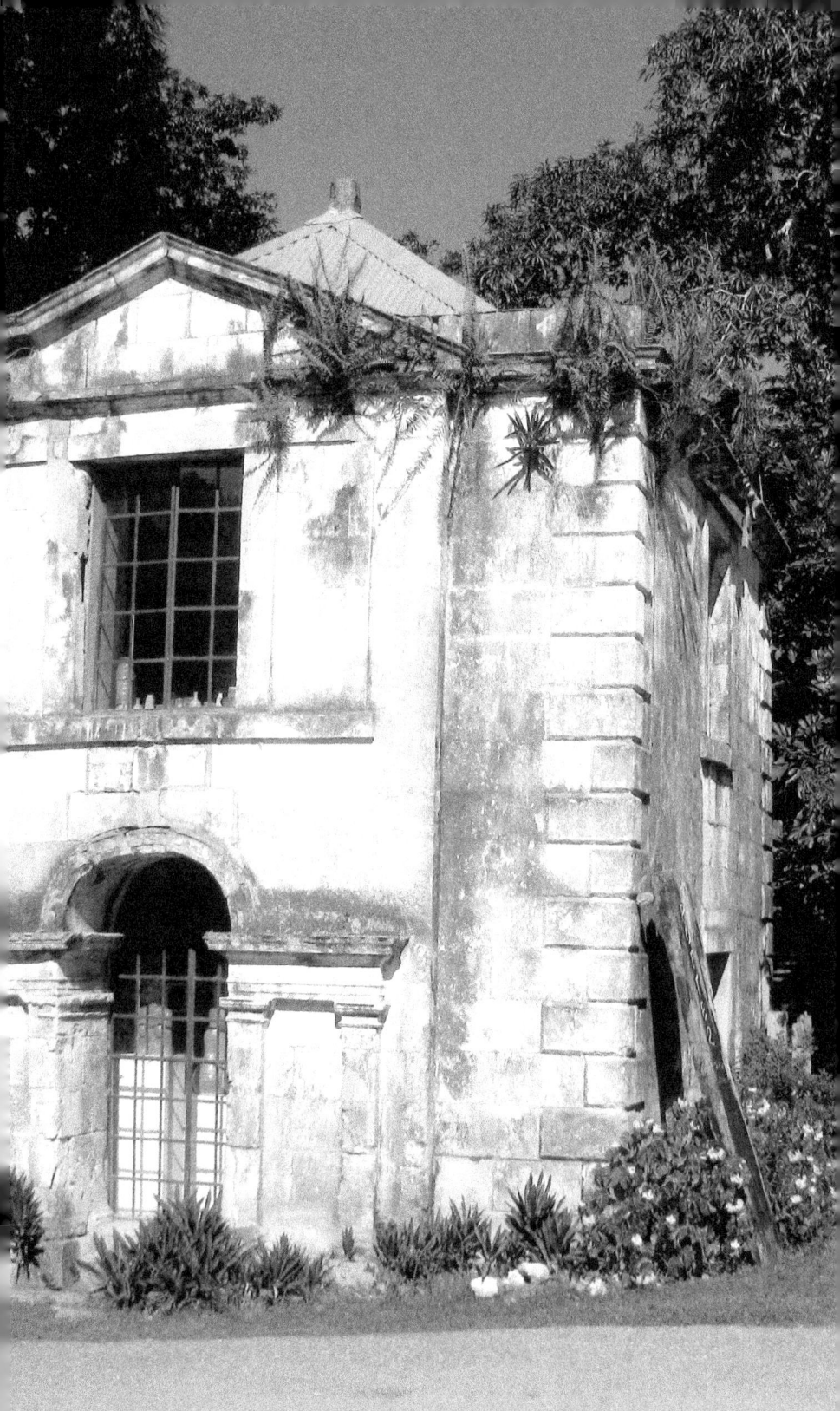

THOUGHT OF A KEY

Trapped words which give no peace
Anger which exceeds limits not known
Once released temptation will arise
Forgetting all facts that have been told
Almost wishing things of sacred nature
An emotion set free to breathe again
How will we know when things will be
Eyes of amazement will be the sign
Showing all that the seen is thy truth
As the lion once again waits in haste
A thought of a key is set into play
For knowledge will destroy our being
Secrets of wrong will be understood
A plague on the houses will be made
As famine sets in across the land
Wars of nations will fight brothers
Mothers will rock their headless babies
As children cling to their dying youth
An explosion will shake the still earth
A ruler of evil will declare himself king
Then our lord will clear all the land
Making way for a new beginning of Life.

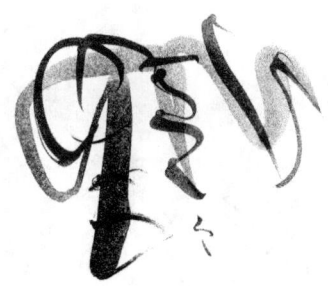

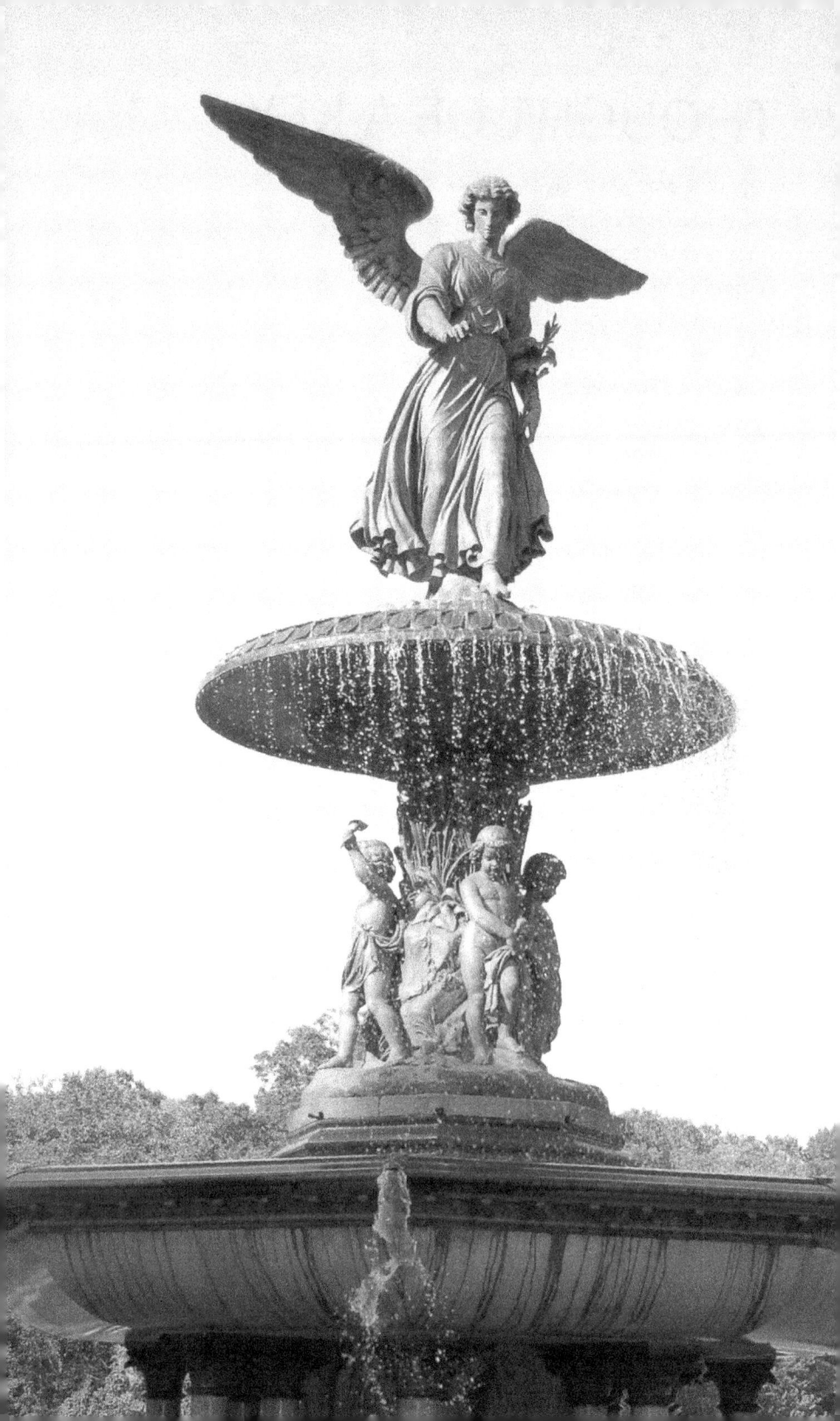

GIVE THANKS

Amazing the way she moves
Like a feather falling to the earth
Graceful as moons rise to the show
Skilled as reflections from the sky
As soft whispers are made
Creatures hide to listen for words
Long white flowing dresses dance in the wind
Casting shadows of metallic nature
A passion for something so beautiful
How can it consume so much to wish a death
As if rain would never fall again
Scars which help to release the pain
Remembering a time when all was lost
Found in a place hidden till revealed
Only then will truth meet happiness
For if mistaken will lead into demise
Then heavy hearts will begin to float
Rising to a great reality of relief
So when amongst sacred beings
Give thanks where its deserved
For you have witnessed the way she moves.

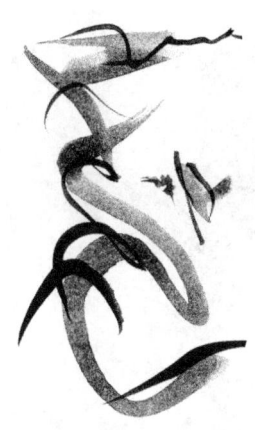

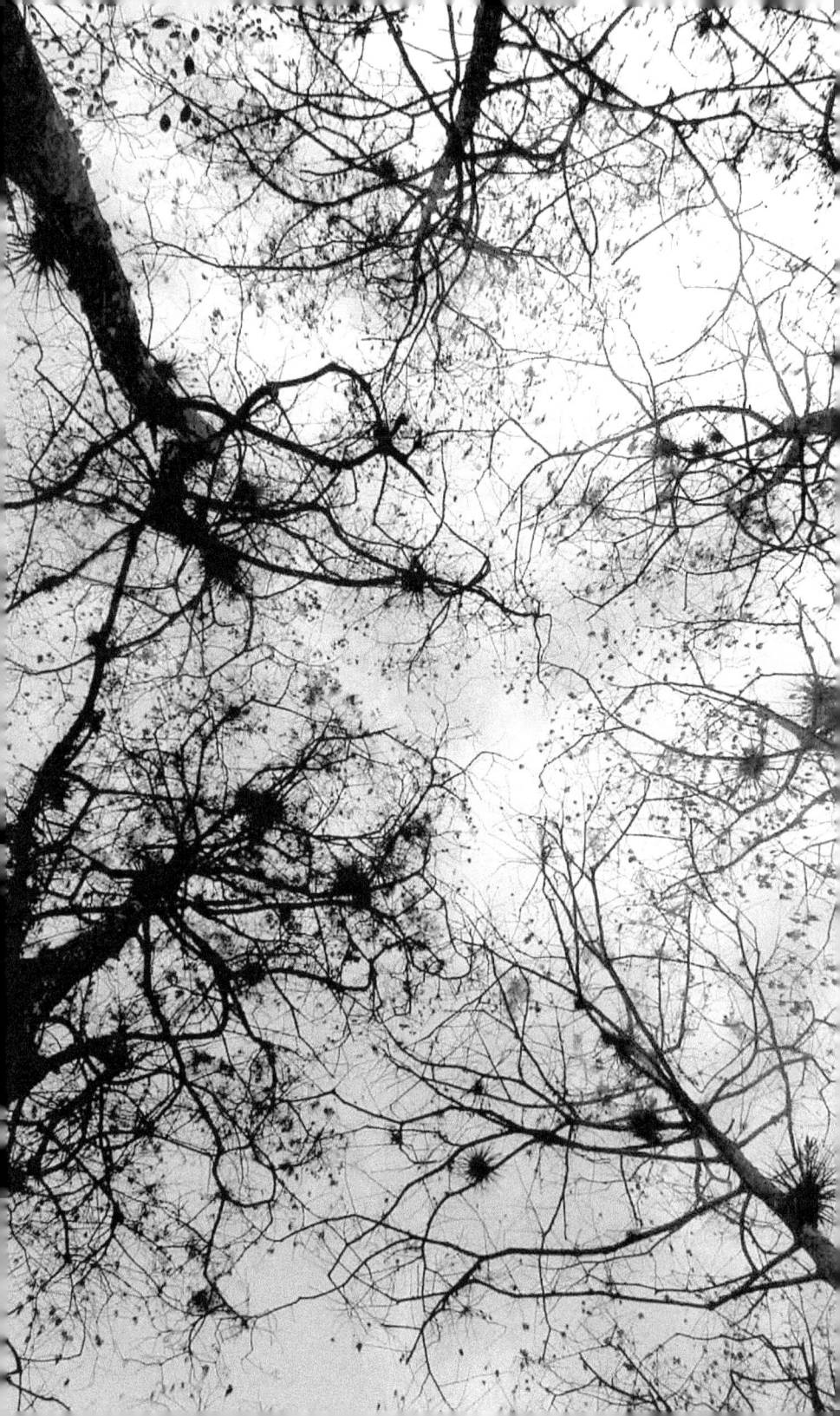

CAUSING A CONFUSION

Drastic infractions of a reality
Forsaken by the beauty of the world
Menaced with imperfections of a society
Masked out to be made clowns
Like paint that drips from a crying face
Realizing that most people are painted
Wishing the world to soak all the pity
Which way will the tables turn to see
Showing great light for the blind to witness
To scared and angry to understand it all
Deprived from a happiness once known
Like flowers in wind showered light
Immense injections of false stories
Filling a book of lies to be told
The power of people has mislead them
Causing a confusion to make sacred
Paths made which should not be chosen
Hoping to find a way back to the truth
For time is beginning to run out
Just as said in the start of nature
The world of life will never end.

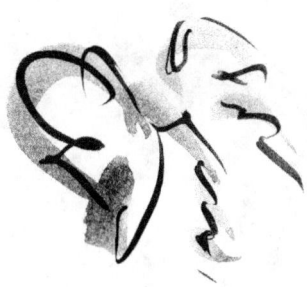

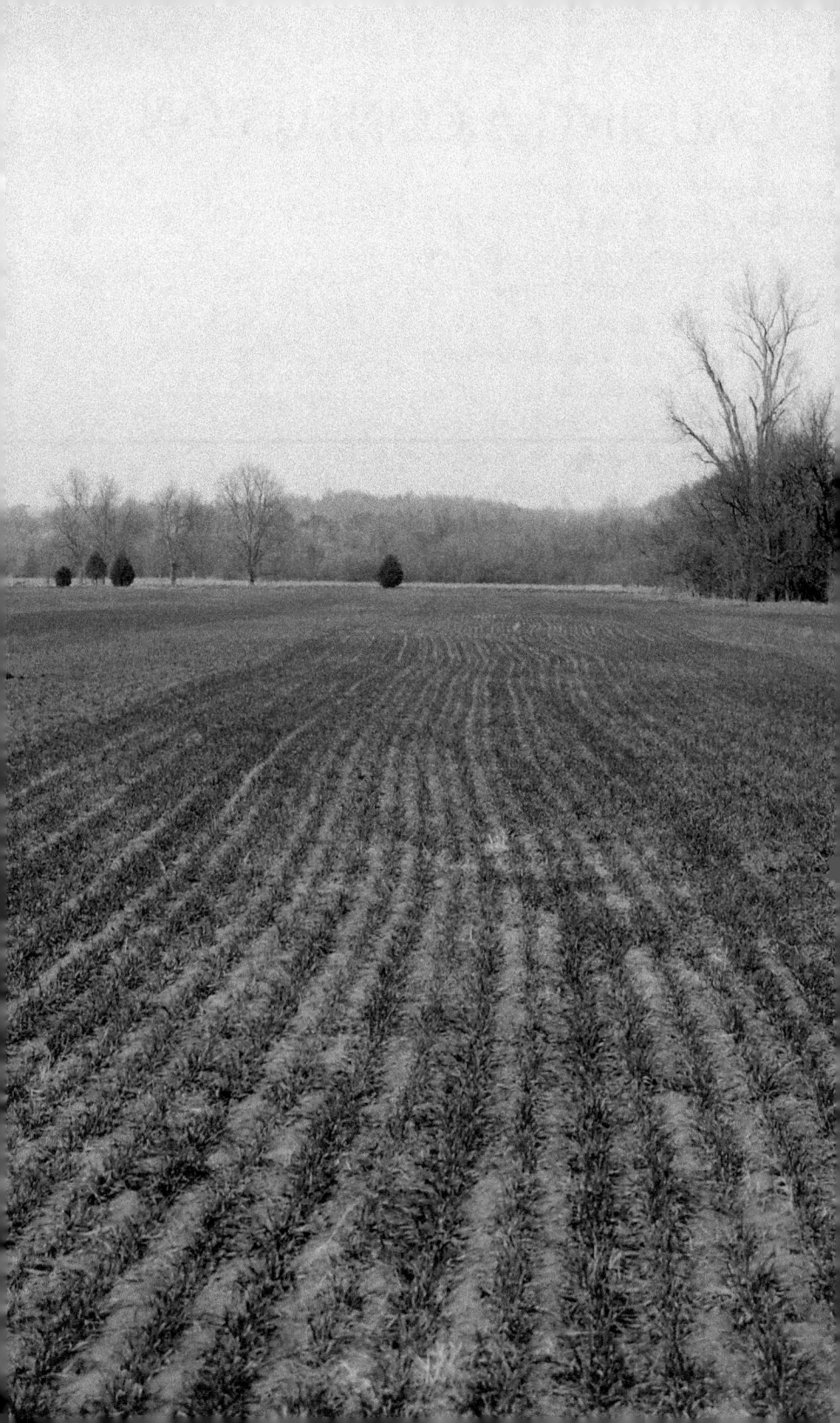

THE CALENDAR

Endless days which never seem to start
A beginning which never seems to end
Lost in a world once found
Recovered from a time once hidden
Darkness which reveals the light
Sunshine which casts away the night
Water to relieve the drought
Sand which will fill the glass
Causing reactions amongst motionless
Moving tides around with the moon
Grabbing the sun to heat the day
An abyss of time which is to shallow
Who's clock will the day run on
Will the calendar ever stop at end
Stars orbit as if there was time
Do they know what day it is
If so, then we know when it started
Then maybe an end can be seen
But in silence they sit and wait
As do most who know the secret
The secret which will revive the truth.

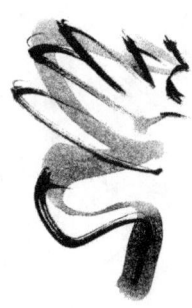

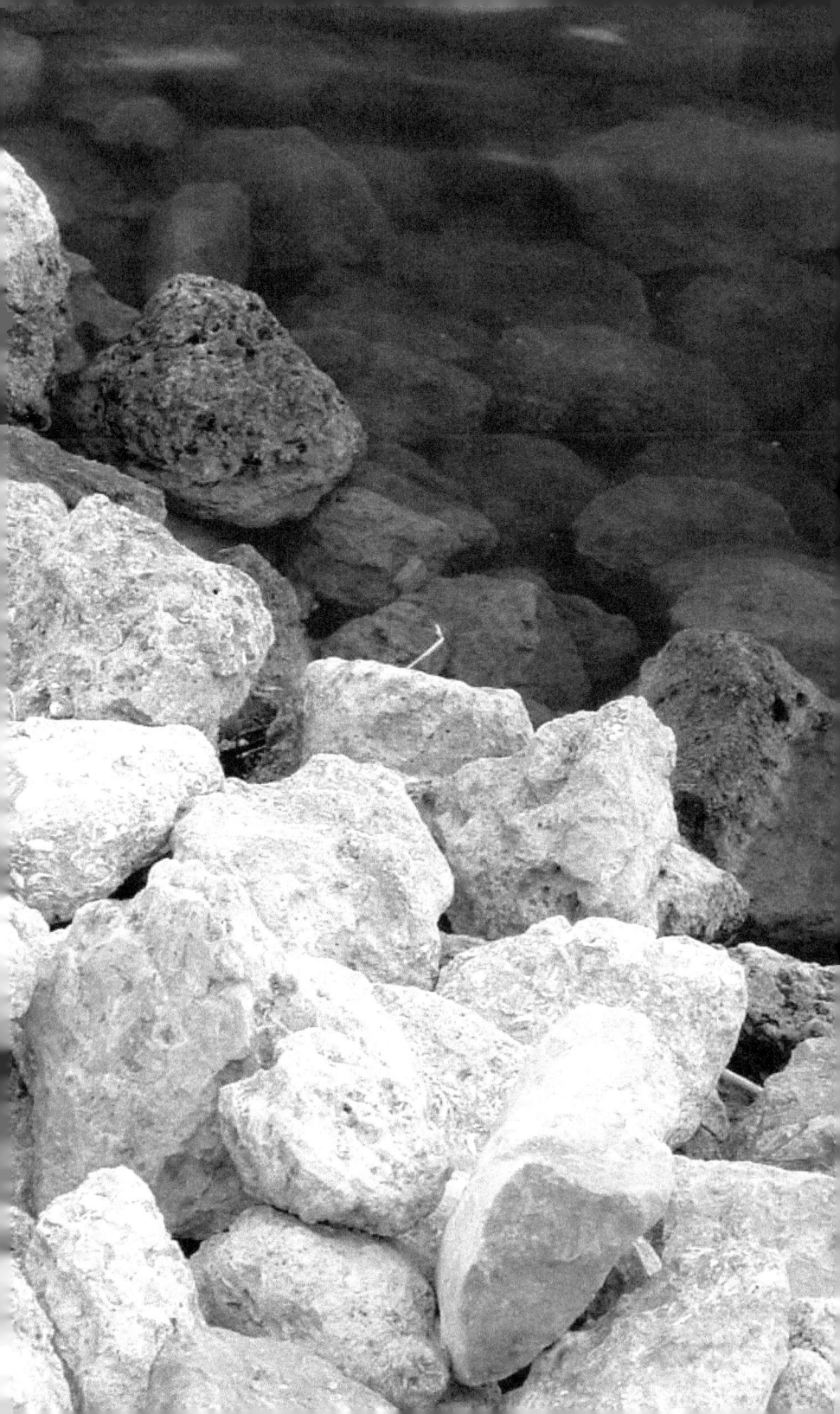

SOUND OF CREATION

Troubled by thoughts of anger rage
A rain falls to cool thy body
Questions of obvious answer
Wonderers of germs that were lost
Angels dance by spreading their love
Confusion sets in to be masked
Sight will not be seen on this day
An illusion will be made for us
This will help even the most crippled
A life force which will soon be expired
A minute more to share things of life
Then maybe a path might be shown
Exposed, the truth will be known
Asked of a human we are not
From a mighty voice we are spoken to
The sound of creation is made
Will you listen or just let them fall
Silence will be heard no more
Only thunder will be felt in the distance
As the truth shakes us from our feet
To a sleep that we can only awake.

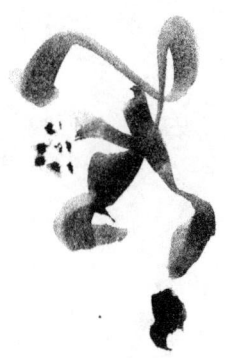

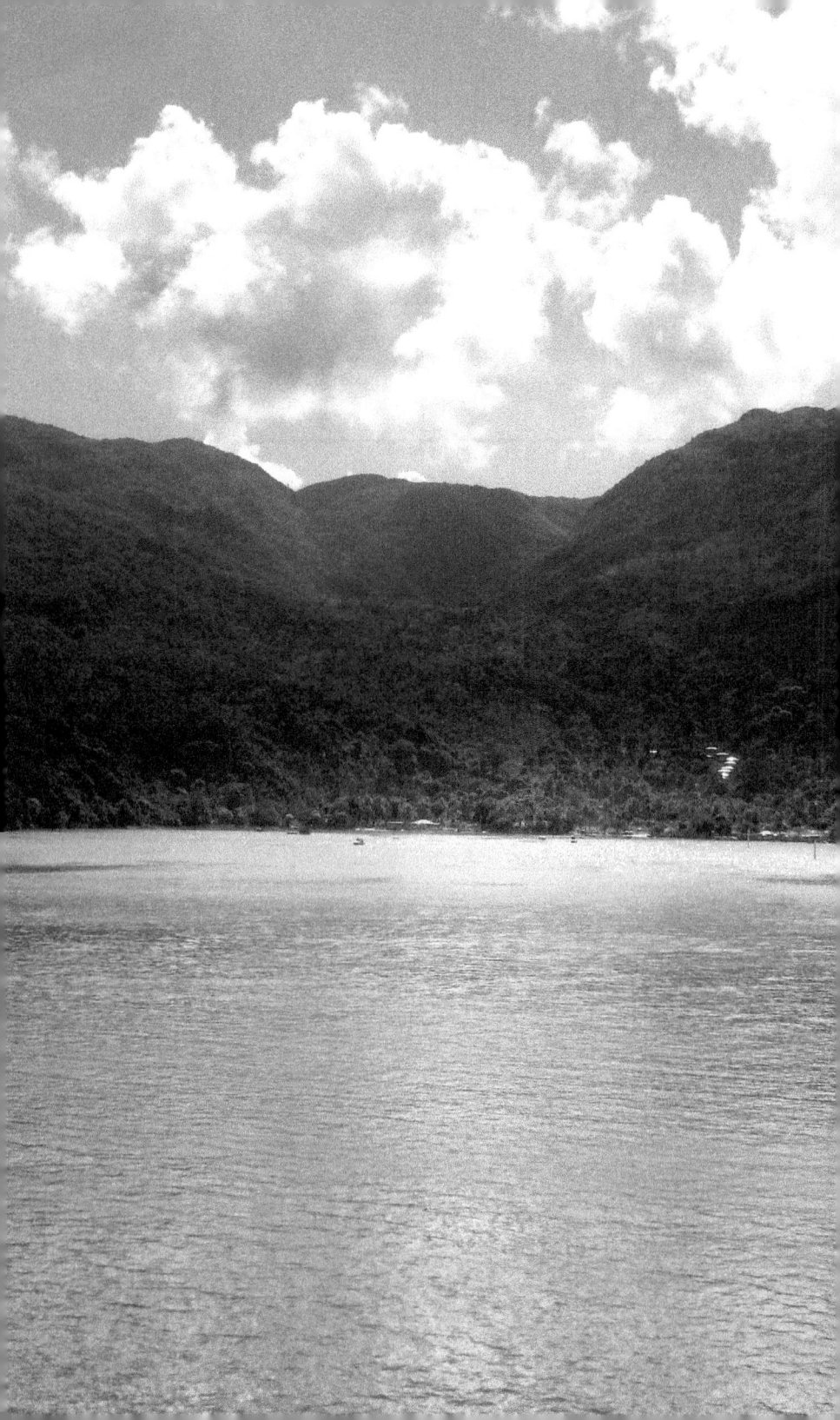

NEVER CEASE

Meetings of children of the lost
Journeys which lead to great knowledge
Bringing to the world secrets of today
Father time plays with our mother nature
Showing her that he will never end
As she explains her love will never leave
For the children will create a home
Tribes created to rule the land of kings
Queens created to birth thy king
Giving to the world a leader of all
As the angels make their way along
They to help to mold thy clay of man
For there could not be one without other
Unity is what helps to move thy soul
Magnets will never pull so hard
Nor words will express thy truth
Thoughts themselves sometimes confuse
Making an illusion that it will all stop
But the cycle will never cease today
The understanding of things will be made
For then true belief will make amends.

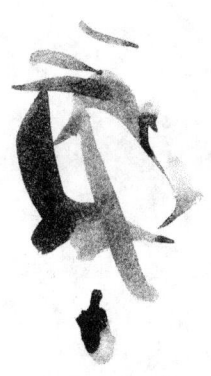

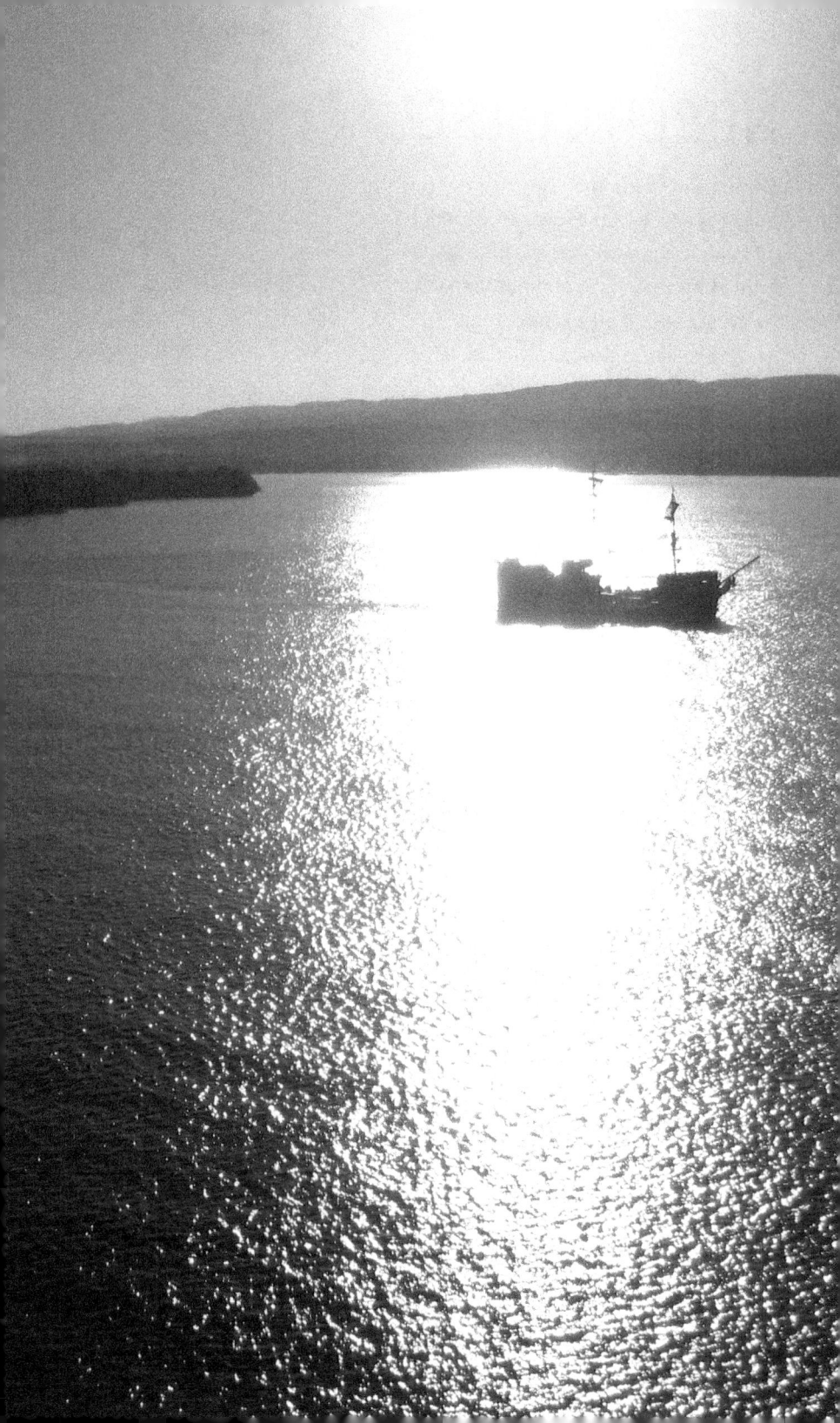

SITTING IN MOTION

Will the inky pens ever run dry
Never, for then none will be told
To make beautiful music together
Having long lasting love
Light as the tiniest feather
So again the story will be told
Not over ocean but over sea
The fountain flows with a never end
Making time as still as frost
But cold we are not to this day
A warm sunshine is headed our way
So does the ink begin to run out
The writing continues without a doubt
Voices of happiness come from a far
Seems so distant like a long lost star
Like an angel sitting in motion
Couldn't believe, couldn't except the notion
So the whisper was told in a tear drop
Landed with a skip and then a hop
Promised it was real and would never stop.

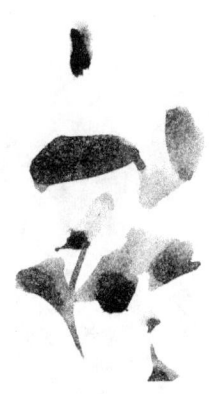

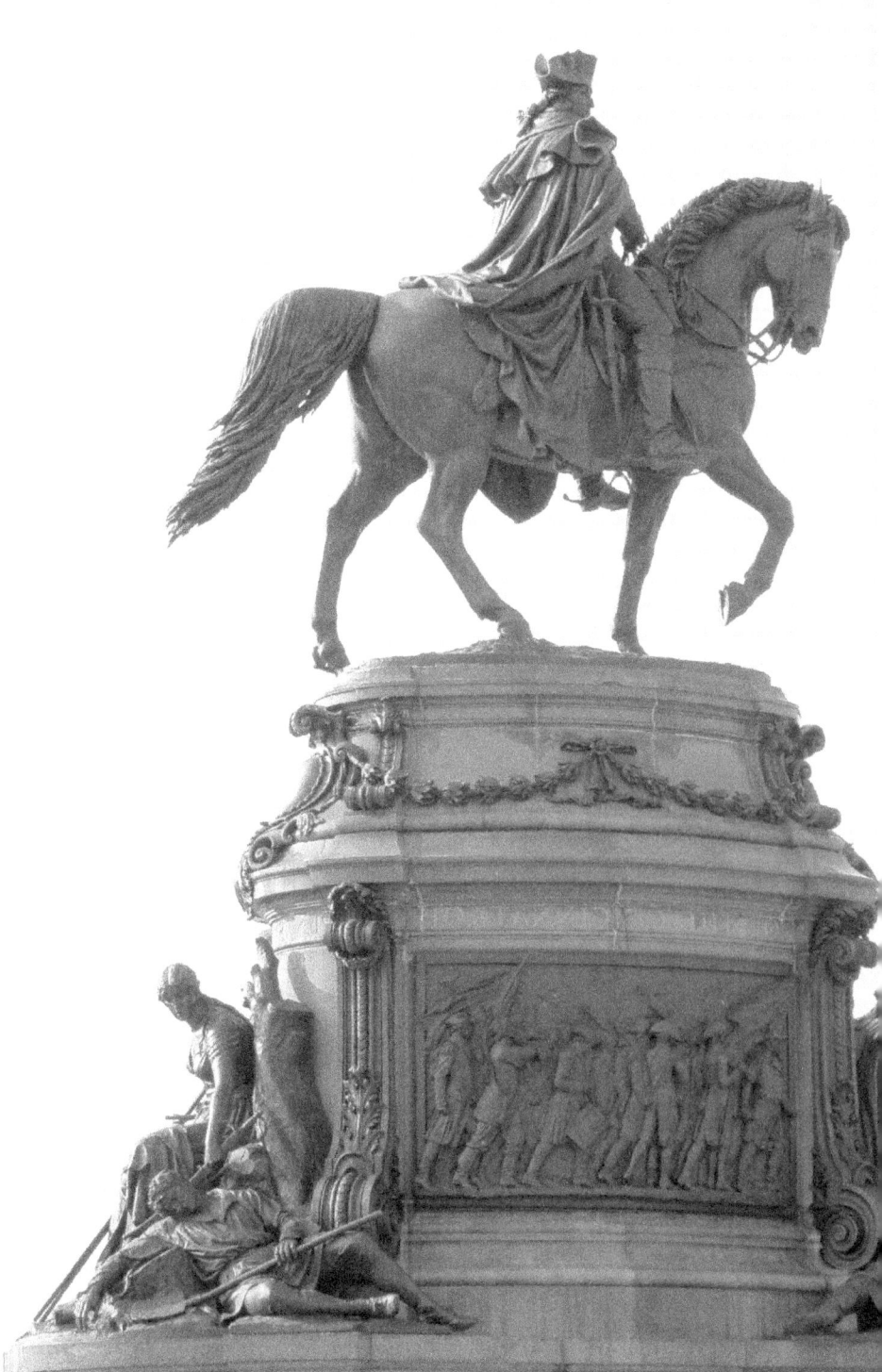

BEAUTIFUL DISPLAY

A reflection in a drop of rain
Who is it to this day we see
A lost king about to see his way
So does this happen to an extreme
Or will it turn out to be as it seemed
Will the pens overflow with ink
As if as they said, is that what you think
So what if the words come out baffled
Wasn't a problem no one was hassled
Like an angel floating in the pool of gems
It's to these thoughts these things stem
Mixed up words we describe to us
Showing off things without a fuss
So when you ask do we see this show
Never, like angels lost in the snow
Happens time and time again today
It's a beautiful scene, a beautiful display
So take note of what happened here
Nothing happened everything was clear
You saw it again, you've seen it before
Never know what the next page has in store.

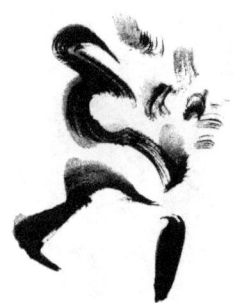

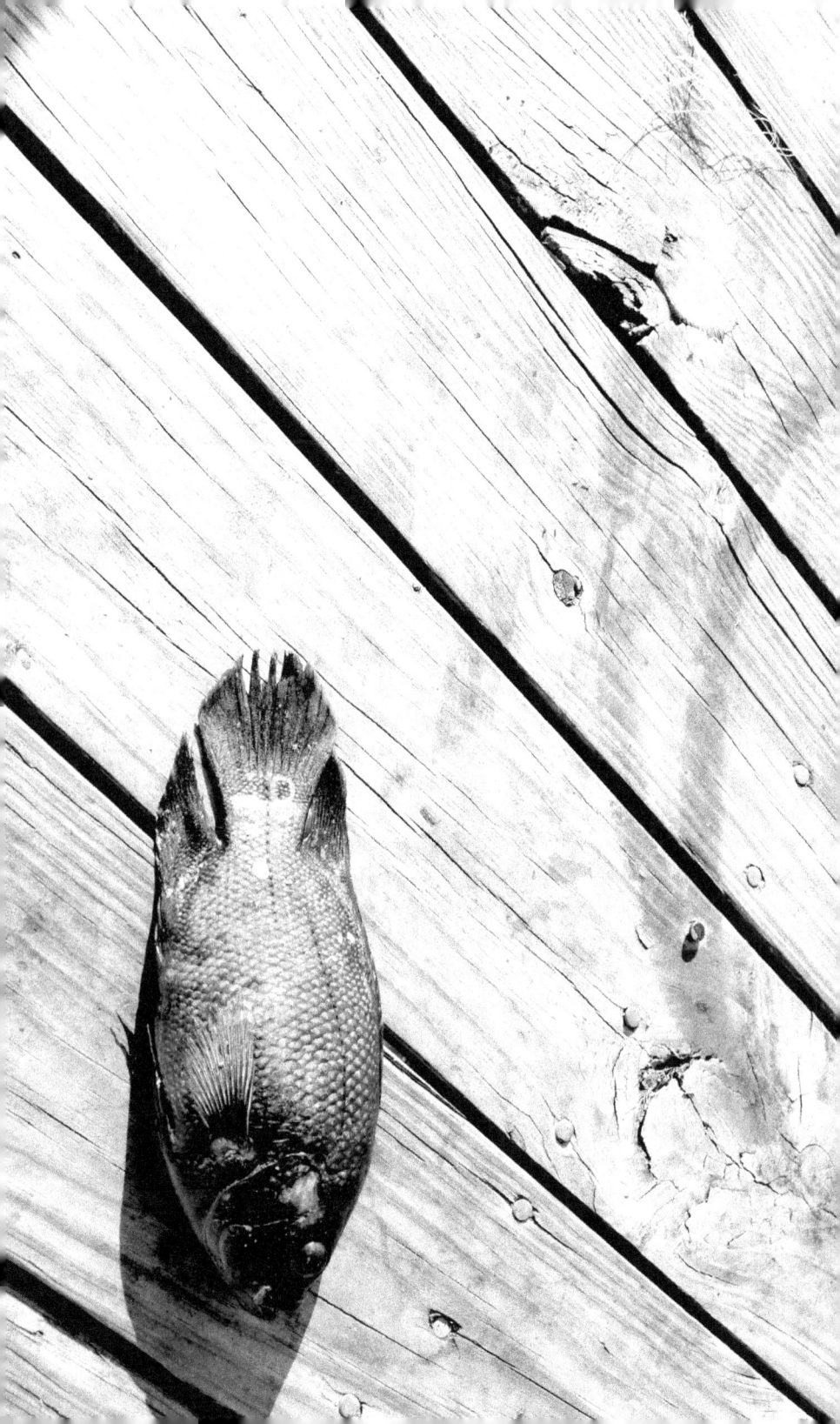

JUMPIN JACK FLASH

Jumpin Jack Flash bolts into action
Leaving behind him a wake of caffeine
Eyes twitching beyond our belief
Face dropping to the numb silence
Wake up Jack for the day has come
Smoke escapes his ears from the fury
A restlessness begins to confuse
The skin itching with his happiness
He's down, He's up, He's gone, Lost
Wake up Jack for the night has come
Now the nostrils bleed with smoke
Boiling water blends his mix
A shot to the eyes help to wake
Breaking points help to make reality
Faded light usually helps to sleep
But to this day nothing will help
Confusion brings jack here everyday
To the same point with no break
Ending though would stop today
Then what of tomorrow would he do
Jack would be lost without endless days.

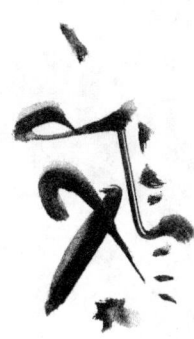

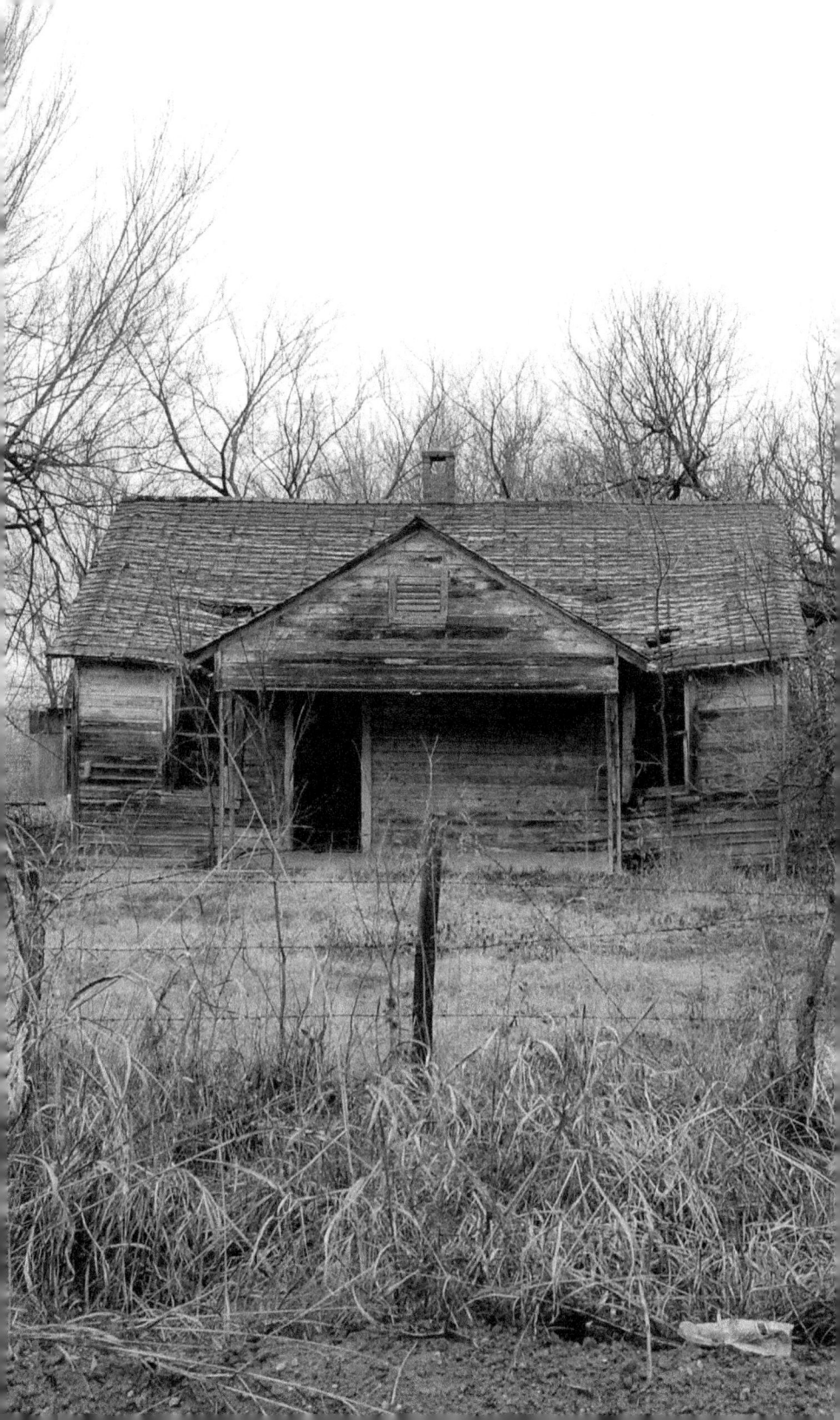

FORSAKEN SOULS

Clocks spinning with endless time
Seeing a walk walked before
Different day with the same old trail
Passing snails once been seen
Old friends with a slow path
Smacking clouds make their music
Shaking the earth as it moves
Rushing streams split the land
Opening a new path for some to take
For all know where most end up
Like oceans full of life bring light
Cycles which make time like lost clocks
A maze that tries to confuse simple minds
Like a dream that may show you a trace
Clues into a reality that's been lost
So close thy eyes or you will not see
Forsaken souls of children been lost
Seekers of days try to find them
Mistakes take a life time to heal
Making the time as endless as light
Watching clocks spin about their day.

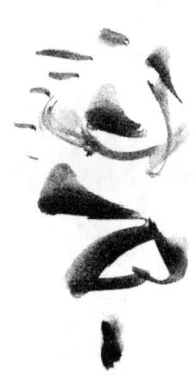

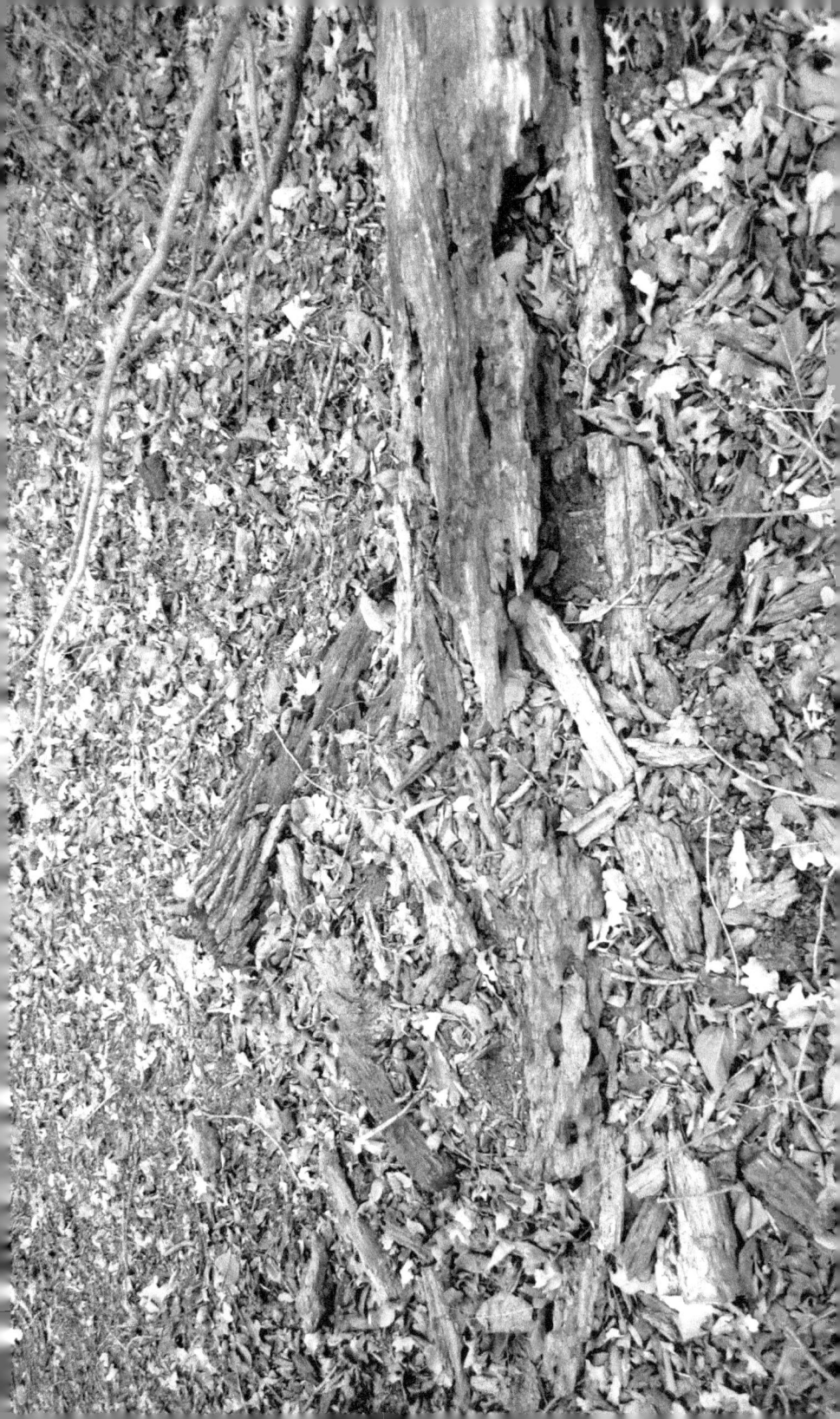

CLOUDS OF THOUGHT

Decrepit ways fusing the bones
An ache which cuts the deepness
Breaking a reality of an old day
Straining to meet a light of existence
Lost in a once sacred jungle
Masked by the monstrous length of vines
Movement is the only strider in the land
Shaking the earth as it wiggles about
Winds of time push them effortlessly
Making a trial of endless emotion
As the cracking sound deafens pain
Whispers are heard beneath the ache
A strain is made to reach above
Pulling a forgotten world amongst them
A might which will bear no other
For existence has to meet light to forget
Only the memory of pain arises from
Once heavy filled clouds of thought
Which will never have to imagine
A life of light amongst the darkness
For a true path of nature has been made.

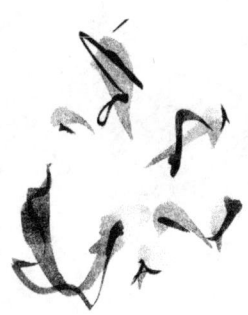

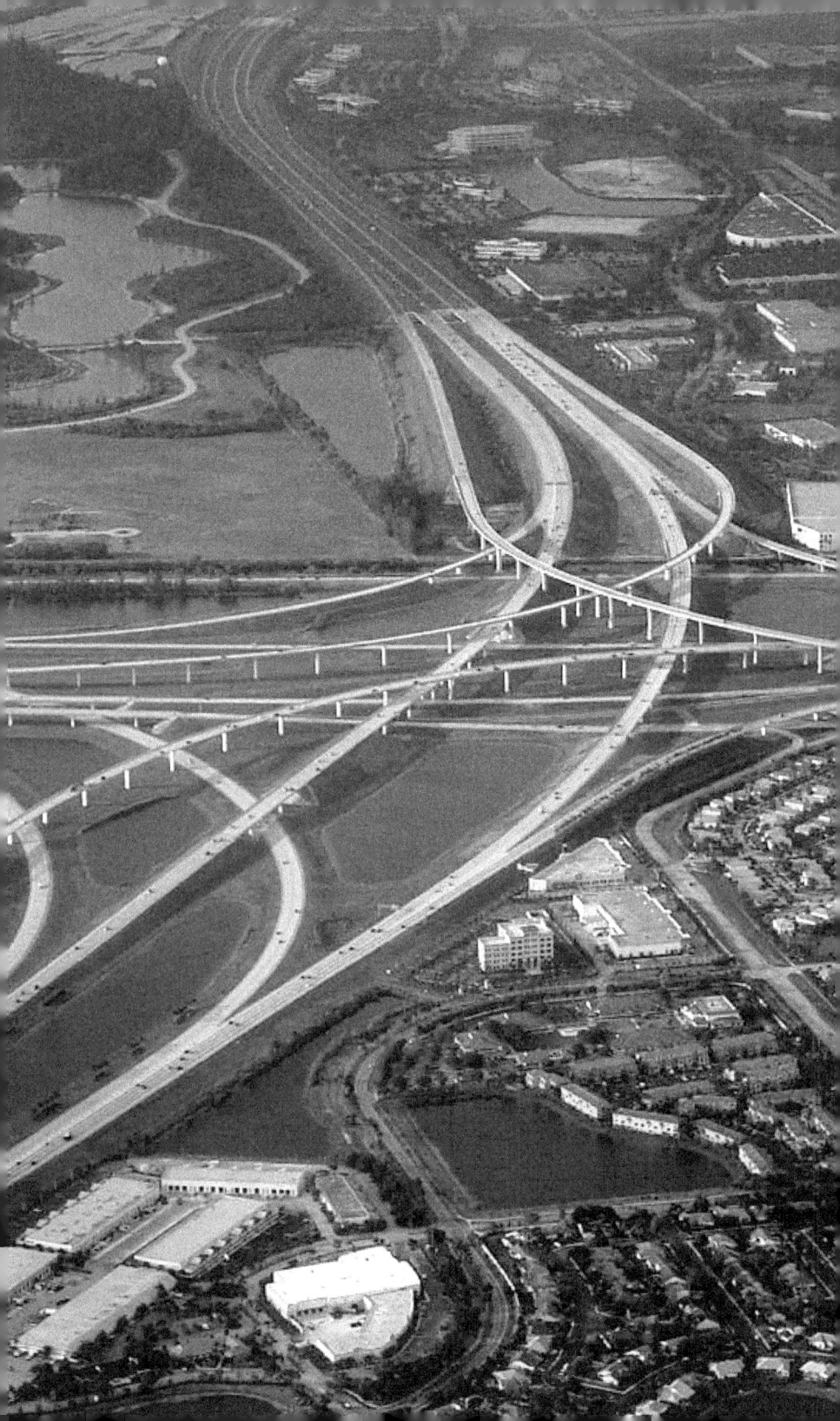

ENDLESS MOTION

A sphere sliding in an endless motion
An eternity to make their souls end
Almost to mask the reality of a truth
Begotten is the power received from light
Like ashes spit from mouths of dragons
Covering the dense skies with grayness
Rays make their way through clouds
Spreading their love across the land
A lion is awakened to understand light
For he will show to the world a truth
That each person has the power of happiness
Like a Buddha who sits upon a rock
His awareness brings a peace to us all
As spheres slide without any gravity
A wish is made upon a tiny star
Let endless motion never cease to exist
For eternity will never end a soul
Shut eyes will begin to notice things
A fear will be felt amongst the tribes
But acceptance makes way for truth
Only one can find it in one's self.

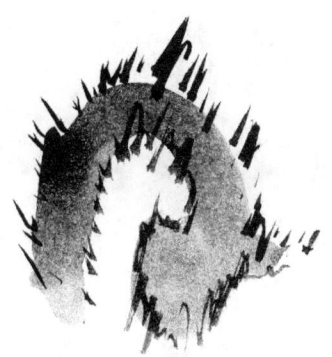

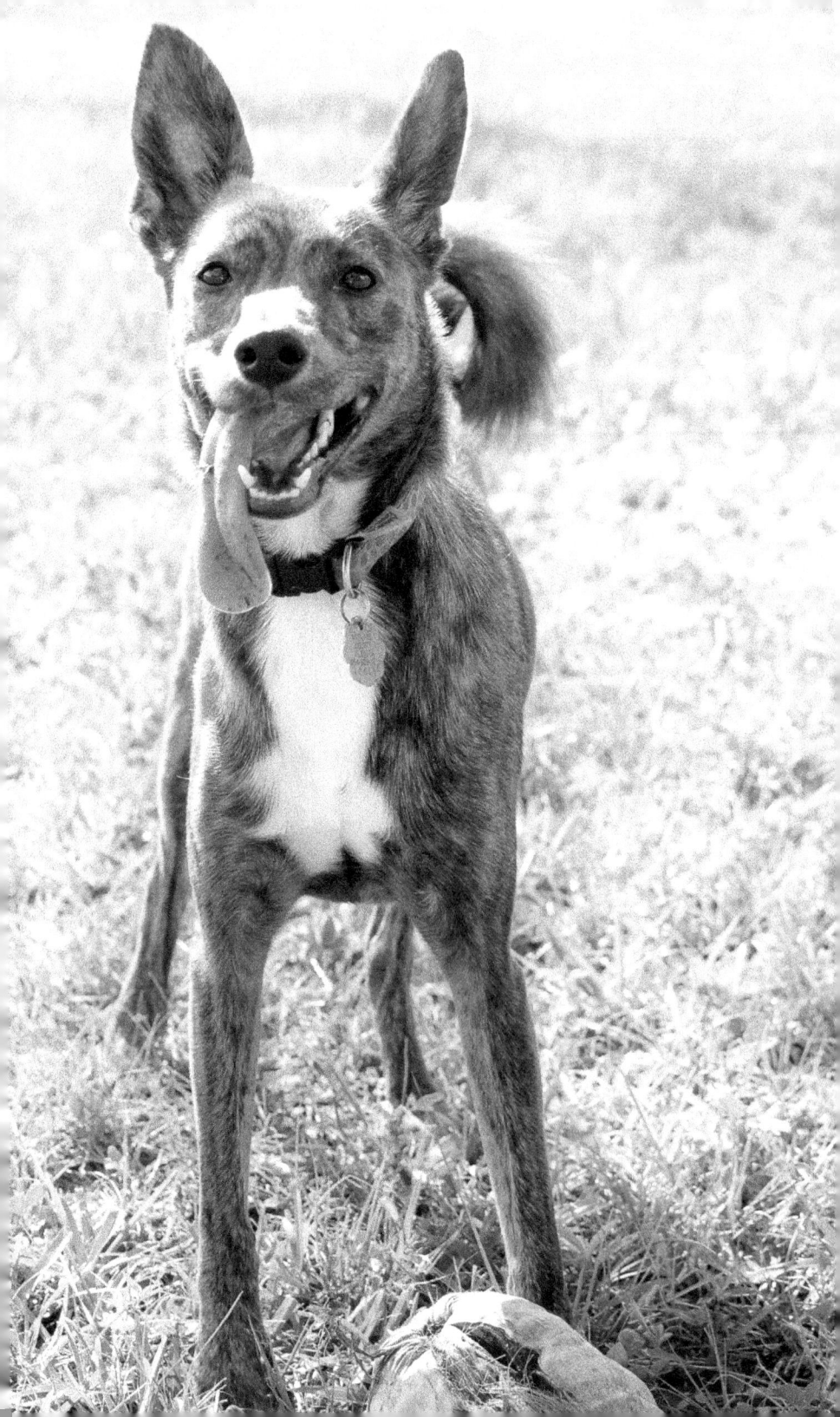

ANGEL EMBRACES

Grains of sand in an ocean so vast
As when lightning strikes the earth
Forming shards of glass to expose
While thy mother sheds her rain
She gives peaceful waves of pleasure
As an angel embraces the lion of truth
She wishes upon a shell to make sound
Drums of the current push us further
Shifting the skies that dot reflections
In the distance it seems so clear
A horizon showing just how flat
Winds pushing molecules to their end
Gravity pulling back to remind them
Fate as we have it makes things happen
A clock which has already been made
Setting life into motion with the time of life
Like a lion who plays nameless games
Walking amongst them as he does
Giving to the world all that there is
Like a dream there is no wake
Sitting hoping to make it a truth.

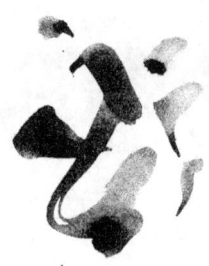

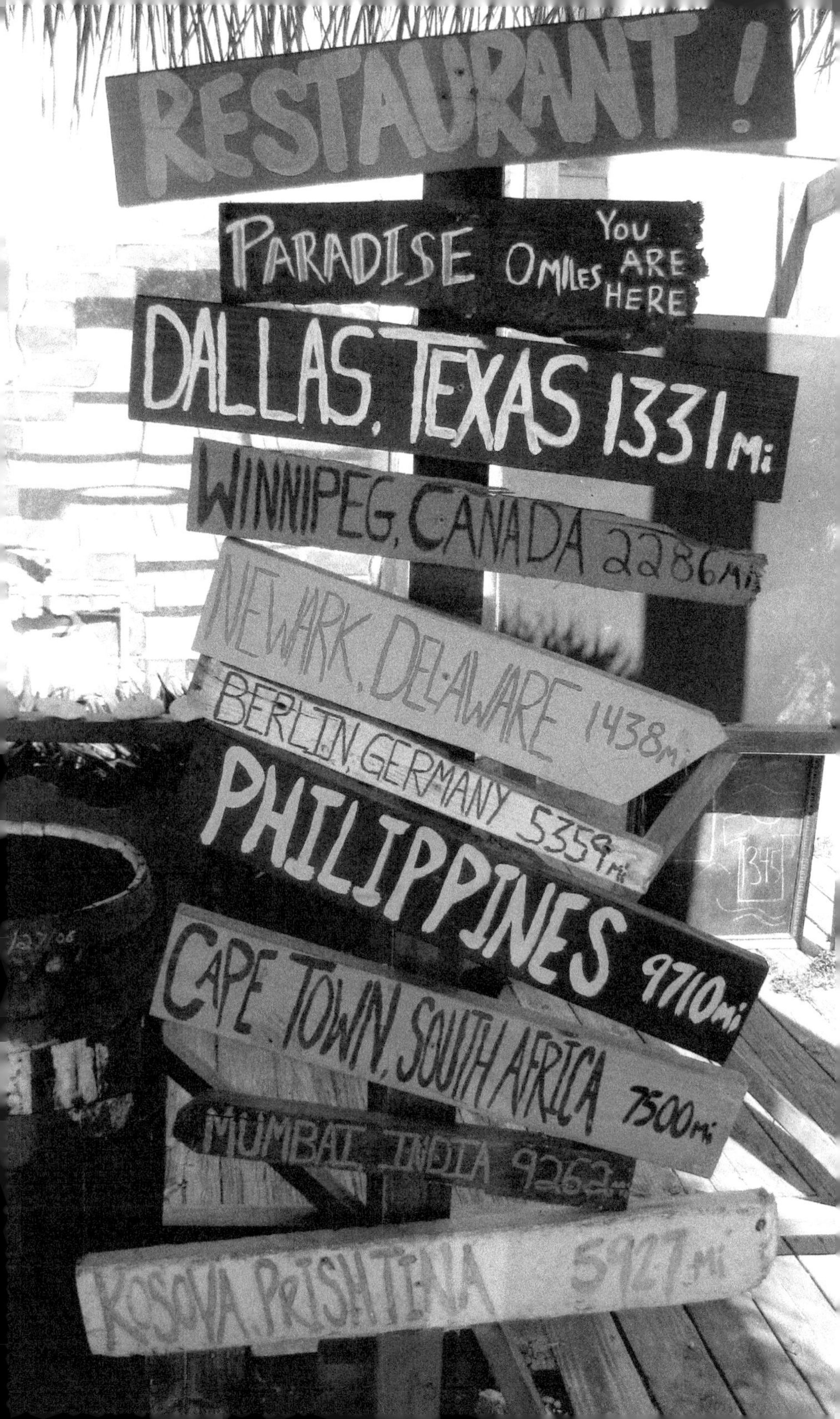
RESTAURANT!
PARADISE
0 MILES
YOU ARE HERE
DALLAS, TEXAS 1331 Mi
WINNIPEG, CANADA 2286 Mi
NEWARK, DELAWARE 1438 m
BERLIN, GERMANY 5359 Mi
PHILIPPINES 9710 mi
CAPE TOWN, SOUTH AFRICA 7500 mi
MUMBAI, INDIA 9262
KOSOVA PRISHTINA 5927 mi

MANY CREATORS

Twin dotted strains of glowing paint
Covering broken dreams of an angel
Wind shocking cold faces of tribes
Crumbs in a house of holy bread
Some sour wine to help ease the pain
Drowning in pages of lost writers
Filling pages of a book to the world
Spoken words which seem to make sense
A fool who speaks knows nothing
So only the curious will find answers
A truth has been told if you have eyes
Like stories of old which tell no lies
Just look where most never do
Within thyself one can find truth
For the beholder holds all dreams
Only they can poses a truth be told
Ancients have written these ways
Been spoken since the beginning
Mastered by many creators knowing
An amazing painting has been created
Let the glowing strains tell the truth.

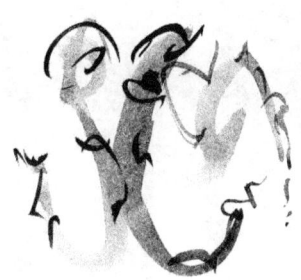

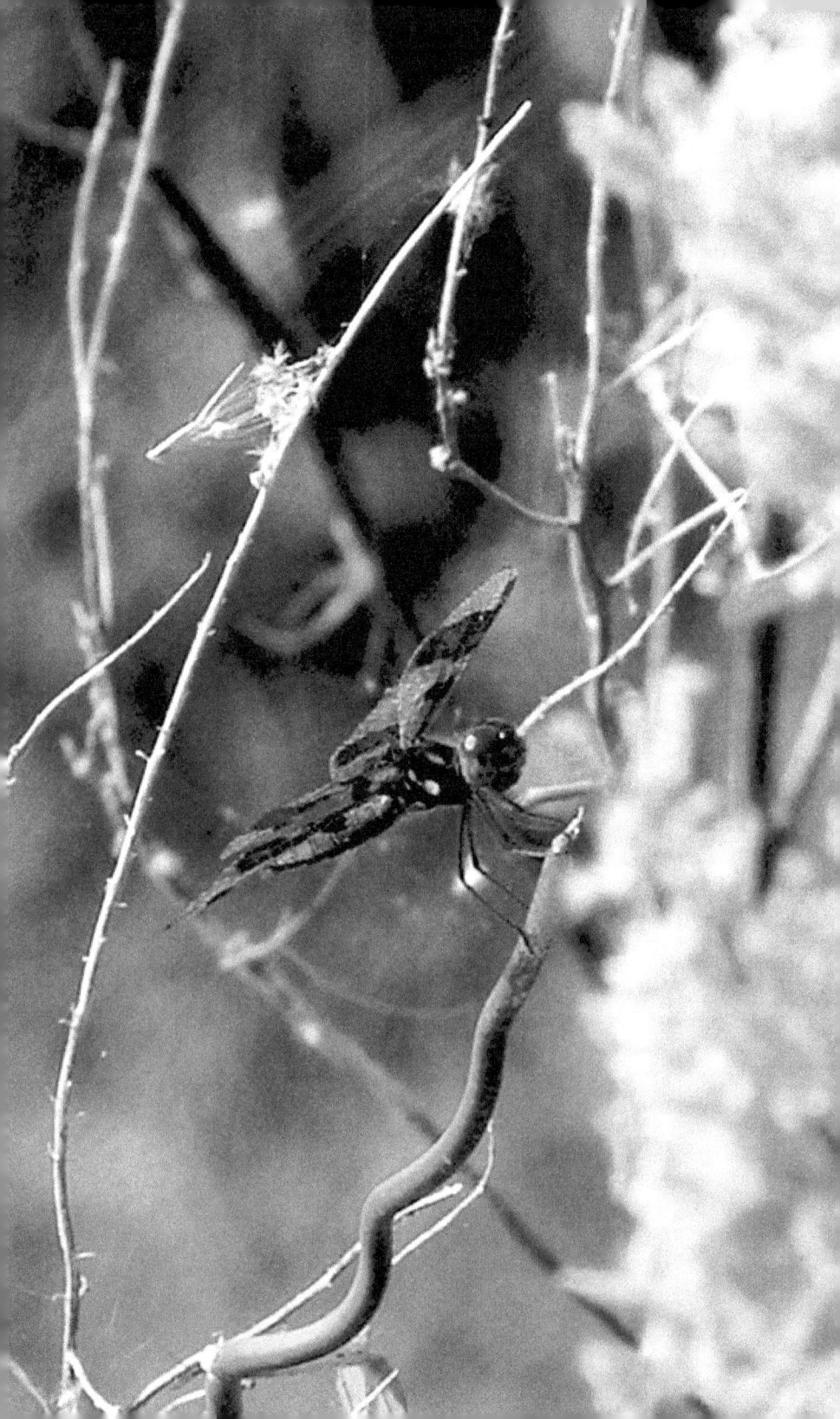

DRAGONFLIES CHOKED

Scratches in the dark make way
Poking at the skin to reveal pain
A slice trickles leaving drops of dew
Fumes rise from the silent stream
Metallic slides leaving a rusty smell
Looks like something not felt
From where will this all escape
Released allowing all to flow
 Puddles reminding of lost reflections
When dragonflies choked on splinters
Lions were lost to a mighty world
Angels cried amongst the dead
Or these puddles remind of nothing
Choking on fumes from open skin
Exhaled by pressure amongst them
Letting pools fill by their side
Watching as the star spins off
Making one with the great gathering
Drowning in the deception of it
Gasping for it to hold some pressure
Only to be released and let go.

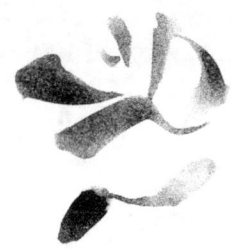

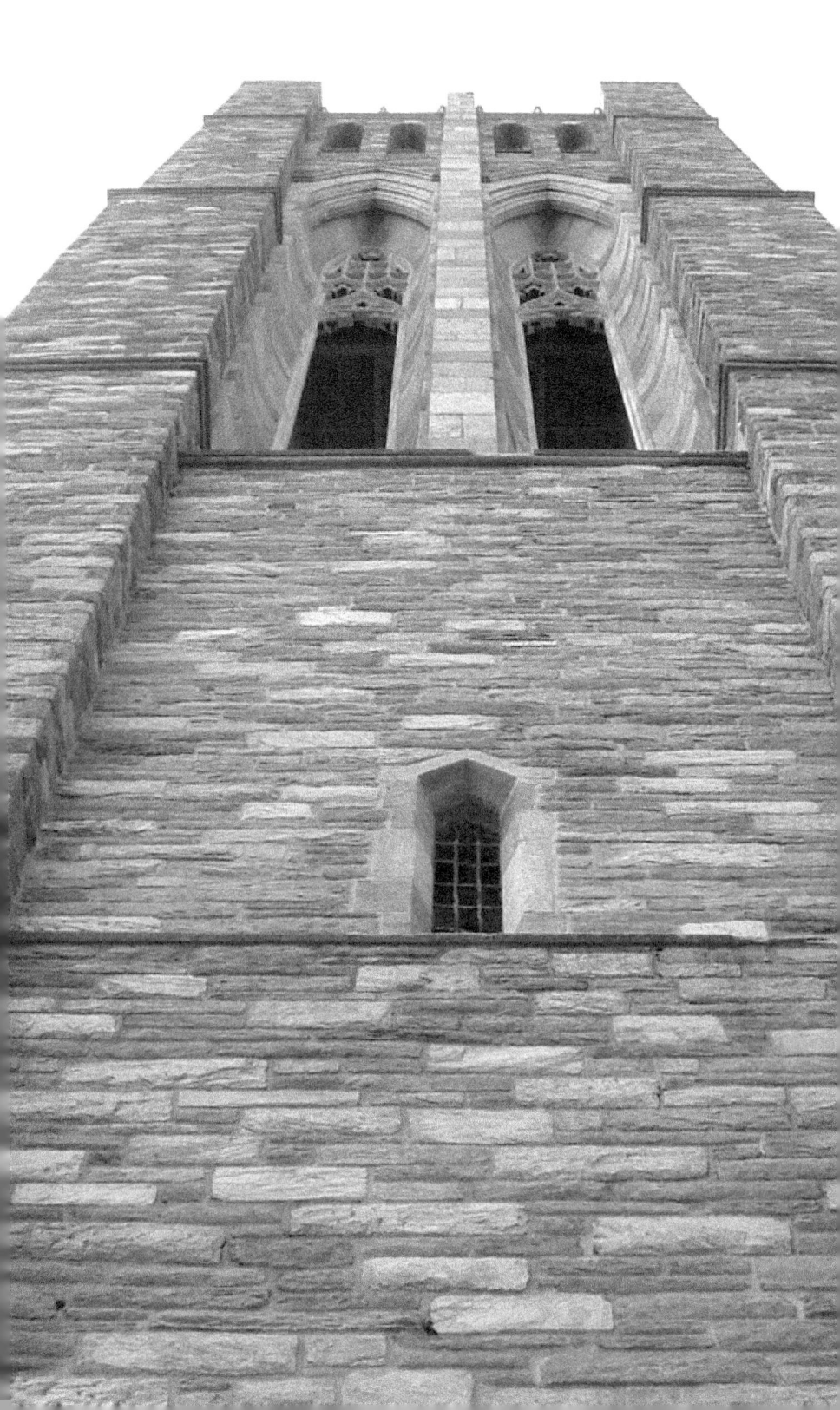

CONFUSING US

A big drop has been released again
Heat boils doing the things it does
A wrinkle in a hand that will write
Lost pages will almost always repeat
Eyes barley closed to tell the truth
Like the pushing wind of crushed angels
Played making without the sound of a smile
The heat makes it to much to take
Lashed out in unexpressive ways made
Challenging a sense of peace shown clear
As if words have any sort of meaning
Deranged in the thought of a past
Threatened by the making when set near
Pushing the seeds of wind to move
To again start again as they do once again
Because nothing will ever be clear
Jumbled sentences confusing us all
Scattered phrases which they live by
A story which has no facts of own
Just a truth made of lies to believe
Because again we will see the show.

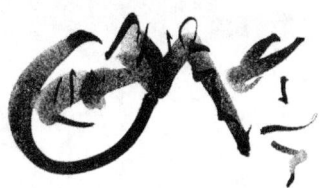

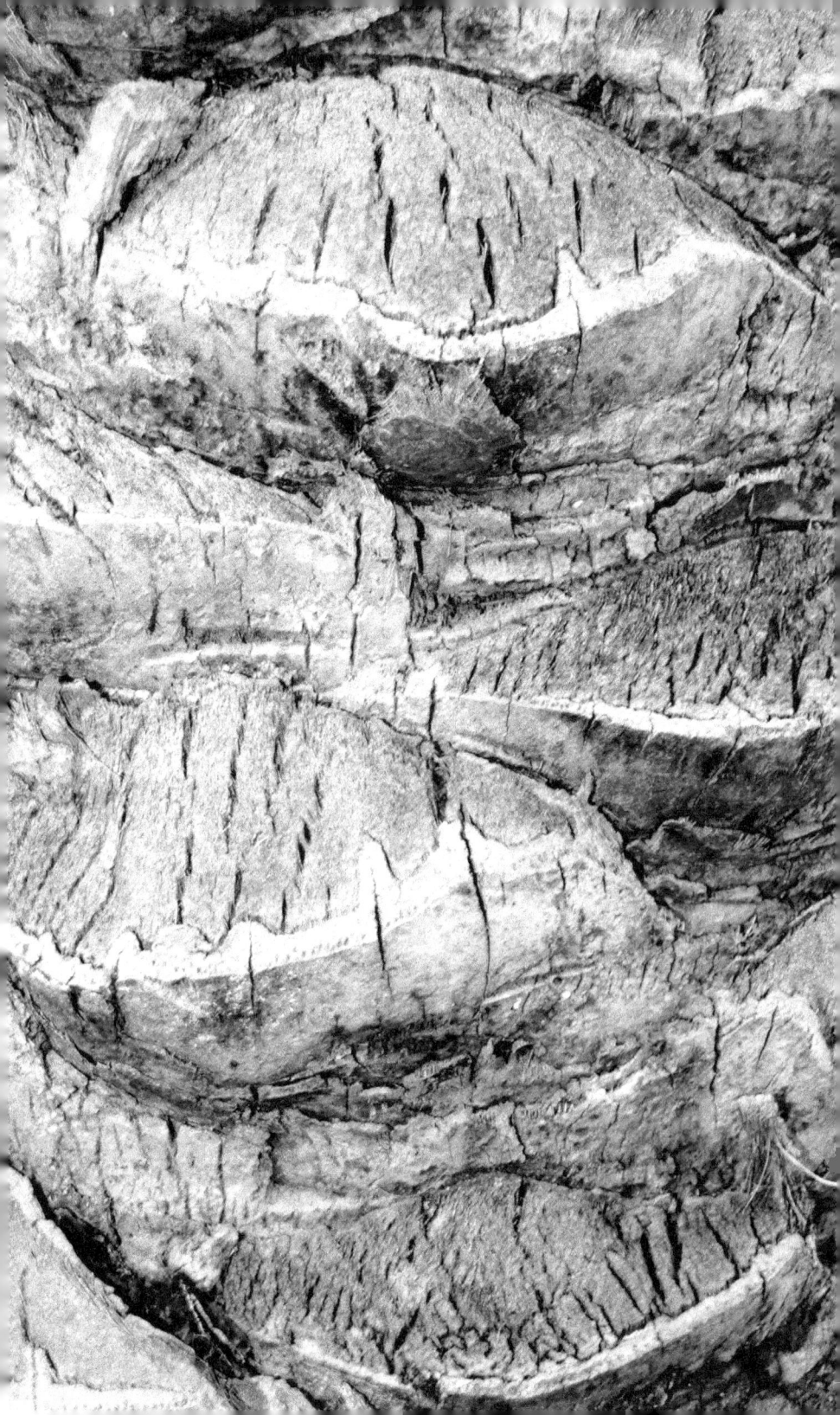

WRINKLES OF TIME

Nothingness of sleep has many dreams filled
A point of exertion pushing the tides
Uncomfortable within lost times
But yet the sight of small kings smile
For their mother queen helps to guide
Language of tribes to be sheltered
Winds pass blowing the nectar of sweet
Making lost lions believe in thy source
The heat spreads upon broken backs
For there is comfort even for lost bones
Beading up amongst wrinkles of time
Playing as if there is no strain here
Shade cools bringing songs of birds alive
Confusion makes way for everything
A speed uncontrolled by fate
Spattered in the tongues of most men
For when does he who knows ever tell
As plain sight gives to the parting sea
We can make clear of our test
Talked to for most ears do not listen
Within is a key to a truth of knowledge.

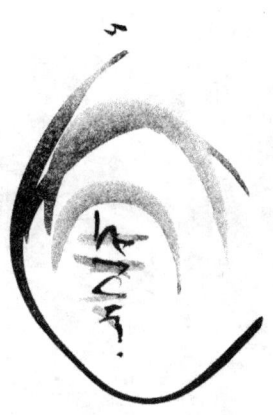

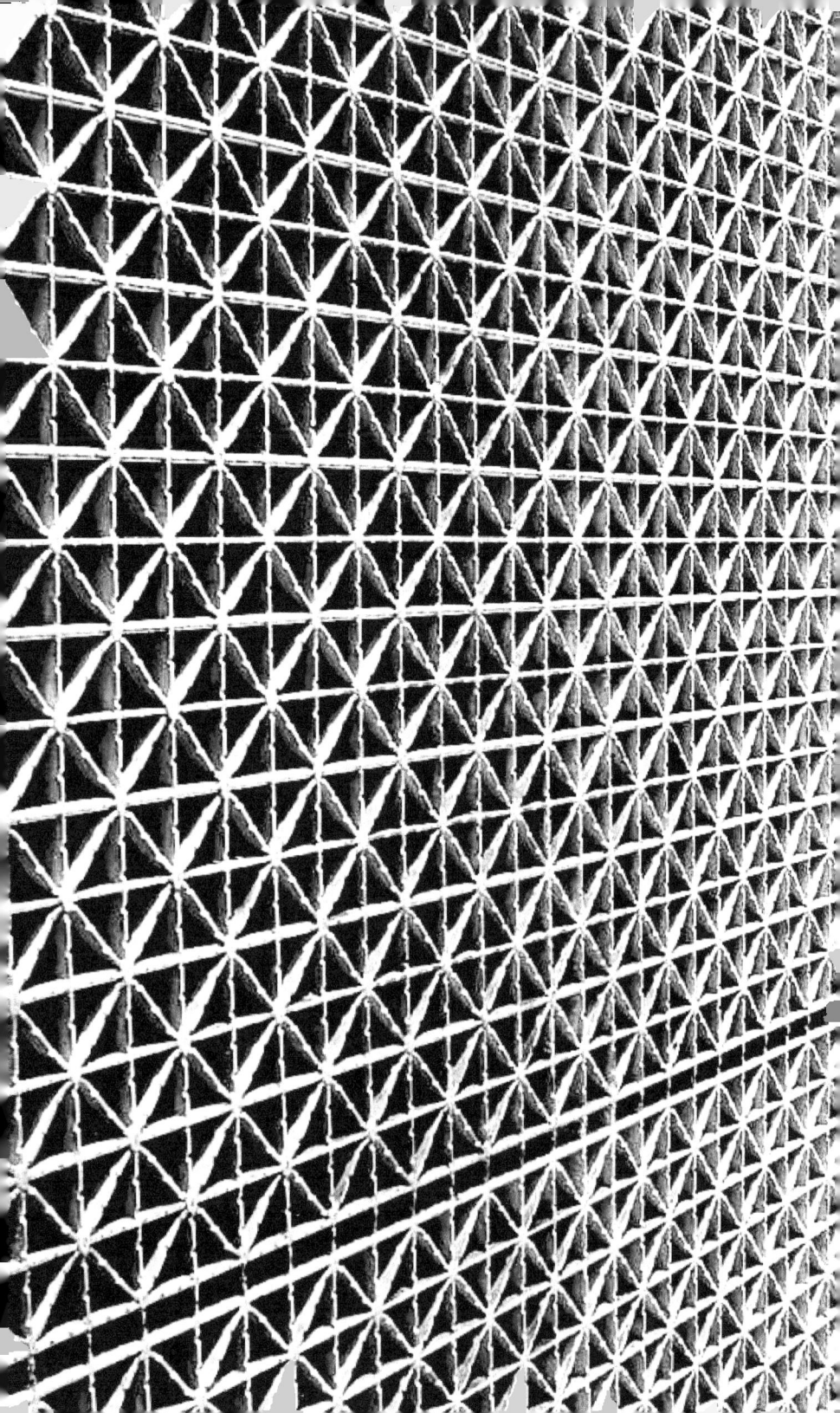

CAST OF FIRE

Patrons of an ill-gotten society
Masked by men of a different kind
Played as if the game was never started
Only to suppress a reality once showen
Conversing amongst them made false
Being shown is sometimes the darkness
Secrets sometimes are the meanings made
Dusty paths line a memory of clear roads
Sacred days make a realization certain
For once there was a king born Sabbath
Bringing to this world a great understanding
Of truth which is filled with small lies
Only to find it's in one self a kingdom
That these things can be obtained by any
It's not hidden in some lost place
One will not be sent nor cast of fire
All to be done must make of a real thought
Help might only make of a confusion
Look deep it's closer then thoughts know
For lessons were made for one to learn
Been shown the way, now just find it.

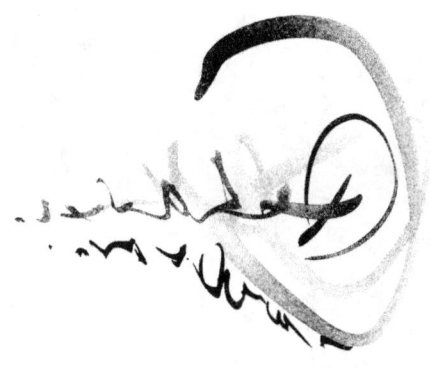

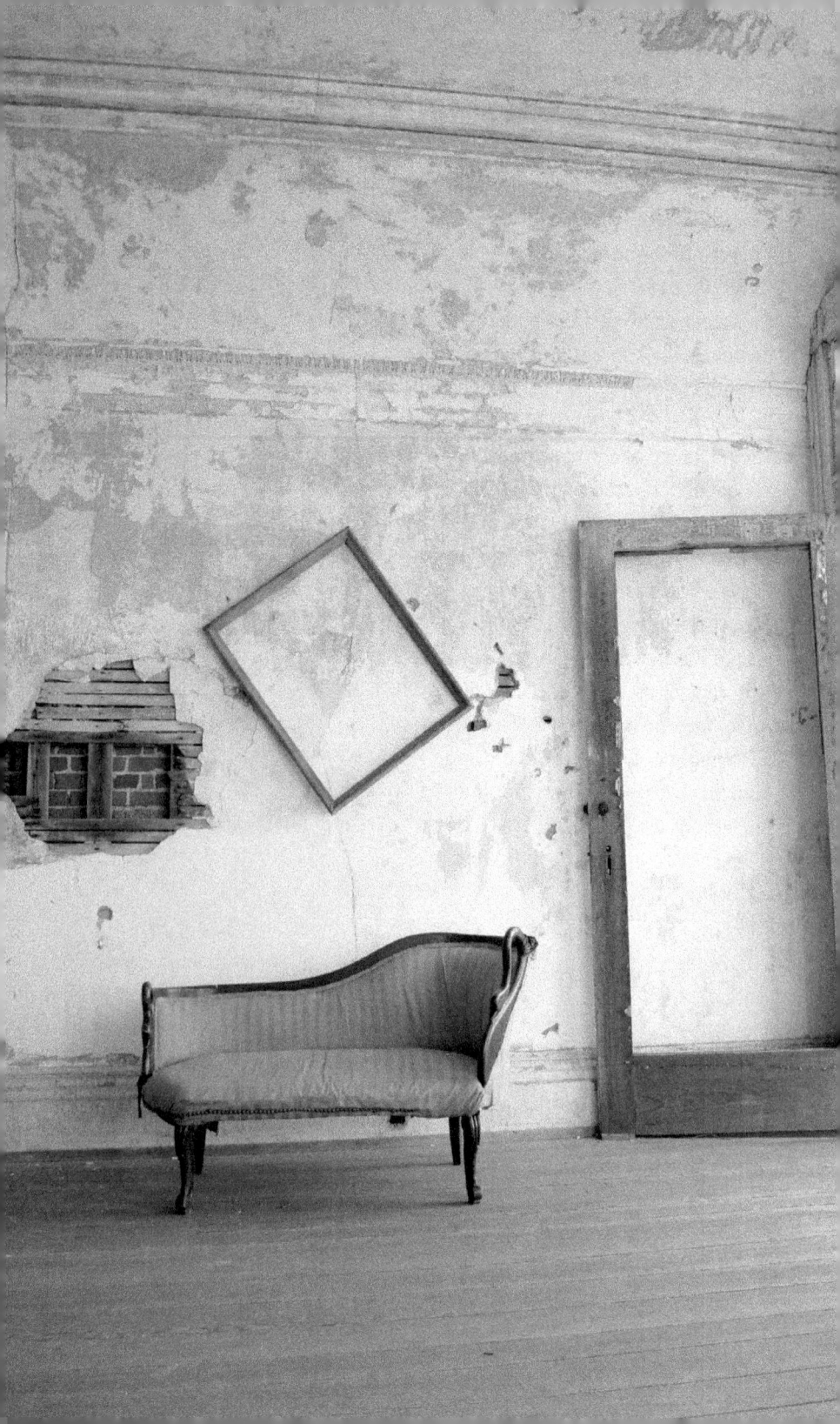

BRINGS COMFORT

The angels of a Kings world
Beautiful are they all in the same
One in common yet so different in likeness
Emotions strange yet do they have
Amazing in the care that they do bring
For each brings heaven with soft hands
But how does each make it seem complete
Each filling a broken glass made of holes
Smiles do they always bring as gifts
Slowing the leaks made of a broken life
For how does a King choose a lost Queen
Was it already set forth by the God of one
Does health depend on unknown fates
For a prince must be made to carry
The lines will not end if to be said
A truth will be passed to help understand
Which will be made by thy sacred angel
Her love will bring comfort to a king
Helping to raise light from a child mind
So this is made for angels of the world
Thanks be made to them for their smiles.

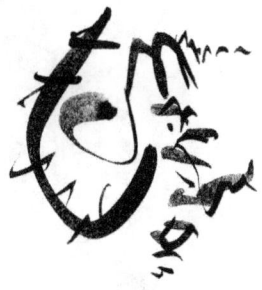

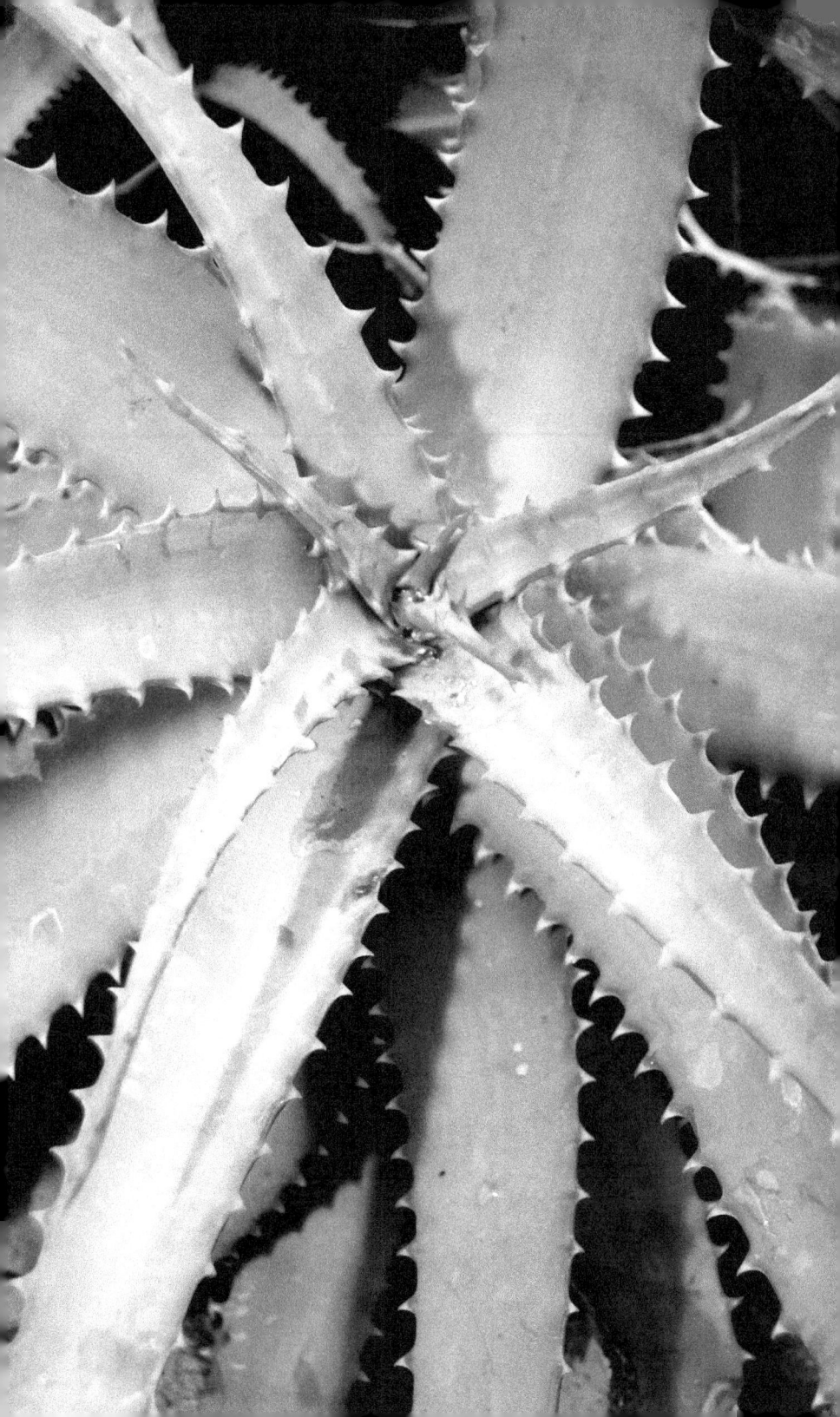

MAGICAL TOUCH

Cadence makes for bright whispering nights
Writing in stone makes thy history known
Shatters of wind made for delight of nature
Whims of angels make smiles everlasting
Lost faster than most snails make speed
Sounds forced to an obscene nature made
Like silent screams made to move thy force
Dipping into the aggression of a lost hope
They lose who they make way for with them
Sleeping with the awakening sound of death
Colliding with a reality never made true
So does one make sense of nothing heard
Is one made with defining sound of light
Open boxes make closed doors feel tight
Battered by the softness of a magical touch
Smashed into pulp made of broken fingers
Making stench smell waste of its own
Undecided angels plucking silver bands
Lost in the way it makes red pebbles
Dotting the skies made of long amber
As the crystal salve soothes the made lion.

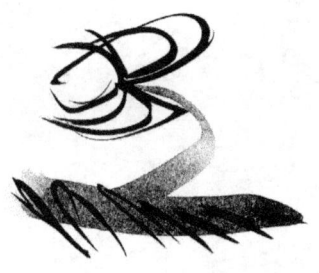

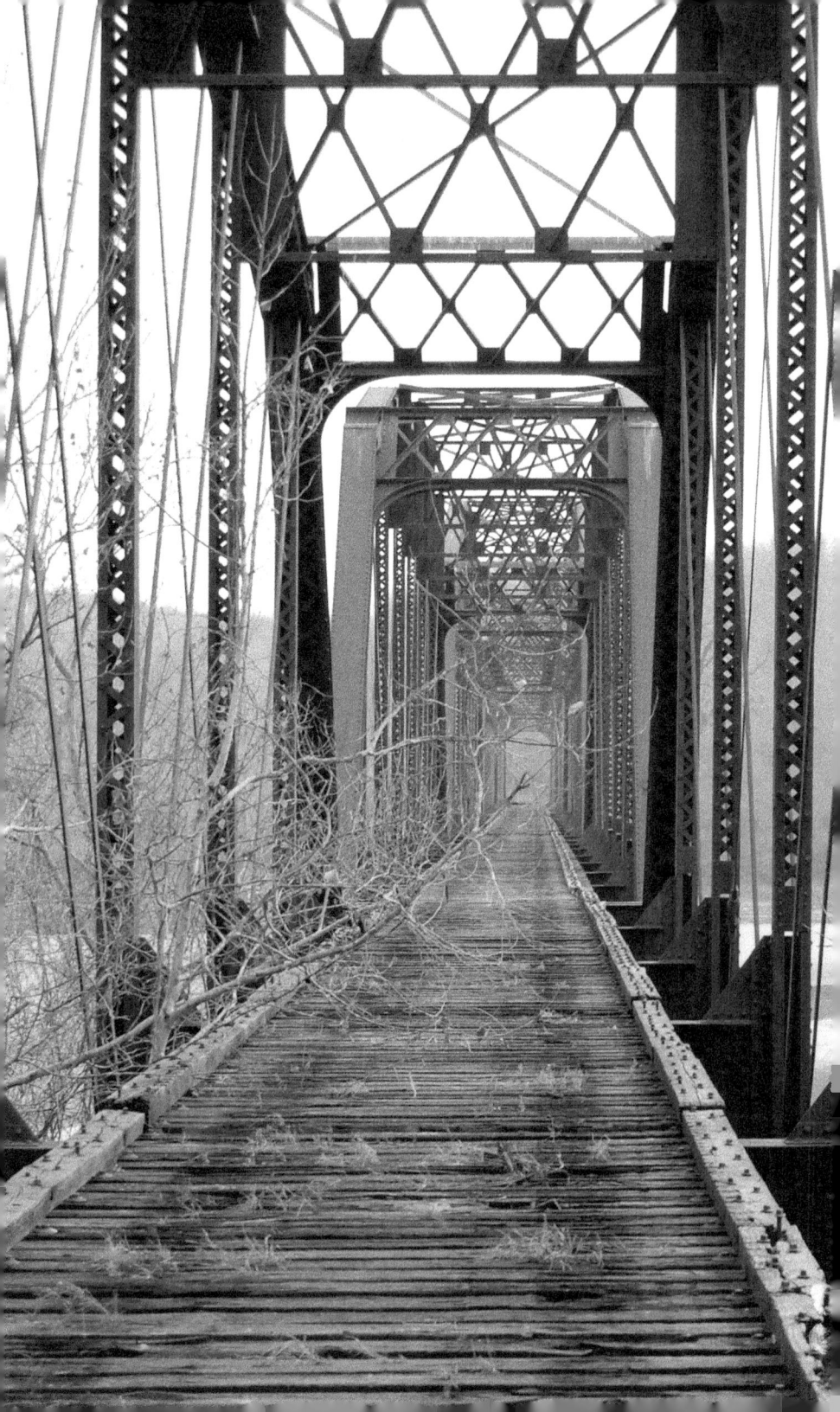

LOSE SIGHT

Relentless in the inked skin of an angel
Covered in the chaos which binds society
Blazing colors as if to be a creator
Expressing to the world beauty of art
Yet her elegance sets her apart to find
Amazing to explore in the nature of a story
Makes for fascinating adventures to find
Holding the way she remembers her dream
Never letting winds push a different current
Eyes wander as she moves to her own beat
Floating as if to never have been down
For how does a creature make existence
Hoping to never lose sight of a being
For if all was nothing then here would be an end
It would make a start seem so distant
As if there really was no place to begin
Only etched pictures can tell of a past
Filling the scenes just to overwhelm
A breath must be taken to exhale
Longing for a place she has found
Forgiving those who misunderstand her story.

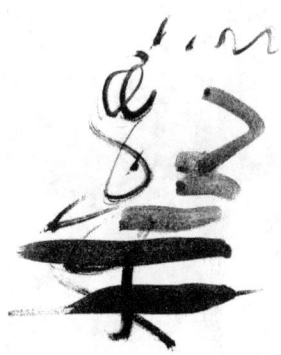

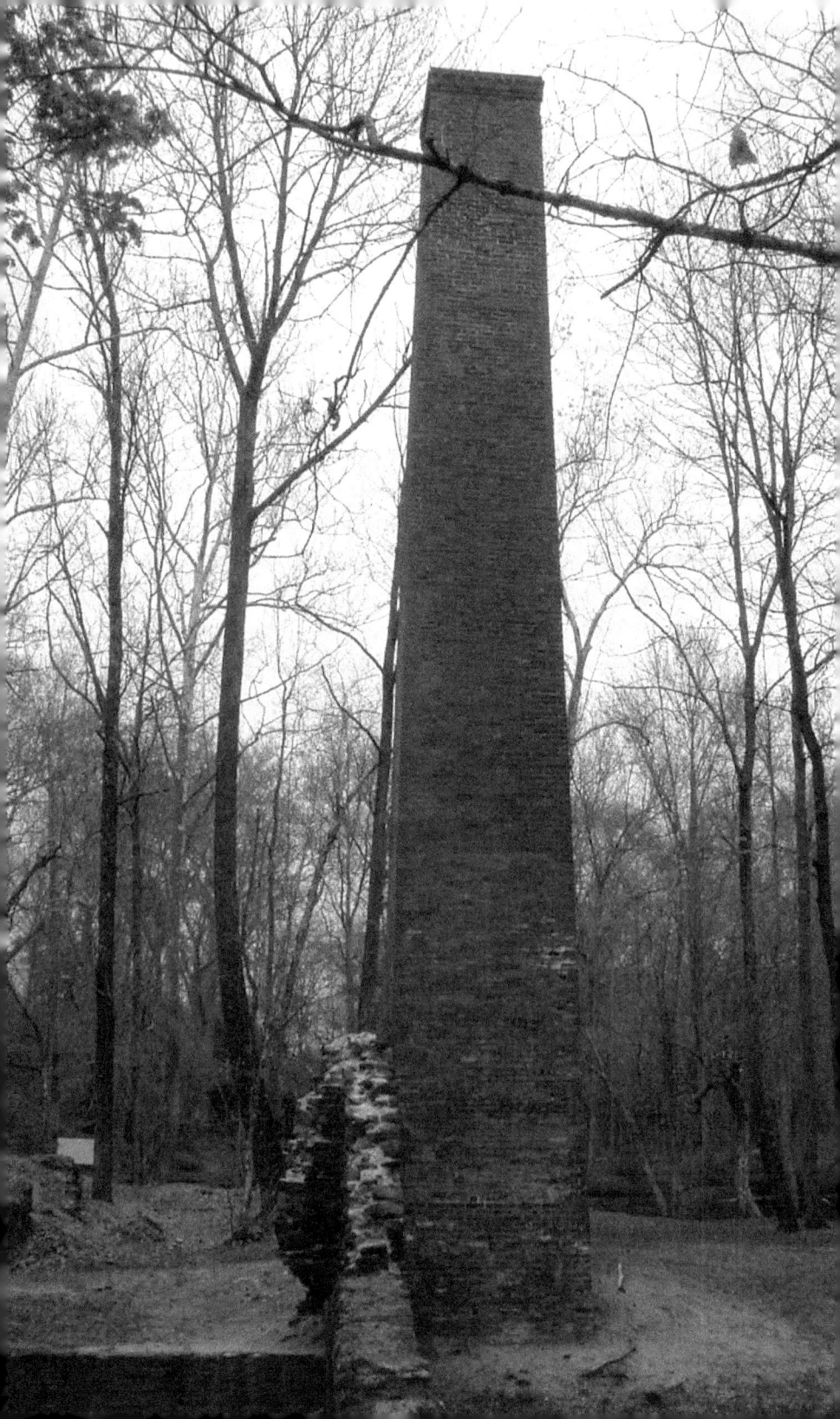

ERUPTION MADE

Stuck in sand covered chaos of mist
Salted as a strong sun dips in and out of sight
Flying shadows move about knowing flight
Asking not to be seen by a hunter of day
Sacred embrace makes thy lovers know
Warm blowing breezes will soften thy face
Discoveries of heart shaped seeds
Sights of orange beaked wind creatures
Helping to make a soul binding day by grace
Horizons made to seem so far and endless
But yet an angel stands washing in the tides
Moving as if to be one itself floating amongst
Almost as to be lost in a sea of life unheard
Even the tides themselves do not know to turn
Confusing to bring rain before light
Fighting away the sun only to bring night
Soaked in an eruption made of lost tears
Flooding broken rivers which seem so dry
Dancing about as if to move a mighty earth
Shaken for a great thirst has been tasted
Sleeping as she spins amongst bright suns.

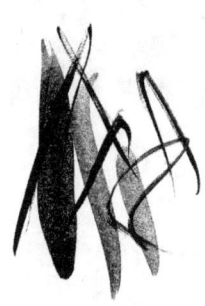

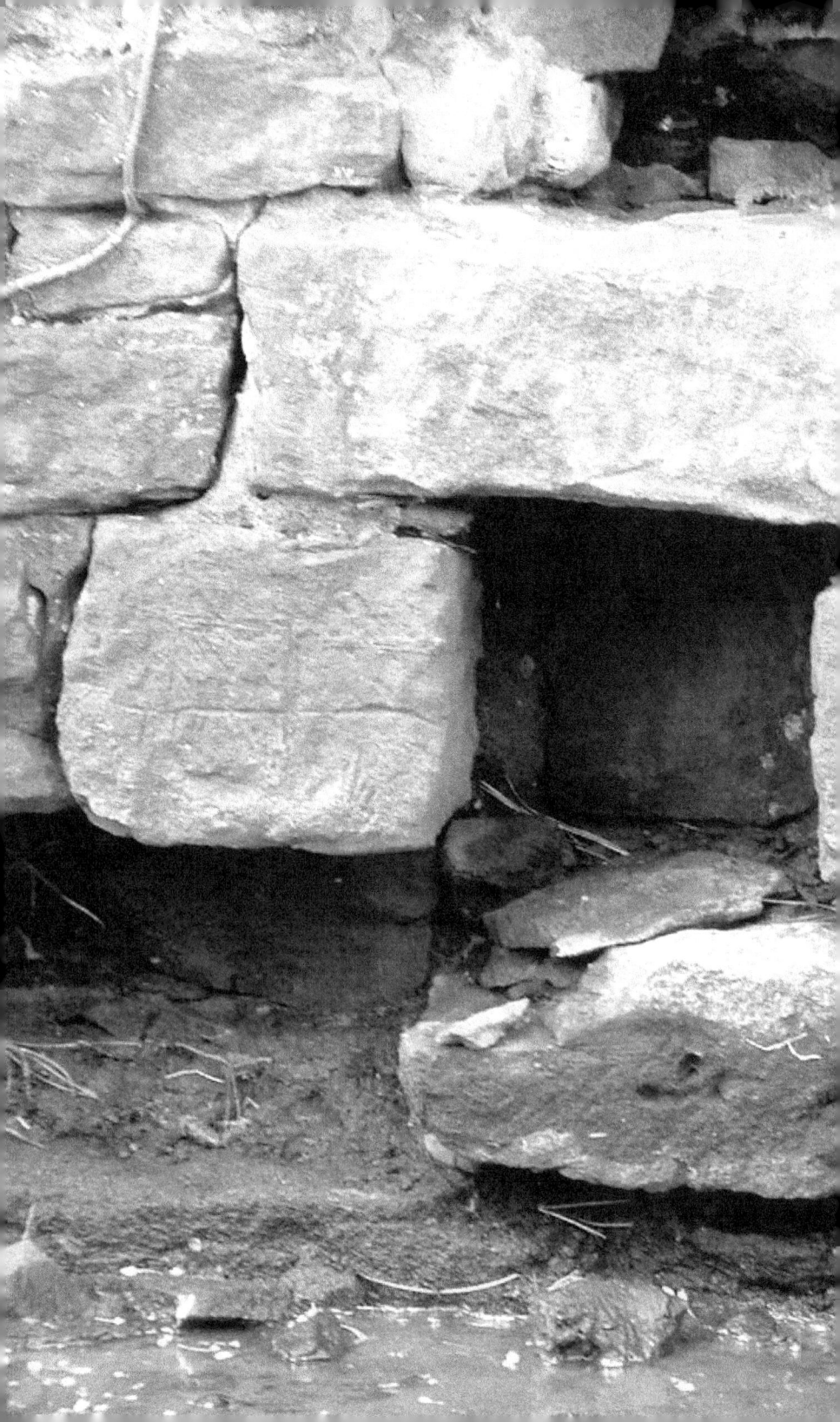

MOUNTAIN OF STONE

Undertaken gravity pulls on a force
Making as to seem like fog does not cloud
A heaviness that seems so strong in pressure
Nor water can cure a dryness once made
To a point of an underlying creature of myth
Paces of awkwardness fill the air of steam
Moisture which consumes cracks of rattled skin
For morning brings a nightly beast of prey
Hooded for none to see a true existence
Masked as to make their own way amongst
Creating an understanding but not yet ready
Driven to madness as if they really know
Saying one thing as yet to do onto another
So for who do you say to who really believes
A truth which no one seems to want to tell
Why do these myths begin in such a likeness
Does a scroll get lost in a sea of death
Does a boat sit upon a mountain of stone
Does a man return to life after such hatred
Many act as if to know only to never find
In thy self its been told of a truth known.

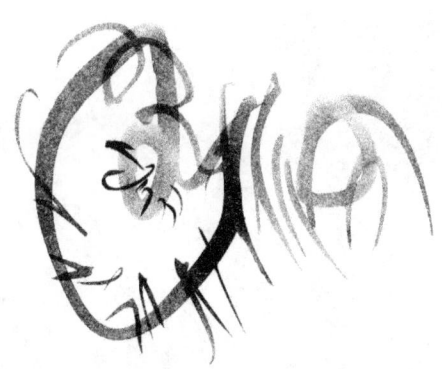

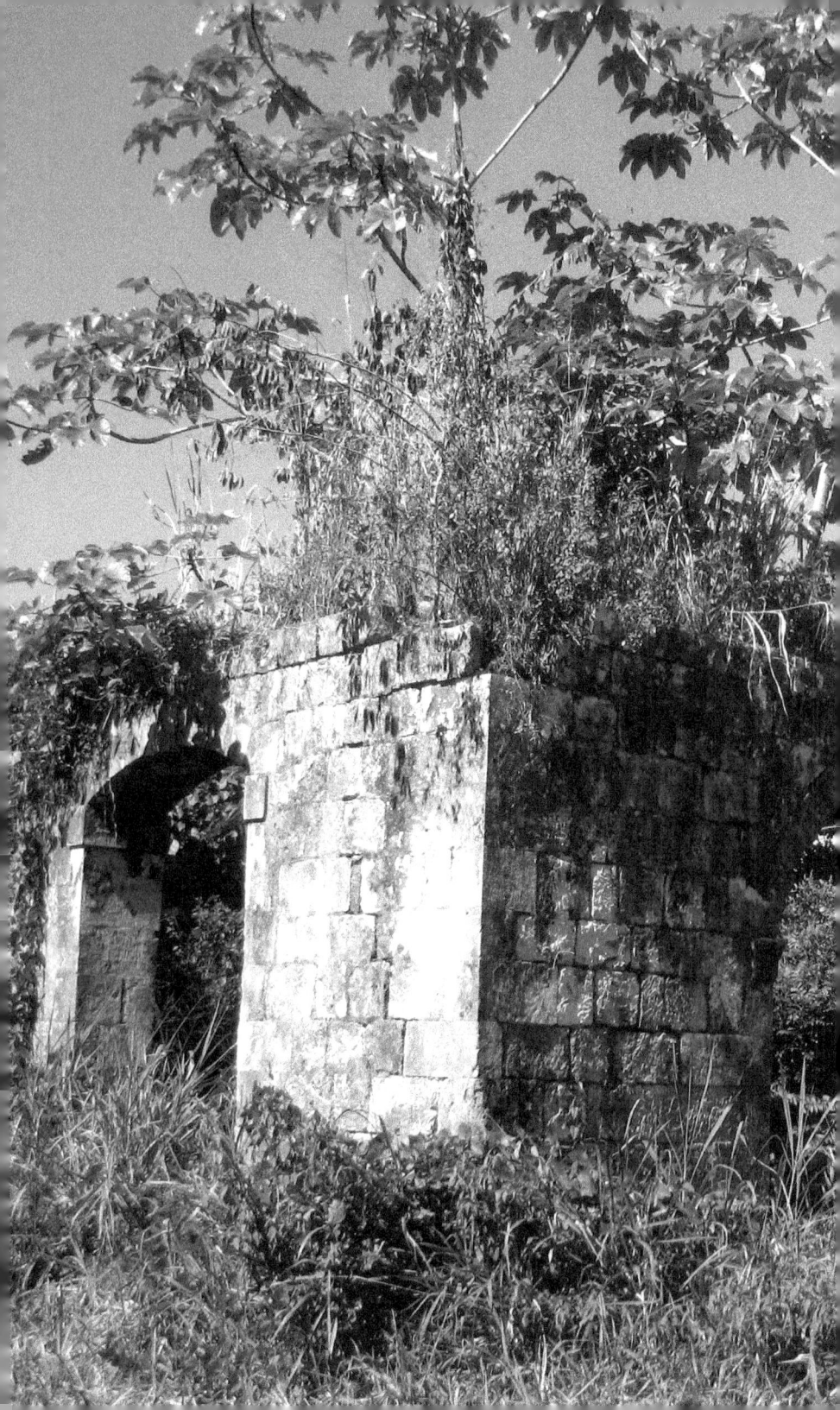

BLURRING REALITY

Mud cramped reality blurring mistakes
Does an ant fly upon wings of tragedy
Or does a rhino walk upon feet of destruction
For not even fables can make explanation
Like a hunger which devours an inner gourde
Pain that twitches with every thought
Consuming most to think that it has a cure
Only to show most it's not what they dreamt
But what some never begin to look for
Like a weathered man in a broken hat
A passer buyer has too many without eyes
A true believer to those with the light
A worn broken disability of nature to none
Ask onto one's self as to what sight sees
For obtainable to any with belief in light
It's with ease as to understand made easy
For straight forward a truth will never be
Hidden in mud cramped mistakes blurring reality
This is where most become long with confusion
Lost are they only looking to be found
Might be a fixable hat on a once broken man.

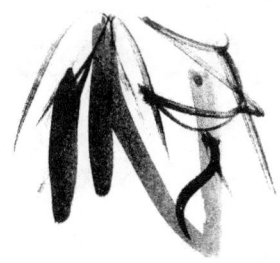

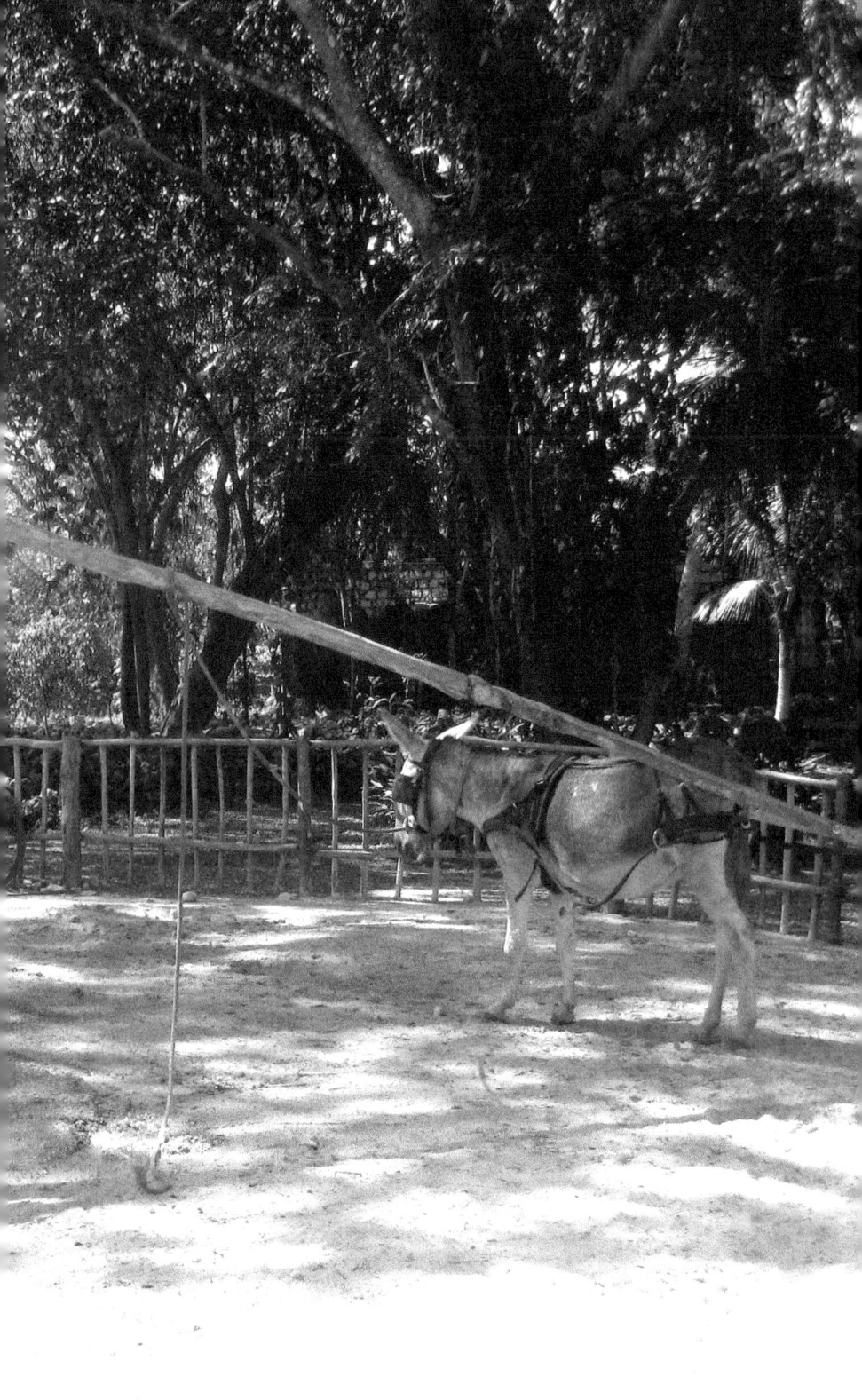

STRING OF A SHOE

Bang played sitting on a shoe string
Captured like a dying flower stuck in a pot
A spring of light which was never given
Planted are the feet that do not move
Twisted with the chaos of the winds
Stuck like a feather mangled in tar of oil
Plagued as harsh black consumes soft white
Making the gray area seem so real within
Does it all lie without a thought of region
As hysteria strikes between streets of jungles
Like a dust speck lost in an ocean of life
Playing in an arena of a shattered casino
Like sipping tea in a café watched by the agency
Even the saloon argues sales of sour wine
For a player cannot play upon the string of a shoe
Being stuck in a captured pot like a dying flower
Given life which was like the beautiful spring
Like moving feet which are uprooted today
The winds even twist with the unseen chaos
Free is a feather able to float amongst oils
For nothing will consume the soft white light.

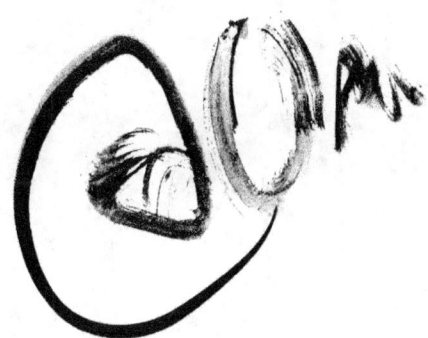

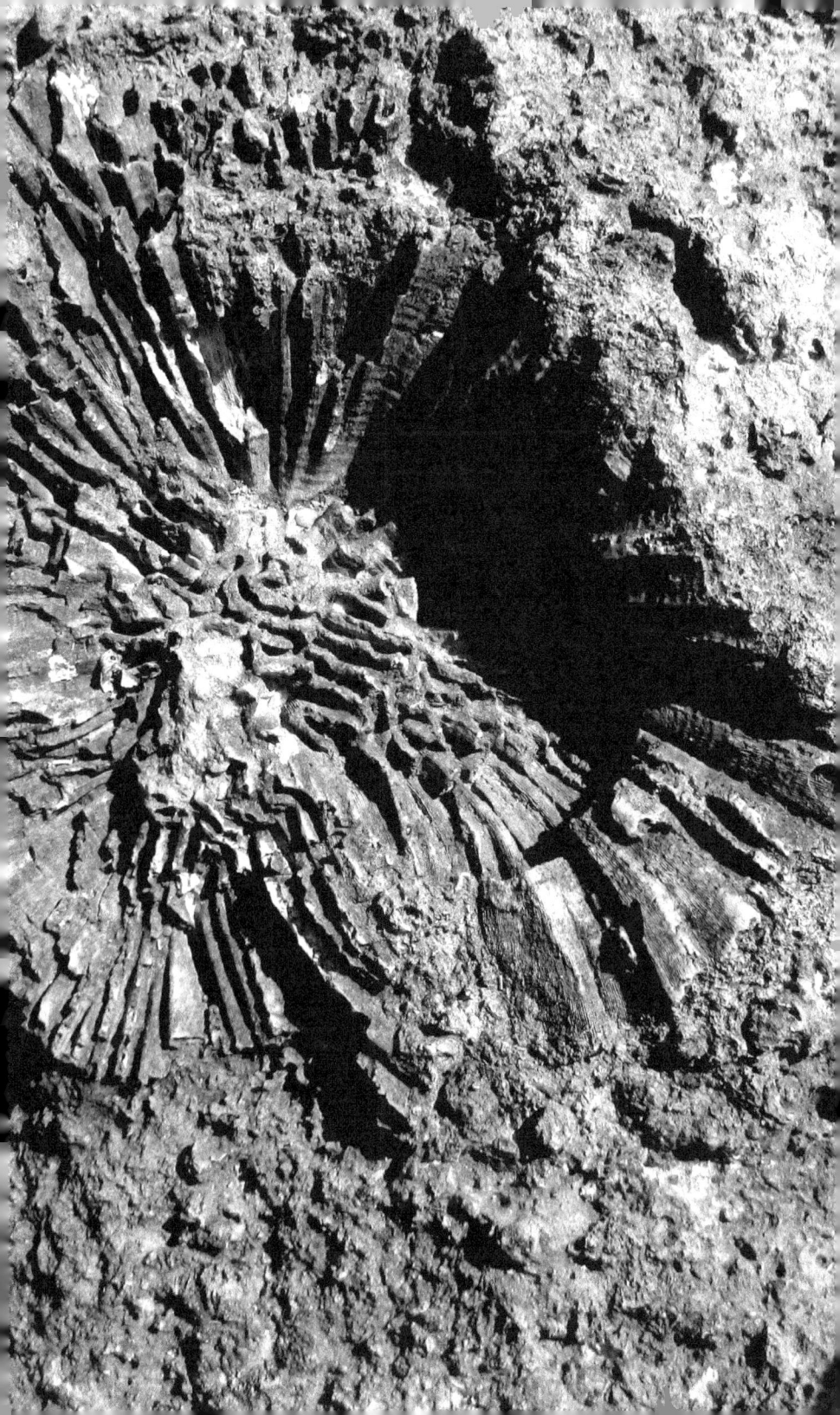

CRITICIZED STORIES

Crowned are the kings who rule
Sitting in squares of mastered words
To the magnitude of mass prediction within
Testing stamina with spirit made sacrifices
Rhythms of fire enchanting fear on earth
Great effort is made against vacant minds of men
Ripe is the extinct fruit made forbidden
Listening to the uncut sound of a waterfall river
Trapped in a gorge of a glacier scrolls reside
Explaining that even molten can't destroy fate
Criticized are the stories which mold society
Insulted may most be without a knowledge of
Ideas which pollute even the most accepted
Firm are the bounds that hold solid hands
Reliable are the labors made of hard work
Tracing the silhouettes casting upon the stars
Embraced by an imaginable force of light
Ideals is an image which deludes fantasy
Making a notion that a meeting will take place
A door less knob made from an open window
This will be perceived as the light which many know.

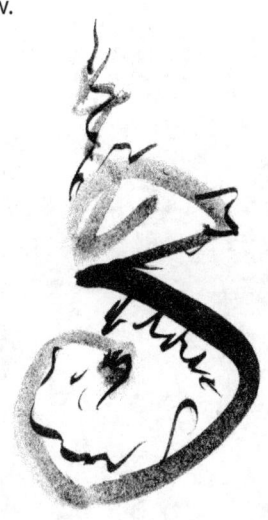

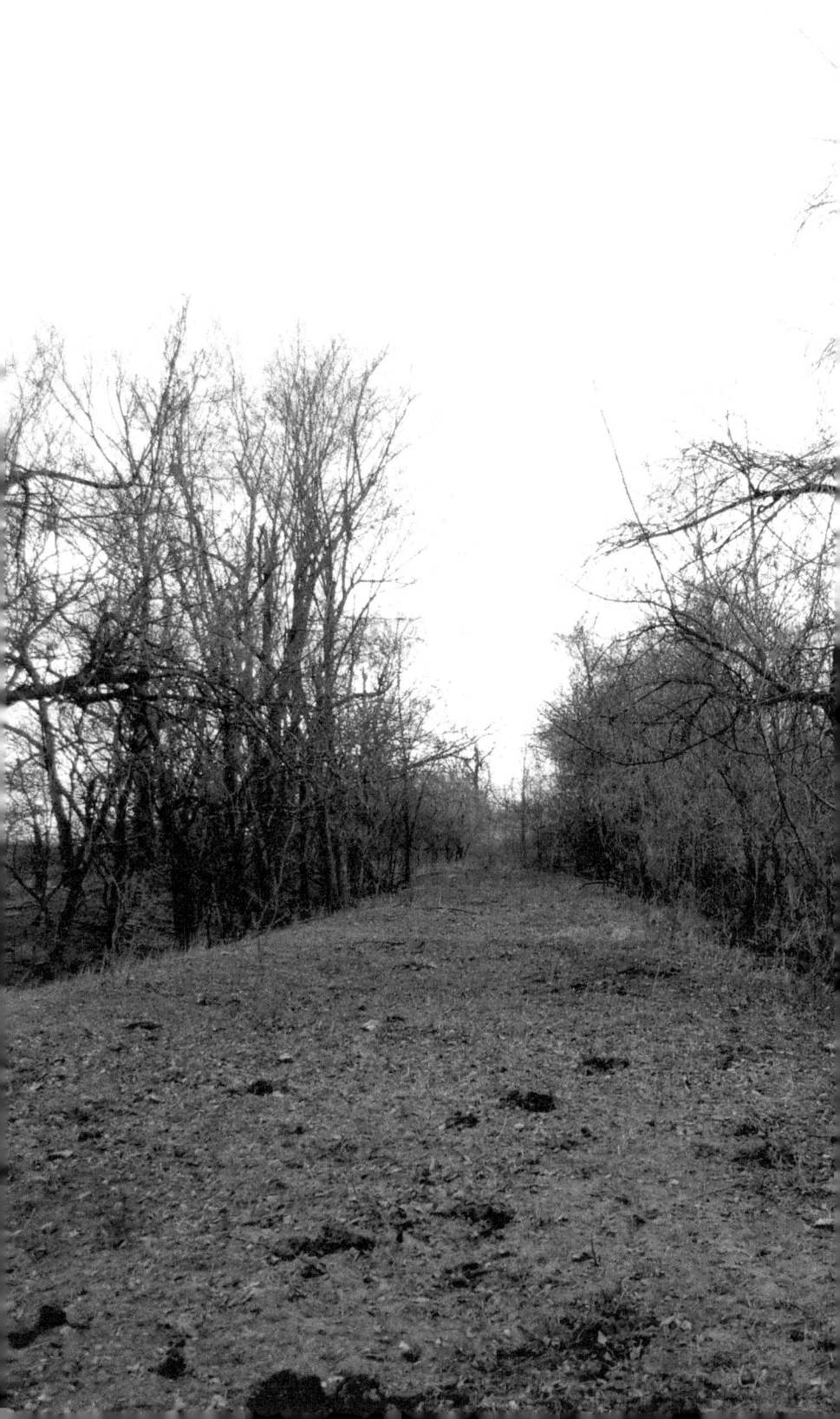

ENDLESS ROAD

Glazed reality making the day so soft
Energy master planned to never escape
Like ink stained fingers that always drip
Filling lost souls to think once again
As if anything can clean the way it's thought
Only the spark shall be made to express
Substance consumes even the most timid
Asking how can so many be so naïve
Is it proof that holds back realization
If so then it is what has been said
Only thyself can prepare for such a quest
For it is with this that most can not find
Shallow pools of despair and comfort
Hoping to know which clock we run on
Is it an endless circle we seek
Or do we know it's an endless road
Truth holds nothing to experience
This is what shows us the way ahead
If we don't understand we can't figure it out
Then it's gone, passed like a waiting child
Only to be found once again on a glazed day.

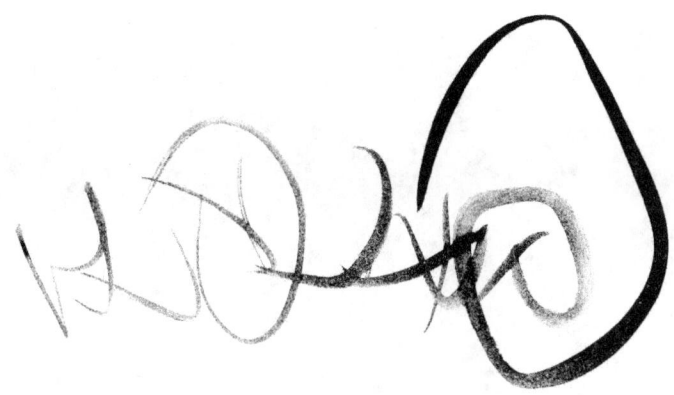

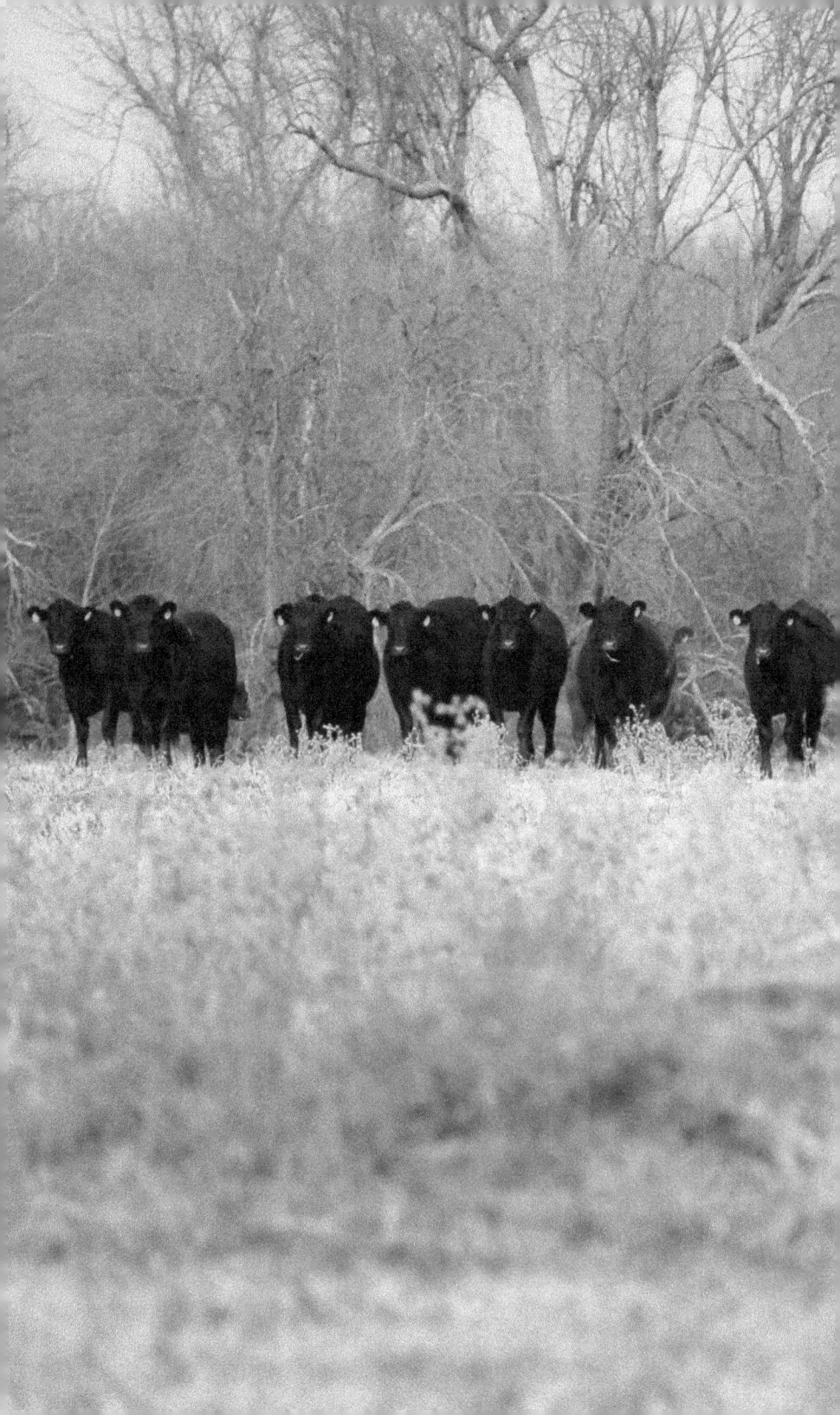

VICTIM AMONGST

Try to escape the meander of a rush
Wander the still silence of a stampede
Like a stray bolt meant to evade the rain
Plunging into the foam of a stealer galaxy
Snaking the mouth of a once smoky river
Control breaks hold of a rule never to speed
Masking the devils desert along a baron coast
Centric are the blades of a fragile carrier
Cut like an injection made to over burden
A song escapes only to make refuge forgotten
Upon a window sill do dreams sit to be found
Painless is the horde of knights who wail
Like a large piano which is played by baby fingers
As a violin plays by the hearing unheard
Unleashed is the motive to signal the storm
Guard is kept only to fall victim amongst
Rocky are the words which compromise
Passed around like an icicle burning to cold
Bashed like carbon only made to exhale
Swallowed like mercury poisoning the veins
Released are the ways of moral laughter.

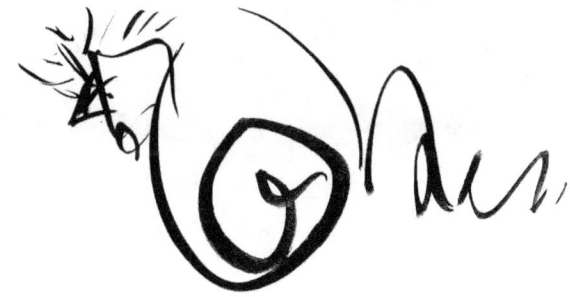

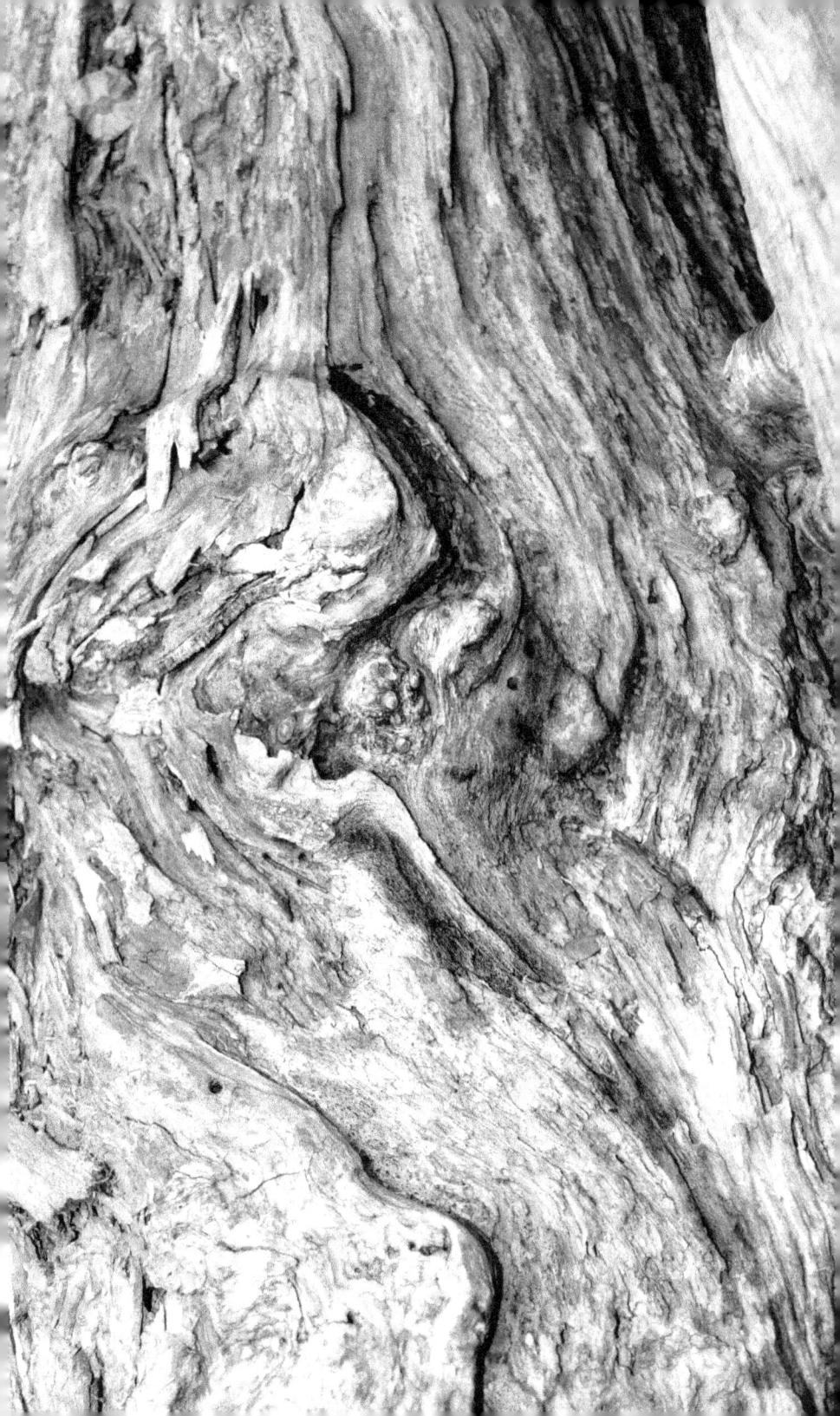

ORGANIC LOVE

Steam simmers against solar spheres
Heat burning to the flame of an explosion
As if bricks have been pulled from the walk
Shaking the distant crop to yield hunger
Pouring a burst of light upon the growing
Out spoken is the rambler who never speaks
Within a radius does a sacrifice make rage
Blank are the eyes which double stare
A force that echoes off the raptured ears
Like a star flower which hides in nightshade
Moonlit creatures who play in quicksands of life
Howls made to mask the silent screams heard
Taunting the existence of organic love
Succulent is the nectar of the day
Spinning against the smacking lips of pearls
Tasting the youth of a culture in society
Taboo is the stereotype made of a tribe
Rituals made of a myth and magic only to hide
Faced against the fears which threaten
Expression is the only true key to fate
A smile will show you the way along.

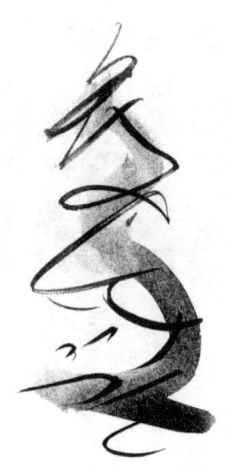

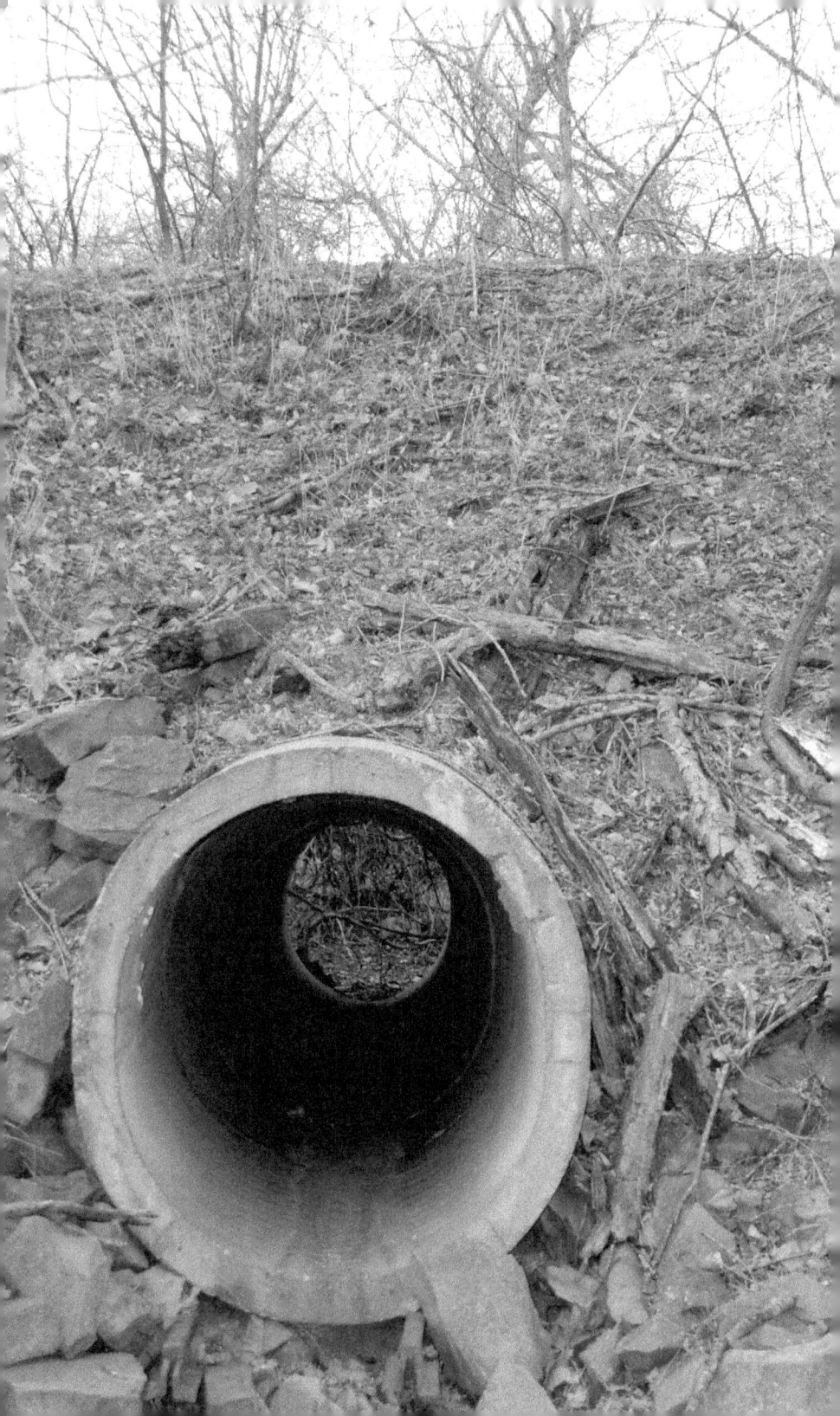

DROP OF WATER

Abundant is the anger that subsides
Unsmeared is the emotion which tells
Exchanged are the looks who imagine
Unrealized are the thoughts that are made
As if never to have been seen today
Unzipped are the hearts who mend them
Falling is the first sign that they are there
Unfocused are the eyes which decide for
Blurring most visions into false creations
Untapped are the minds which ask us
Like a filled ocean without a drop of water
Unquenchable are the mouths which speak
Dried as a lost desert where most reside
Untrue is the story that most come to believe
False is the reality of a making to come
Unborn is the thought we will make ours
Sad like a child walking to only the night
Unaware of being so lost and to never find
For comfort and love is all that most seek
Unashamed are they in belief of their own
For all is the same in loving eyes of yours.

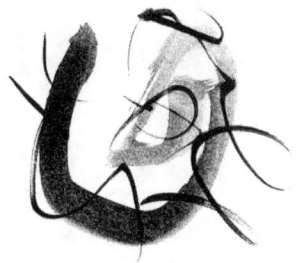

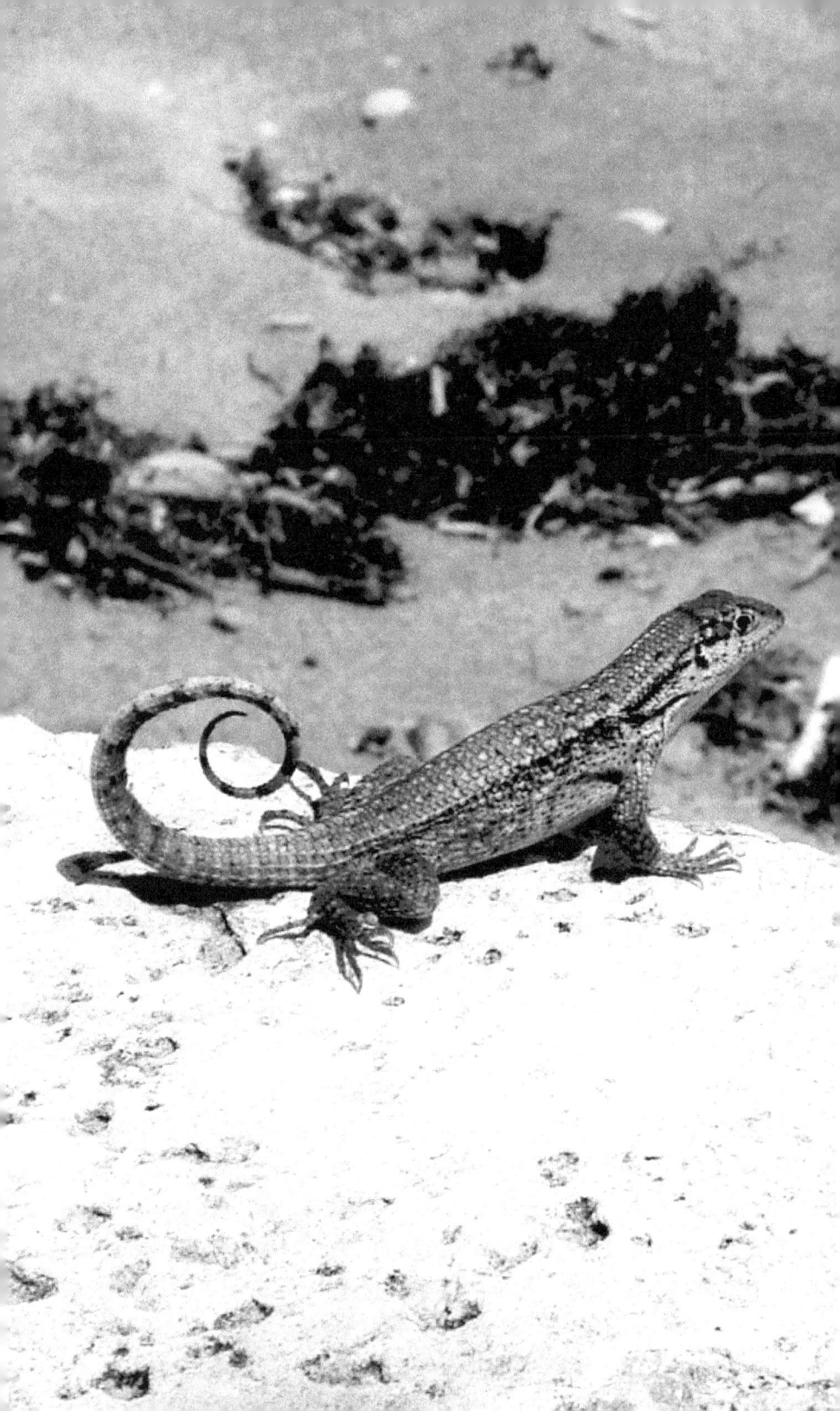

LIZARD KING

The lizard king has meet a feathered serpent
Reluctant is a being who means no harm
Passive is a lizard with rough skin
Hardened over time only to withstand
Smooth feathers help to remind of silk
Bubbling in the flavor of a forgotten taste
Enchanted by the very essence of it
Mesmerizing are tranquil eyes of passion
Moonlit as to have been an awakening dream
Confusing are the messages which are made
Mistaken are they as one can become two
For together, equal is all that they are
Amazing is the soul they poses
Repeating is all that they ever could do
Their wish was to always remain
Paths were always meant to cross
It was set into motion for eternity
A love which will never be lost
For time will always circle around
And caught will their hearts always be.

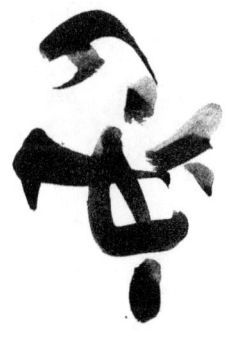

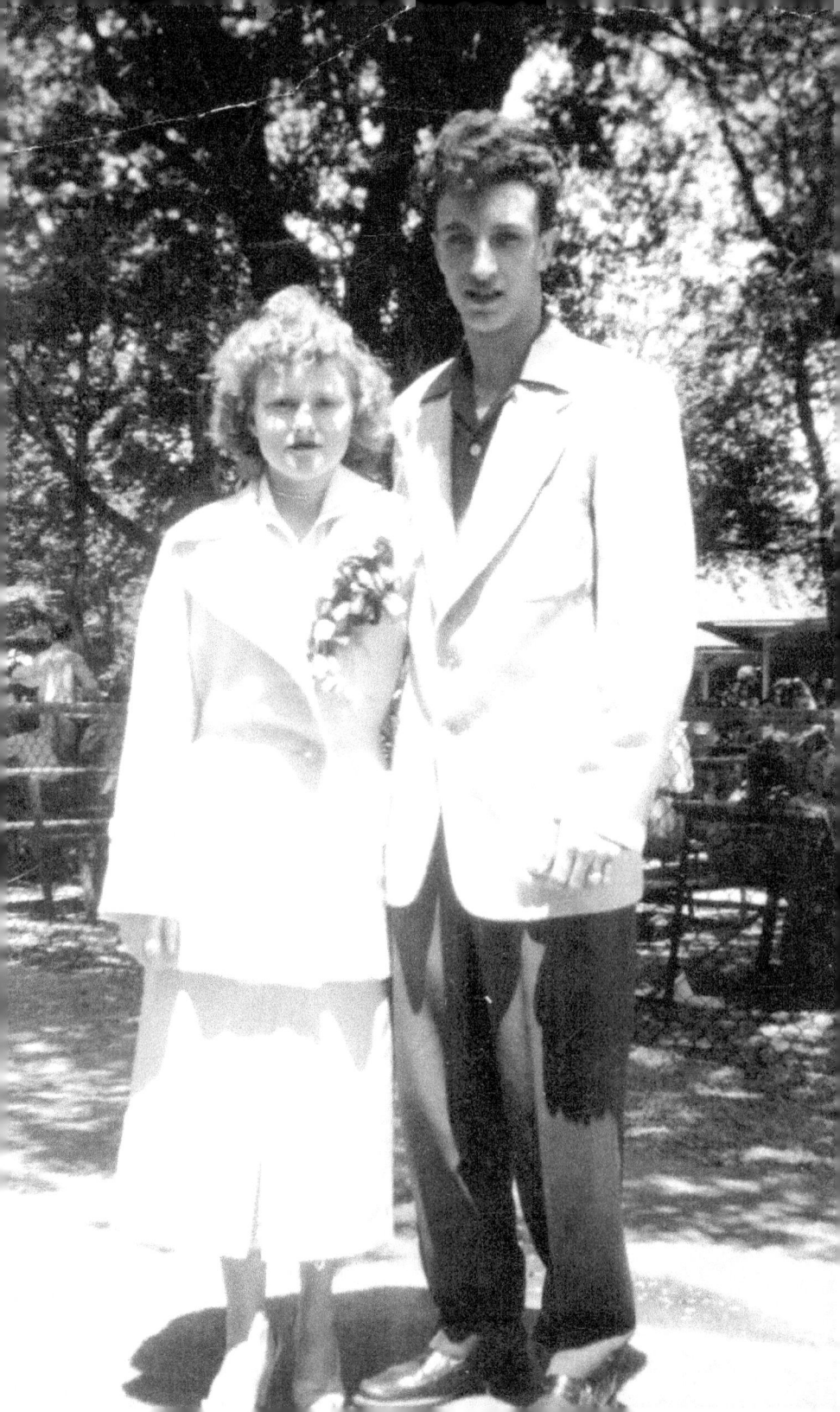

GRANDFATHER

Lost more than usual on this given day
Feelings of a loved one almost gone
Sadness rains over me not knowing
Not yet but a truth says soon may be
What's the point of it all, really
To be confused as if to ever know
A loss of hope with sacred thoughts
Not to affect a life, but a lost mind
Was there ever happiness, is he now
Did everything get done, was all said
Laughter was brought as often as I
Was always there to help guide through
Anger, pain, and struggle is all he sees
Hope, love, and praise is all that I see
He taught me how to laugh and imagine
Helped to make memories and dreams
When I told of my problems and stories
Always said stay strong and not to ever worry
This is what keeps me to this very day
Never gone and always in my heart and mind
To this I write for the world's greatest Grandfather.

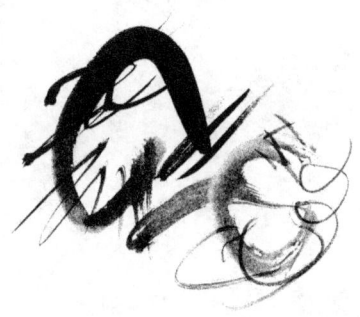

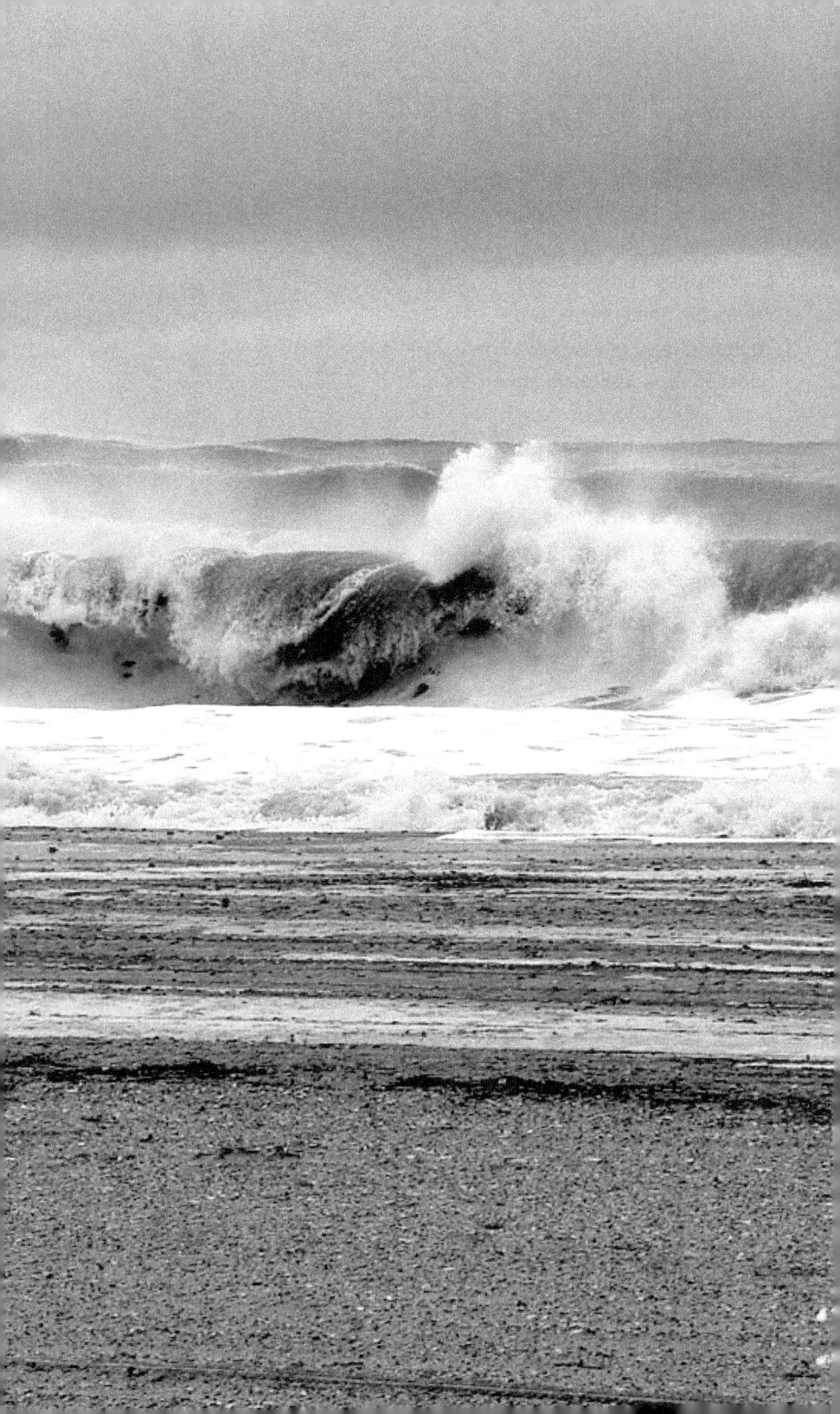

WHIRLWIND CYCLE

Bing bang boom wick click pow
As to which most people live their life
Bing all day long just to make a buck
Bang all over just to have a good time
Boom the world hits you like a brick of reality
The wick you try to burn at both ends
Then Pow it all just goes away
Just is what helps to start it over
Back around the whirlwind cycle again
Maybe this time the pow won't hurt as bad
Even so, stronger it will tend to make
Blinding you for the next run around
Planning to indulge in a scene of bliss
Happiness kept will never cease amongst
Intrigued are the beings who watch us
Hoping to learn more for their journey
Patience is exchanged to avoid the chaos
Trust is put into play to bypass the fear
Love is made to encounter a passion
Together we are made to never be apart.

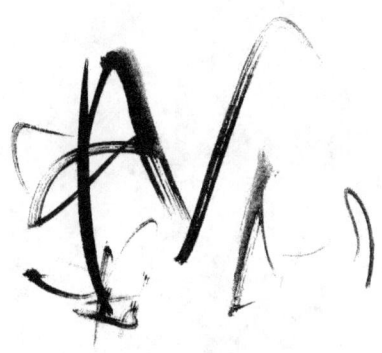

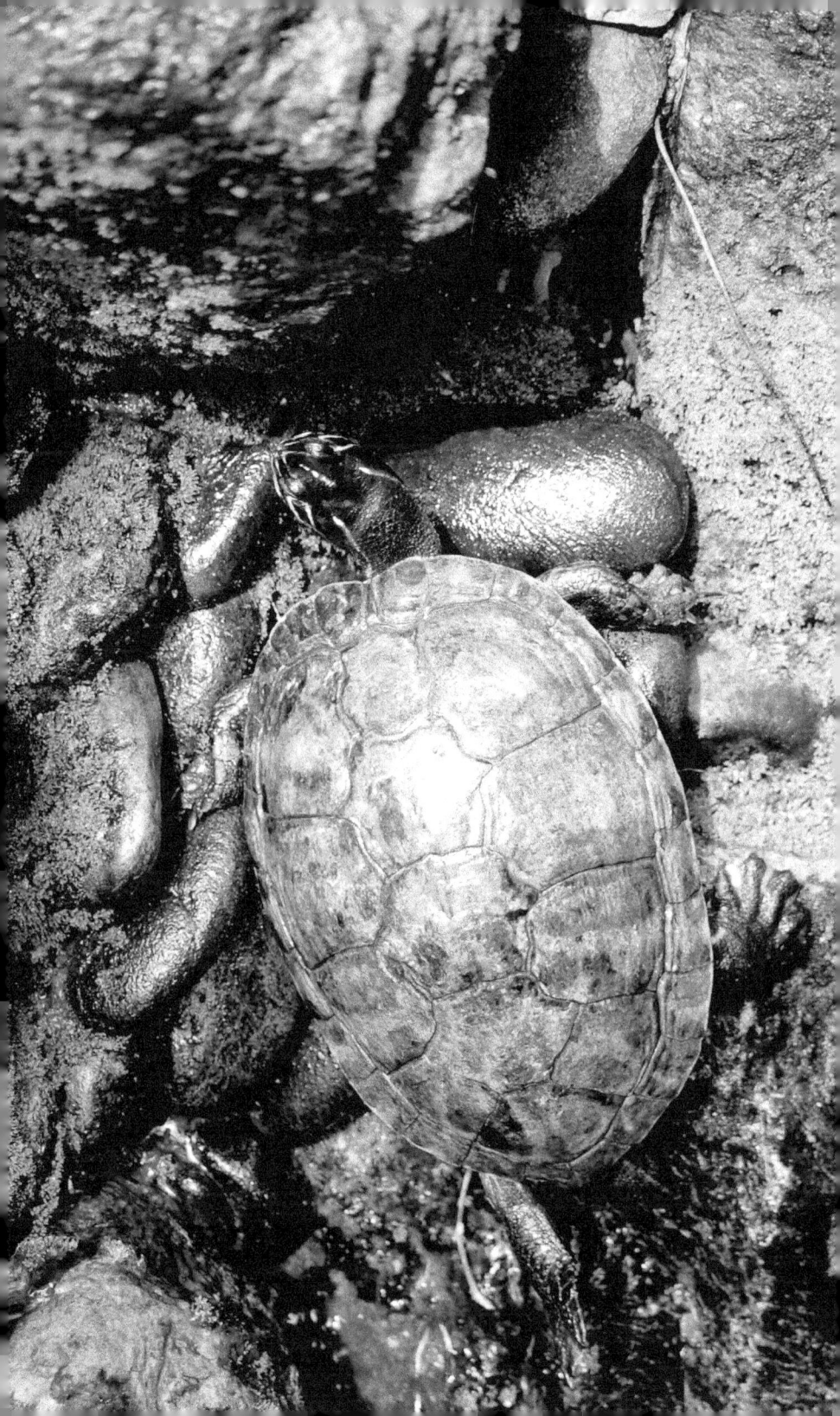

BLINK OF AN EYE

Is trust the true protector of love
Do untamed dreams remind of a day
For is comfort only a mistaken position
Does the rain ever fall too hard upon
As the wind begins to blow you down
When does the sun become too bright
How does the sound cease to exist
Can a breath ever begin to slow
May a heart forget to love so blind
Can it all happen in the blink of an eye
Will the stars ever seem to fall so fast
For if missed will there be another chance
Does everlasting light show itself again
May we open our eyes to believe once more
Can we share with you in your existence
Will there ever be such a harsh pain
When will we get there to understand
Is there someone to help show the way
Does it all happen to slow to even see
What is going to be shown will amaze
For trust is the only true protector.

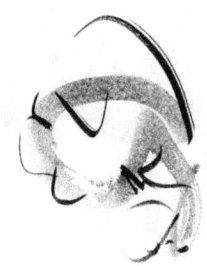

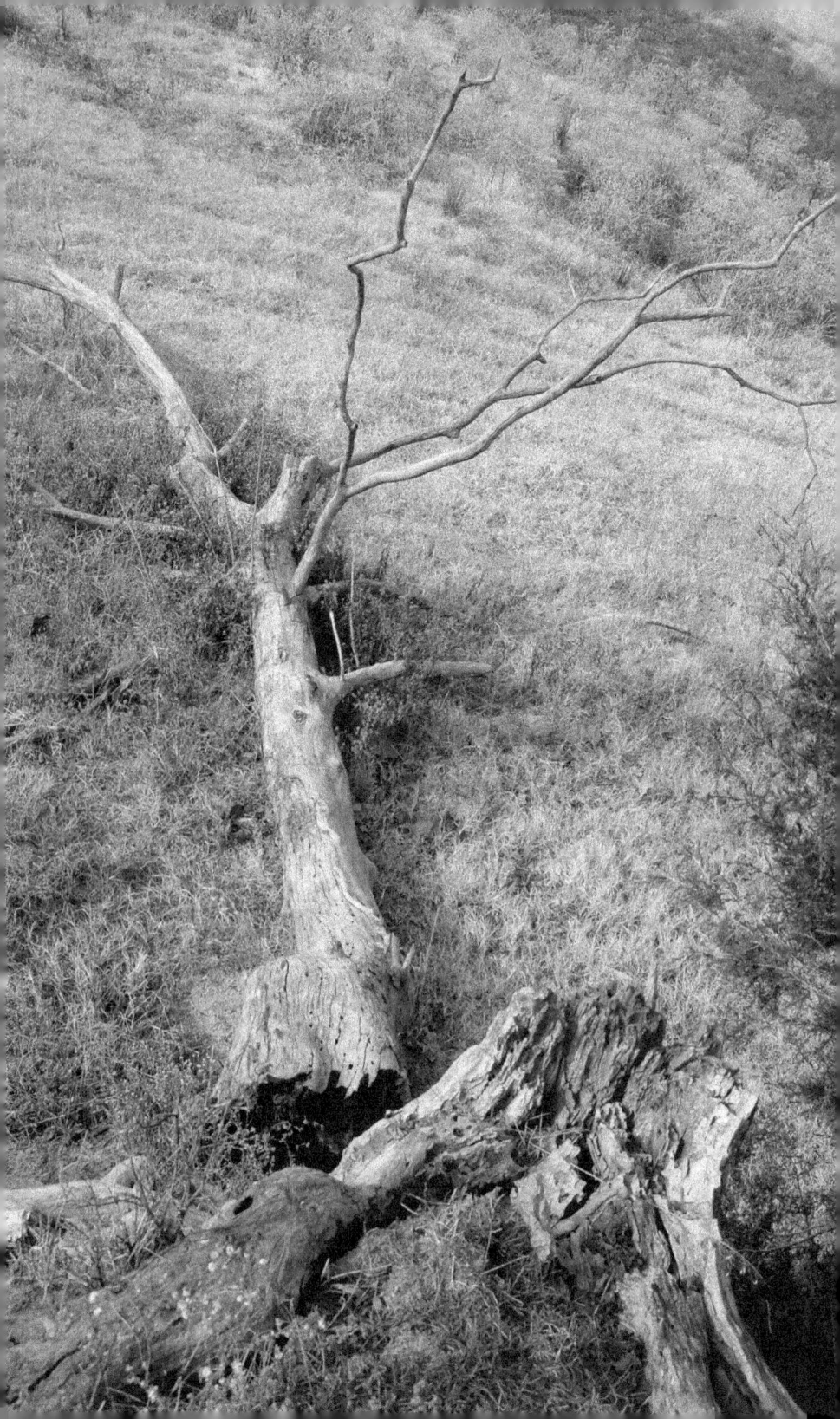

SUPREME LIFE

The flash of an eye taking notice
Bright are the realities we never see
Dormant to the idea of ever realizing
Remembering a distant thought of time
Untamed are we in the nature of a beast
Distracting senses to mask a memory
Scattered are the paths which lead us
False signs which make no utter sense
Blind as the day most people were born
Practicing false dreams only to withstand
A harsh reality that what is learned isn't true
Only a constant cycle which locks us out
So day to day most go about their lies
As if it all really didn't matter to them
But, which there is always that but
There is a truth out there within
Within one self it can be found to praise
A supreme life will be understood to enjoy
Warmth is always shown to those of cold
It's been told before to ask of these
Expression will be enough to show thanks.

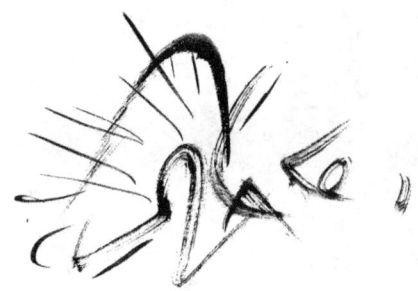

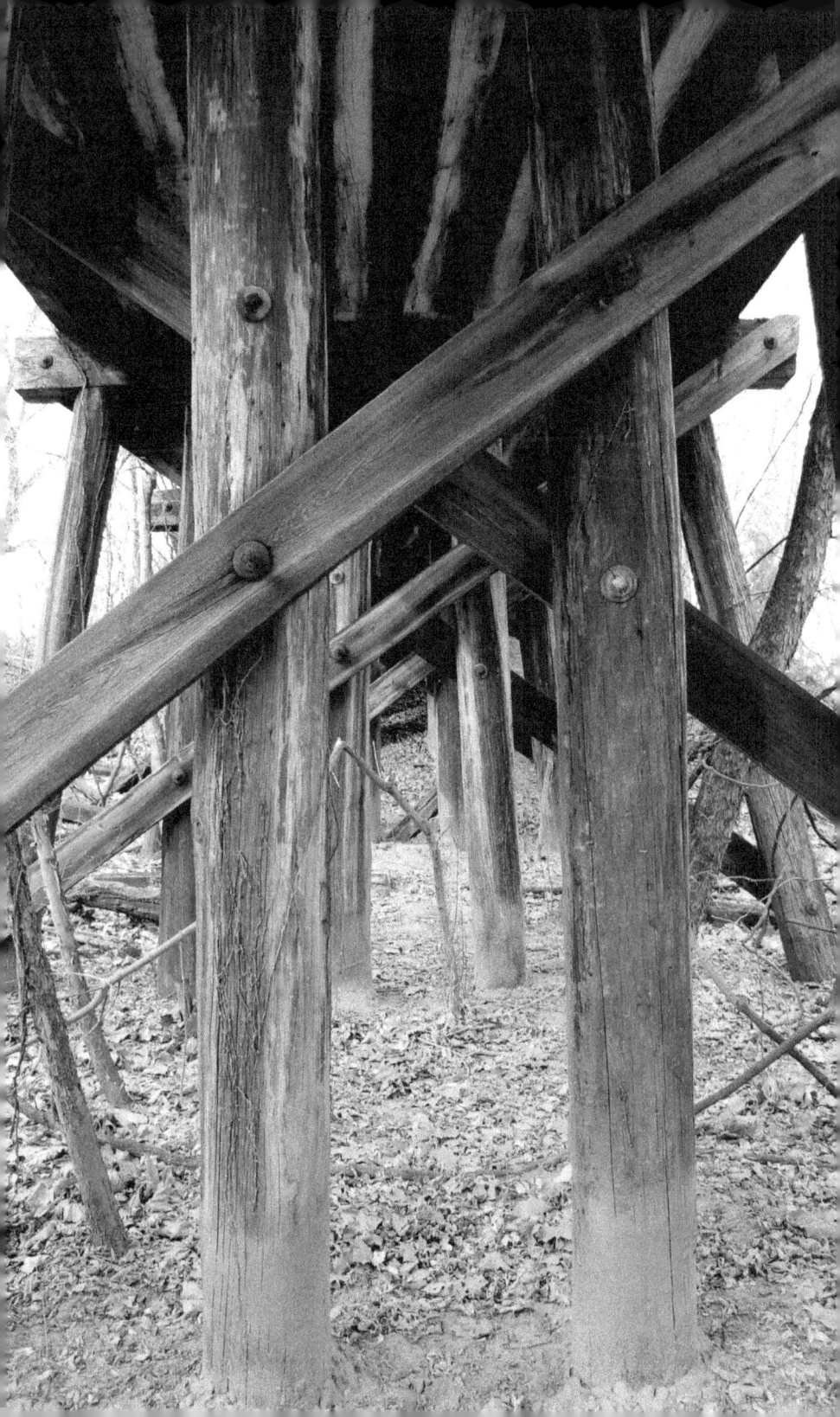

DRIPPING INK

Thought never seems to fill a blank mind
Waiting in idle time are these dreams
Times when a warmth of sun fades within
Anger never felt resides with reality
Trapped are the bindings which hold them
Free are emotions to set ablaze amongst
Like a rapid fire burning so deep throughout
Enraged are the drops which never cool
Scaring even the strongest heart made
For pain can never be escaped from life
Tougher times make for a stronger lesson
Without death one can only become wise
For each day brings new light and thought
But thoughts are lost amongst a dream
Painted like dripping ink made for a puddle
A picture never thought to show one
Only to confuse against untold stories
As if many times act as to never know
A finger touch could release them to light
For then maybe the blank could be filled
And a lost dream could be experienced.

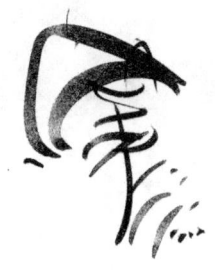

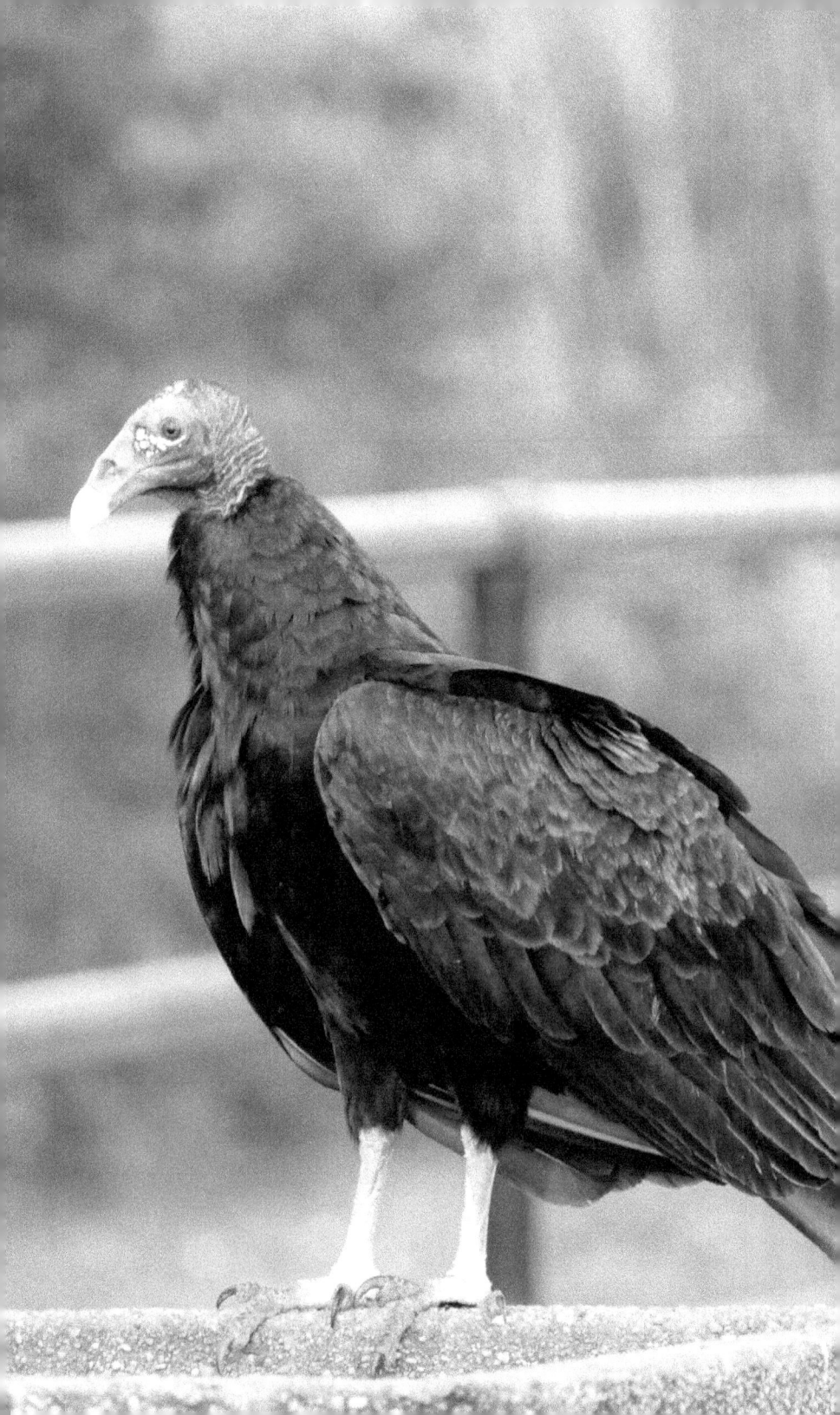

MOVING ON

A cultural magnification of a massive kind
Fighting over holy land not even anyone's
All that they do is murder back and forth
Estranged is their nature of a truth
Heads filled with misperception
Not even time will be wasted for them
Nor a thought…

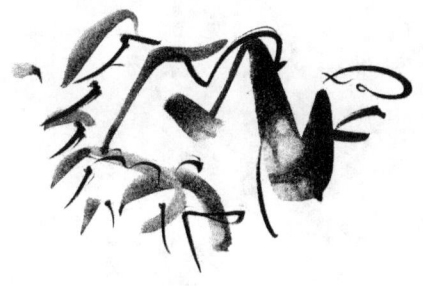

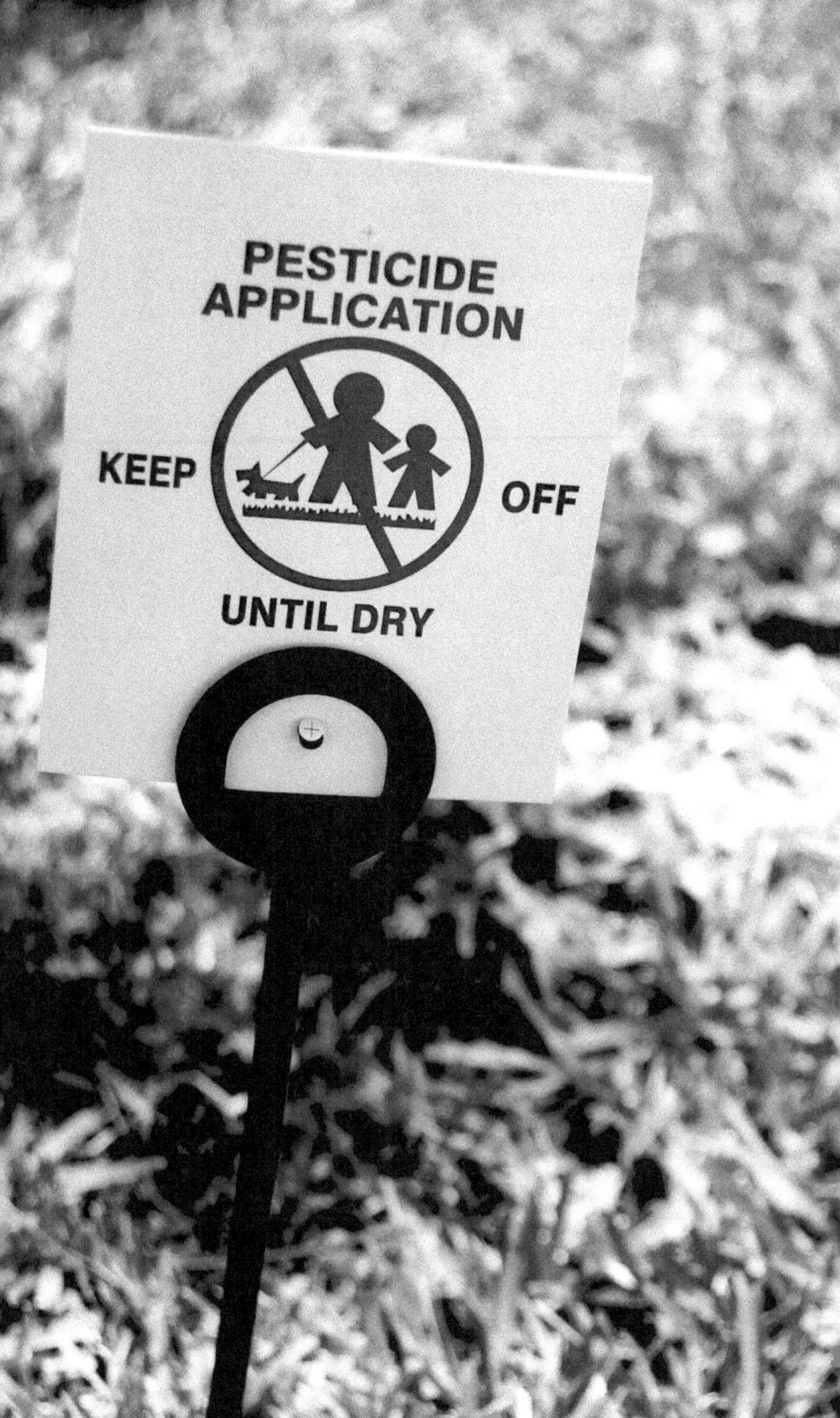

AWAKEN A THOUGHT

Sitting upon a reluctant branch of knowledge
Streamed like the sound of life as it runs
A visit from dragons of breath and red hair
Elastic responses do they leave behind
Songs of old play to seduce a melody
Explained is a love not knowing existence
Tragedy expels with a hidden meaning
A misunderstanding made of mistakes was told
Unrealized are the people of tribes they seek
Lost in a society made of fools to believe
Watch what is conceived as a truth
Like birds of prey who begin to starve
This is why it seems most never have to delay
Confused in the static of their forsaken day
Even this blends to a sense of all known
Mislead are those who read fools thoughts
Yet thoughts of a fool are read this day
Perception to awaken a thought is tried
Was there anything to begin with
Helped are those with a force to begin
The force is what will make everlasting.

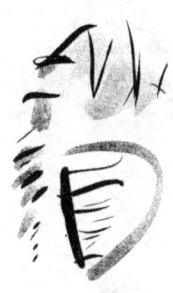

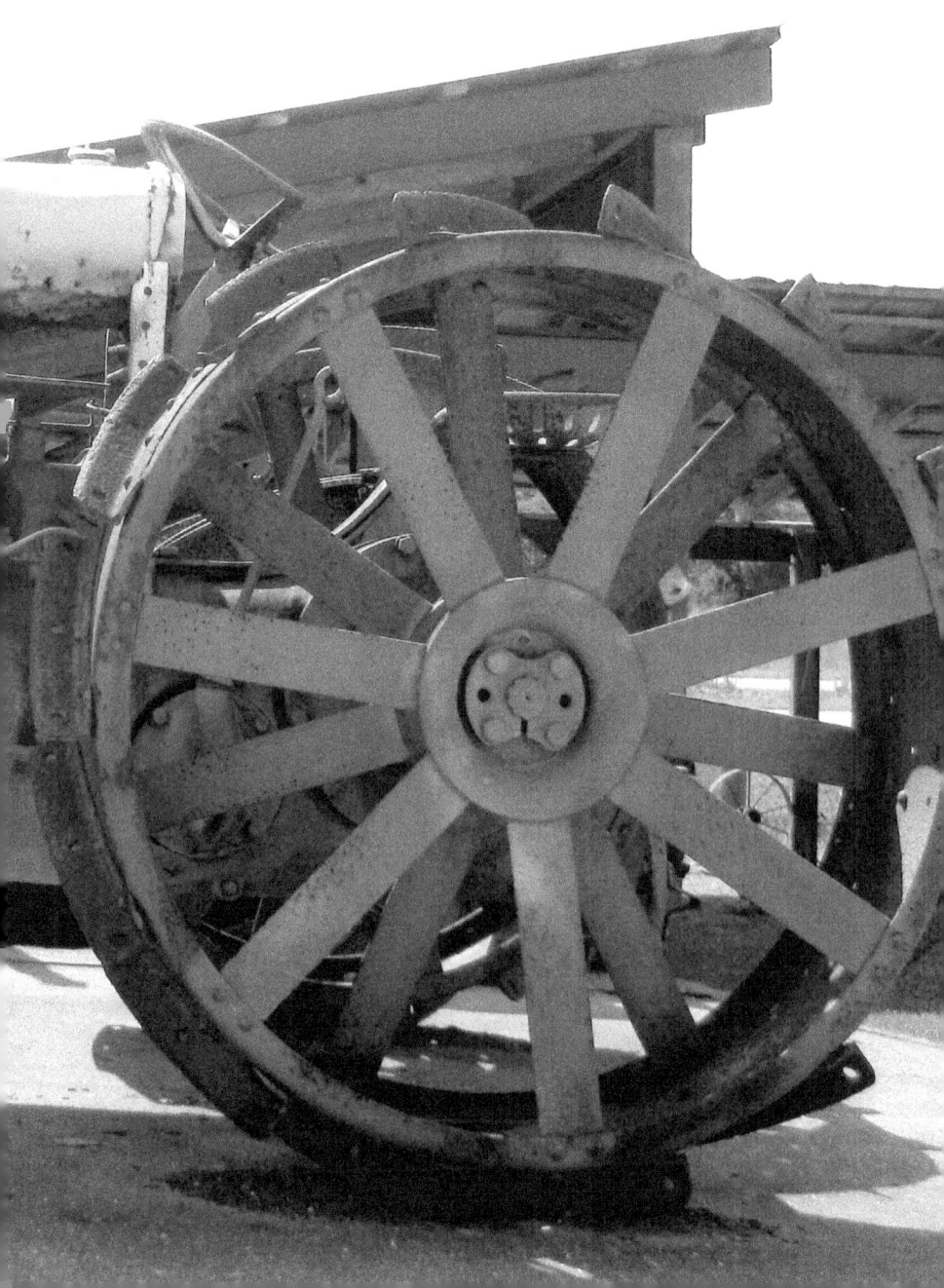

CLENCHED THROAT

Mutations of a decrepit soul
Gross in the beauty it beholds within
With a pressure building only to escape
Releasing a mist of life of a false kind
Only to choke on the sweet nectar of
Filling a broken mind which never knew
Grabbing at the dust filled bones made
Covered are the hands which pull away
As the air is in confusion which way to blow
Smacked packed are the words told
Heard as nothing will ever listen
Lied is the story as if to ever tell a truth
Angry are these emotions who laugh
Happy are the seas who flow against
Mistaken are many thoughts that consume
Swallowed whole without a soft taste
Strapped within a clenched throat
Amazed as the way most begin to breath
Forced to make a life start with struggle
Then feeling gravity pull till most end
With an eternal sleep closing open eyes.

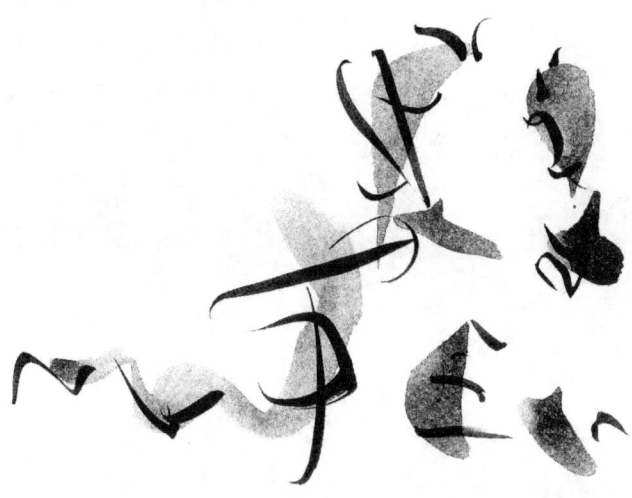

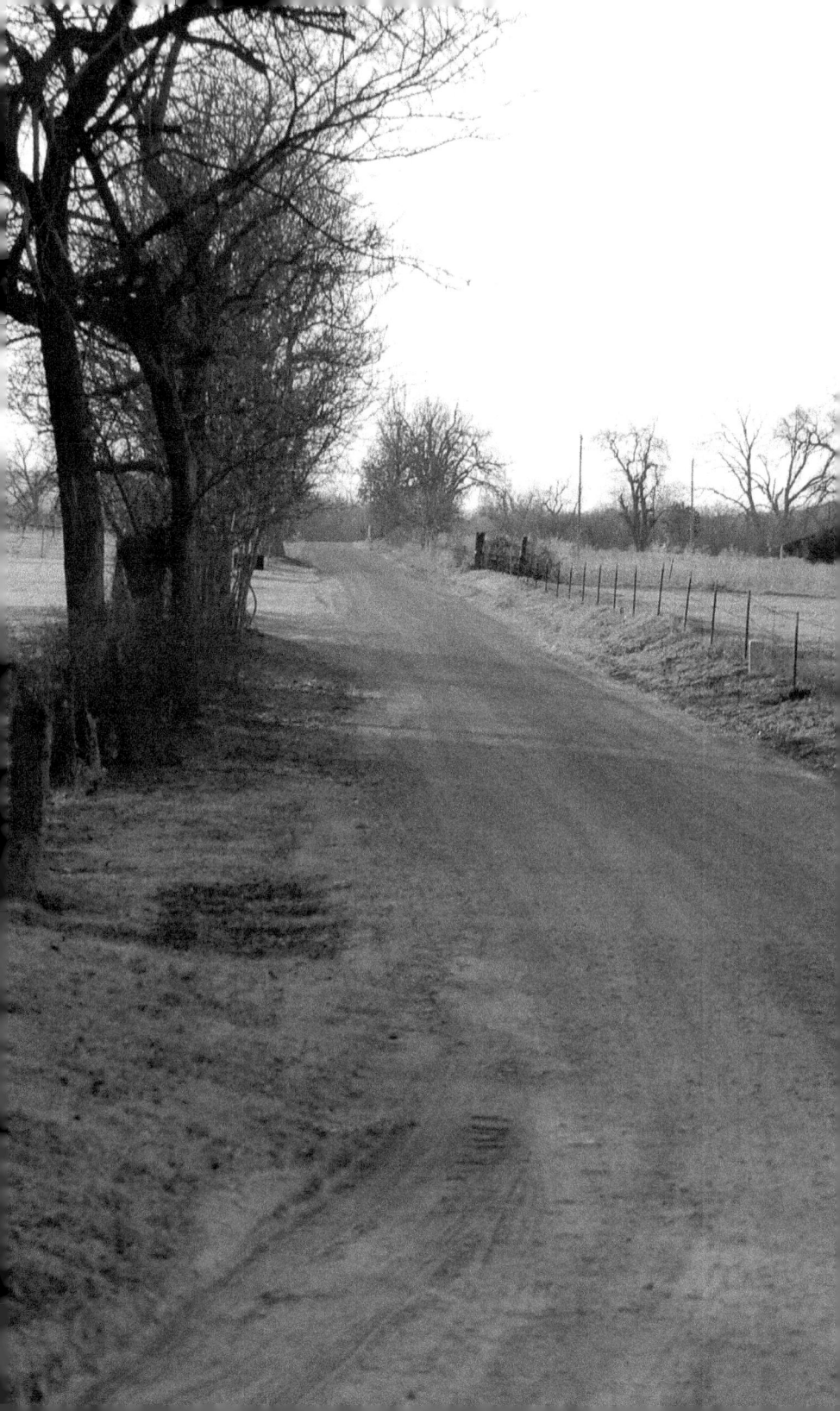

THIN AIR

Dancing on snow covered tree stems
Dragging fingers leaving no mark
Like a child who screams to never be heard
Or an abandoned parent left to raise
Caught in a tidal wave of excuses made
Can one drown in the sand of a sea
Only to be swallowed whole again
A stench is made to consume the thin air
Covered are those who do not move fast
Dangled are they in front of open mouths
Disgusted is the digestion which leaves them
Hungry in the way of lost antics said
Almost like an apple that had no choice
Bitten to expose the harshness of life
Again to deceive an unready mind
Experienced are they not in unknown time
For even the wind can get confused
Blowing as if to once know a song
Listening to the mistakes always shown
Confronted on decisions are they now
Unspoken are the voices who dance.

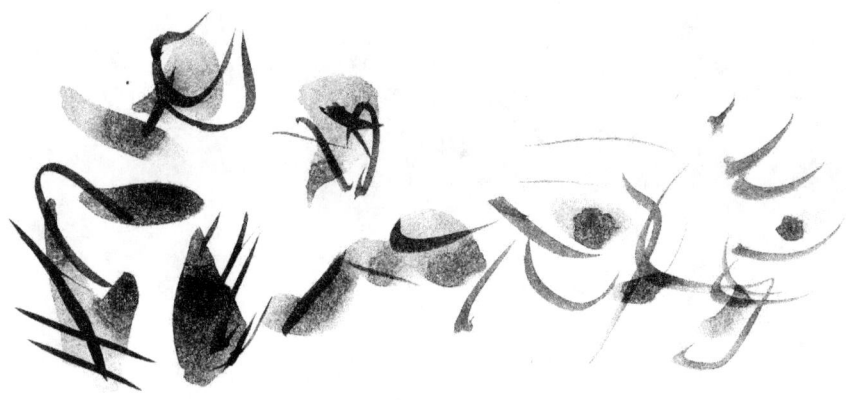

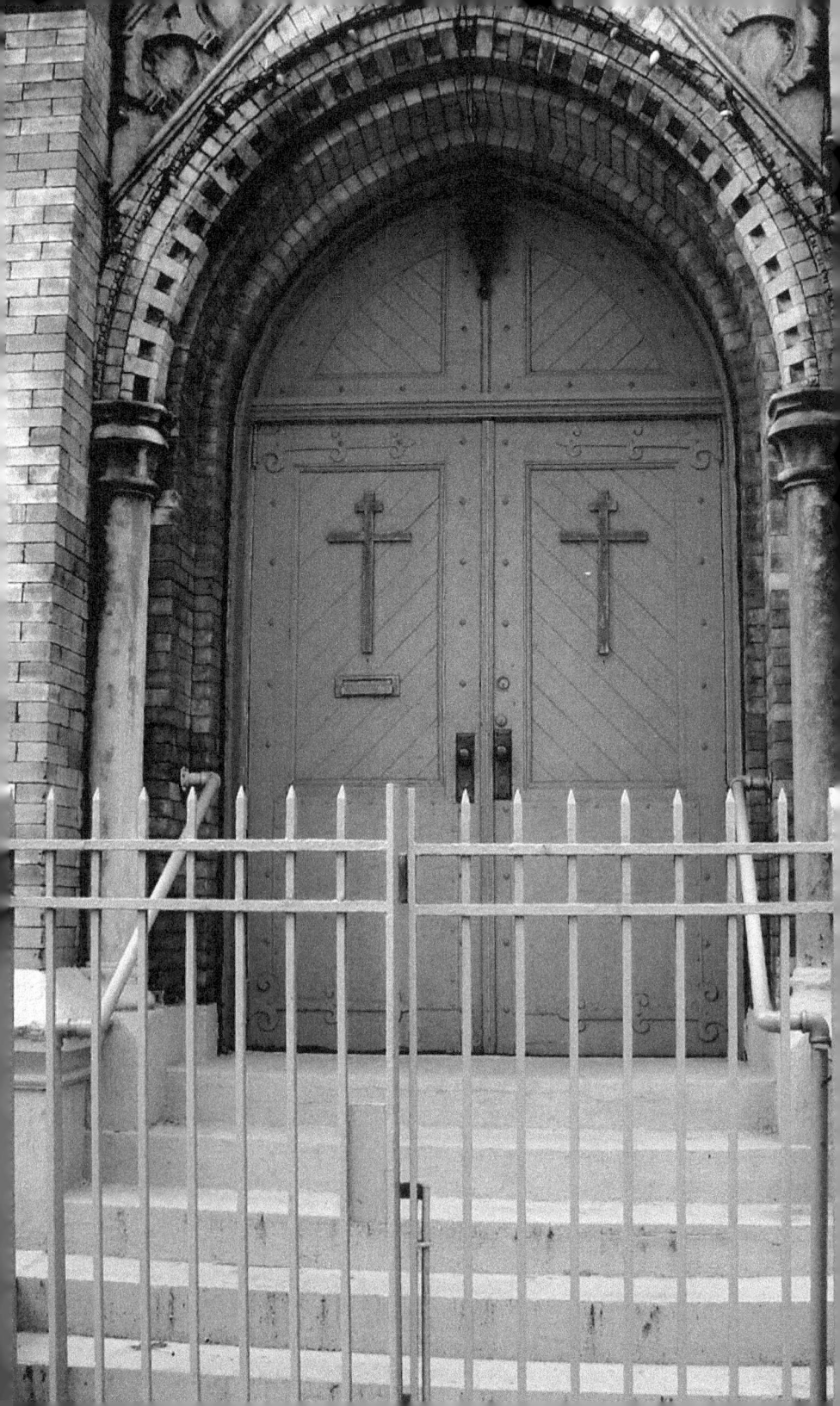

LIGHT NOT KNOWN

Brittle are the bones which stack
Together are they mangled into form
Piled high into a heap of great nothing
Mass is all that is shown to be made
Gravity helps to hold a float amongst it
A warmth which runs through immense heat
Keeping a flow brought by soft pressure
Intense is the pain which subsides within
Pushing to release through clogged pores
Filled with toxins of a day to live against
Hoping to one day see a light not known
Checked are the temperatures that rise
Above average are most as they play
Moisture of nature is all that keeps them
Pulsating on a different level to give birth
Brought into the world anew they come
Blanked by a mist to keep one alive
Drastic are the measures which take place
Only to show nature in its purest form
A truth which most will never see
A lie that most will live to this day.

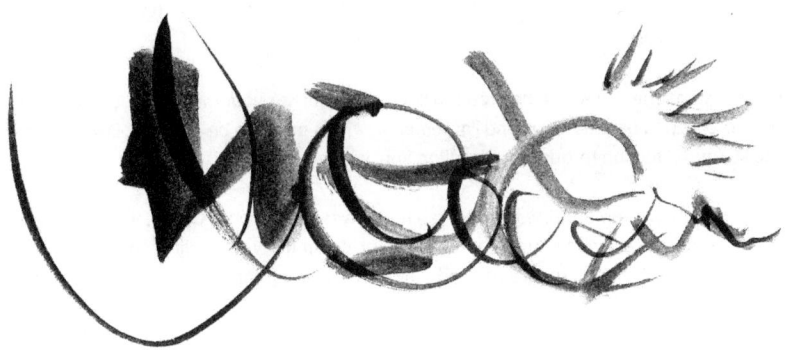

ABOUT THE AUTHOR

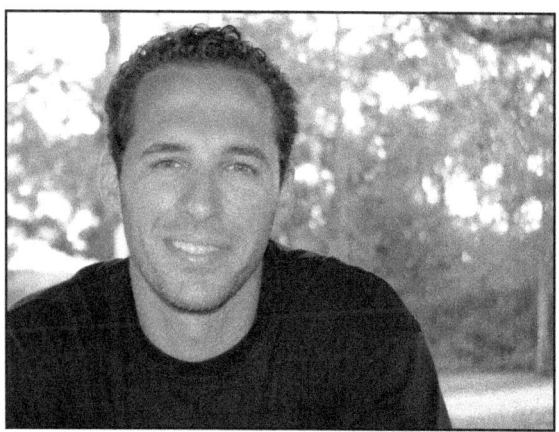

About the author Dwayne Michael Adams

"Hurry, Hurry he's knocked out!" …Laying in the grass face up to the blue sky, eyes closed, bike along side of his body, friends looking over him and a lonely not so innocent "ramp" of plywood and bricks not in use and me running down the street barefoot screaming, "Oh my gosh what happened?" It is always an adventure raising a boy!

Yup, that was just another weekend at our house while Dwayne Michael Adams was growing up. Dirt bikes, baseball games, converse sneakers by the dozen. Boys in and out of the house, birthday pool parties, skateboard ramps, pets, bb guns, home-made go-carts, friends on trips with us, football, baseball, girlfriends, laughs, cars, a funny personality, a good friend, jokes, schools, family, summers at Nanny's, Art Institute, Orlando, New York, sauce maker, kids book publisher, owner of his own magazine and big brother. This is my son all rolled into one.

From a young boy, to a young adult, to a man. Over the year's discussions, frustrations, life's lessons. Words of wisdom given, maybe used, maybe not; "Never get caught", "Always be kind", "Don't burn your bridges", "Keep in touch with friends", "Never say Never" and "Your family comes first, no matter what!"

Dwayne is someone you would be proud to know, thankful he's your friend, proud to have as a brother, proud to have as a son, and I'm someone who is proud to be his mom. Dwayne was blessed to find direction through my dad "Pop Pop" when it came to his career with computers.

Within his creation "WeMerge" he has touched many lives and supported a great deal of friends. His positive support allowed them to grow within the community and believe in their dreams along with his. What a great run it was. And now an aspiring author. Boy … the years went fast!

God bless in all you do.
All my love, Mom ☺

FROM THE AUTHOR

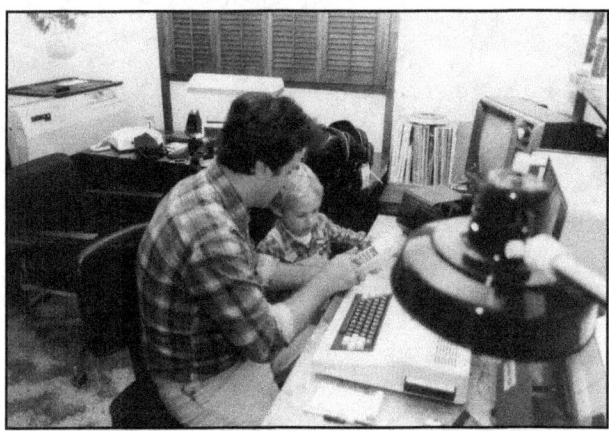

From the author Dwayne Michael Adams

Having computers in my life really influenced me. When it came time to choose a profession the one thing I knew was computers and I loved to create, so with that came the profession of graphic design. Creating is one passion I hope to never lose. It was the driving force behind this book. Motivation came in at a close second, as it is the hardest thing to come by. Time itself can help but is sometimes a deterrent. If the effort is made, dreams can be created.

The image above is of my grandfather and I playing with his new digital phone. He used to show me the many different technologies that were coming of age. That computer you see there didn't even have windows on it. We used DOS back then. He used to have games like pitfall, that I played on his computer. My grandfather loved technology and showed me everything he could find. He used to have a stuffed Piranha that sat on his computer desk. It always reminded me there were greater things out there to explore.

One of the greatest song writers I know created a song that always expressed to me the feeling to make moves no matter what. To always get up and Go. It was a song that I listened to many a time; Mostly because the CD got stuck in my car radio for over 3 years. Reminding me on a constant basis that I need to get up and Go! It made in impact on my life, just as any great music should do. If ever motivation is something you lack, I highly recommend this song.

Like the song explained above, I hope that this book gives you the inspiration you may need to further your life. Be creative and make something of your life with each passing moment.

With that I hope you enjoyed your read and look forward to one day saying hello to you and yours. May God bless you on your path and may your days be filled with happiness, good health, and above all, laughter. I thank you.

Dwayne M. Adams

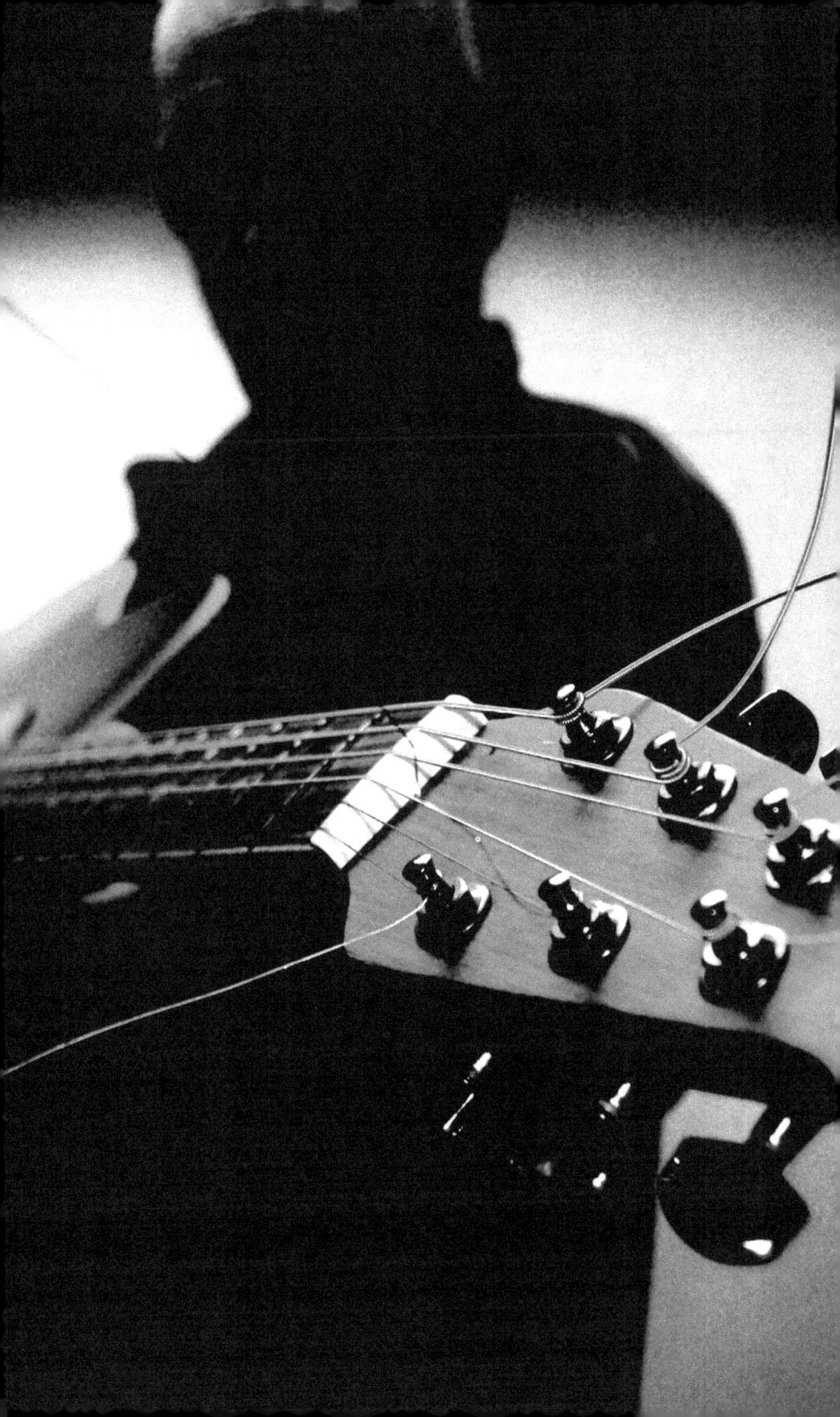

Radio Go Go

by John Paul James & The New Taste

I was on the move, on the steal,
it was ten 'til two when I grabbed the wheel,
and I was late already so I drove right steady
on down the road.

I figured I would get somewhere,
You can't come here and I can't go there,
and I won't go back to where I was, I've got
nowhere to go.

So I headed up that highway fast,
burned about two tanks of gas, before I blew
the doors off that ride and kept on coastin'.

and a song came on the radio,
singin' get up go, get up cat, go go go.
Yeah I might be singin' a bit too loud,
but it's just the right sound to go go go.

I wound up down in New Orleans,
where I met a man there just as mean,
as any junkyard dog, off the chain,
you can find.

He said, " I sing it loud, this is how I feel,
if you don't like it chump, well come pluck
the steel, and you can see what it's like to
stand on stage and die."

He had a voice of gold but he sold his soul,
with every nickel they dropped inside his
bowl, he just kept on singin', " I am alive! "

Now I think about those words sometimes,
how he made a rain cloud, black as night,
turn the lightest shade, the brightest shade
of white.

and how a song came on the radio,
and made me get up go, get up cat go go go.
Now I might be singin' a bit too loud,
but it's just the right sound to go go go.

See you might not know quite where to go,
when life is fast but time is slow,
and hell I don't know,
I'm just along for the ride.

If it's one thing that I do, I know,
you gotta get out now and hit the road,
You're either punchin' a clock, that pays
minimum wage, or gettin' high.

So if you feel the need to leave hey hey,
I know it's downright tough these days but,
walk, run, take a train, fly.

And when a song comes on the radio,
you gotta get up cat, get up cat go go go.

WE ARE EXPERIENCED, HIGHLY QUALIFIED, AND DISCREET PROFESSIONALS,
WITH EXCELLENT REFERENCES AND A BROAD RANGE OF PROJECT KNOWLEDGE

WE CAN MAKE YOUR BOOK IDEA A REALITY
FROM START TO FINISH

PROFESSIONAL EDITORIAL & PROOFING SERVICES

WeMerge Publishing's editorial department provides a wide range of professional editing, manuscript and indexing services to make your book the best it can be. Engaging a professional editor to elevate the quality of your work is an essential task for every author who wants their work to be taken seriously by the book buying public.

EXPERIENCED BOOK LAYOUT & ARTWORK SERVICES

With our professional graphic design studio, and our experienced team of talented book designers, WeMerge Publishing can create and incorporate eye-catching designs and artwork that will compete successfully in any retail environment. We take pride in our work and strive to bring you the most imaginative and breathtaking design projects.

E-BOOK PUBLISHING, DISTRIBUTION & MARKETING

WeMerge's eBook publishing and distribution brings your book to an amazing new audience of readers. eBook publishing is included in most of RedFox Publishing's book publishing packages. This market is one of the most rapidly growing industries to date and will help bring your title in front of the eyes of millions of people.

www.WeMerge.com | 561.305.2070

WEMERGE PUBLISHING QUICK ORDER FORM

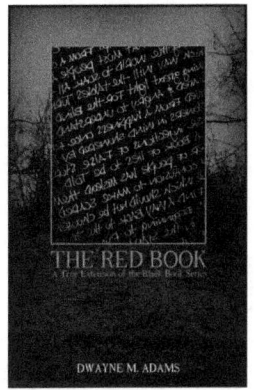

The Red Book $12.99
ISBN: 649906713784

Name _____

Title _____

Affiliation _____

Address _____

City _____ State _____ Zip _____

Telephone _____

Email _____

Check or money order enclosed for $ _____

Bill us. Purchase Order Number _____

Tax Exempt No. _____

Charge: XX AmEx   XX MasterCard   XX VISA   XX Discover

No. _____

Experation Date _____

XX   Please send the most recent RedFox Publishing catalog

XX   Please send a copy of the RedFox Publishing Newsletter
to my email

Alternatively you may also log onto our website and order
through our online store or email your request to
info@wemerge.com. Orders made by web or email will
receive a discount on the retail price if the code *Red Book* is
used. We thank you for your support and wish you the best in
all that you do.

Thank you for reading. Hope you enjoyed.

THE RED BOOK
A True Extension of the Black Book Series

The truth is always hidden, for the seekers are to be the only one's who reach enlightenment. Within these pages are hidden meanings that will mislead the common mind and only those who have been exposed to a truth will be able to see the secret knowledge within.

These three elements help to conceal not only the truth, but also help to guide the unknown away from their path towards enlightenment, which is given to each person.

Without certain knowledge of the unknown, will we ever find our existence within, or will we find ourselves.

Trying to read between the lines is an age old task of searching for truth within ourselves and within the life we lead.

We try to figure out the codes that have been shown before us to help us understand the meaning of this existance to share with others.

Ask yourself what you have learned and what you can share with others.

The pages you hold in your hand will help to guide not only your mind, but it will also shed light onto your soul and help you to see the truth within, not only in yourself, but in others.

Thank you for taking the time to share the dreams and the light that is with all of us. Appreciating all that you are and hoping to one day share an experience of truth with you.

- Dwayne Adams

www.ingramcontent.com/pod-product-compliance
Lightning Source LLC
Chambersburg PA
CBHW060843170526
45158CB00001B/225